ABC of
Alcohol

Fifth Edition

ABC series

An outstanding collection of resources for everyone in primary care

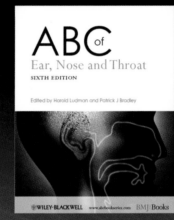

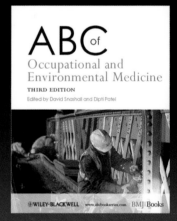

The *ABC* series contains a wealth of indispensable resources for GPs, GP registrars, junior doctors, doctors in training and all those in primary care

▶ **Highly illustrated, informative and a practical source of knowledge**

▶ **An easy-to-use resource, covering the symptoms, investigations, treatment and management of conditions presenting in day-to-day practice and patient support**

▶ **Full colour photographs and illustrations aid diagnosis and patient understanding of a condition**

For more information on all books in the *ABC* series, including links to further information, references and links to the latest official guidelines, please visit:

www.abcbookseries.com

WILEY Blackwell   BMJ|Books

ABC of

Alcohol

Fifth Edition

EDITED BY

Anne McCune

Consultant Hepatologist,
Department of Hepatology,
Bristol Royal Infirmary,
University Hospitals Bristol NHS Foundation Trust,
Bristol,
UK

WILEY Blackwell

BMJ Books

This edition first published 2015, © 2015 by John Wiley & Sons, Ltd.

© 1982, 1988, 1994 BMJ Publishing Group
© 2005 by Blackwell Publishing Ltd

BMJ Books is an imprint of BMJ Publishing Group Limited, used under licence by John Wiley & Sons.

Registered Office
John Wiley & Sons, Ltd, The Atrium, Southern Gate, Chichester, West Sussex, PO19 8SQ, UK

Editorial Offices
9600 Garsington Road, Oxford, OX4 2DQ, UK
The Atrium, Southern Gate, Chichester, West Sussex, PO19 8SQ, UK
111 River Street, Hoboken, NJ 07030-5774, USA

For details of our global editorial offices, for customer services and for information about how to apply for permission to reuse the copyright material in this book please see our website at www.wiley.com/wiley-blackwell

Designations used by companies to distinguish their products are often claimed as trademarks. All brand names and product names used in this book are trade names, service marks, trademarks or registered trademarks of their respective owners. The publisher is not associated with any product or vendor mentioned in this book. It is sold on the understanding that the publisher is not engaged in rendering professional services. If professional advice or other expert assistance is required, the services of a competent professional should be sought.

The contents of this work are intended to further general scientific research, understanding, and discussion only and are not intended and should not be relied upon as recommending or promoting a specific method, diagnosis, or treatment by health science practitioners for any particular patient. The publisher and the author make no representations or warranties with respect to the accuracy or completeness of the contents of this work and specifically disclaim all warranties, including without limitation any implied warranties of fitness for a particular purpose. In view of ongoing research, equipment modifications, changes in governmental regulations, and the constant flow of information relating to the use of medicines, equipment, and devices, the reader is urged to review and evaluate the information provided in the package insert or instructions for each medicine, equipment, or device for, among other things, any changes in the instructions or indication of usage and for added warnings and precautions. Readers should consult with a specialist where appropriate. The fact that an organization or Website is referred to in this work as a citation and/or a potential source of further information does not mean that the author or the publisher endorses the information the organization or Website may provide or recommendations it may make. Further, readers should be aware that Internet Websites listed in this work may have changed or disappeared between when this work was written and when it is read. No warranty may be created or extended by any promotional statements for this work. Neither the publisher nor the author shall be liable for any damages arising herefrom.

Library of Congress Cataloging-in-Publication Data

ABC of alcohol. – Fifth edition / edited by Anne McCune.
    pages   cm
   Includes index.
   ISBN 978-1-118-54479-2 (pbk.)
1. Alcoholism.   2. Alcohol–Physiological effect.   I. McCune, Anne.
   RC565.A23 2015
   616.86′1–dc23

                                 2015000043

A catalogue record for this book is available from the British Library.

Wiley also publishes its books in a variety of electronic formats. Some content that appears in print may not be available in electronic books.

Cover image: © iStockphoto/ersler
Cover design by Andy Meaden.

Set in 9.25/12pt Minion Pro by SPi Global, Pondicherry, India
Printed and bound in Singapore by Markono Print Media Pte Ltd

1   2015

This book is dedicated to Douglas, Cameron and Hamish for their unconditional love and support and to my late dear father, David.

Contents

Contributors

Jane Alty

Consultant Neurologist, Leeds Teaching Hospitals NHS Trust; Honorary Senior Lecturer, University of Leeds, Leeds, UK

Eric Appleby

Formerly Chief Executive, Alcohol Concern, London, UK

Rachel Bradley

Consultant in Elderly Care, University Hospitals Bristol, Bristol Royal Infirmary, Bristol, UK

Adrian Brown

Team Leader, Drug and Alcohol Liaison, Alcohol Specialist Nurse, St George's Healthcare NHS Trust, London, UK

William Christian

Consultant in Paediatric Emergency Medicine, Bristol Royal Hospital for Children, Bristol, UK

Jeremy Cosgrove

Neurology Specialist Registrar, Leeds General Infirmary, Leeds, UK

Anne Frampton

Consultant in Emergency Medicine, Bristol Royal Infirmary, Bristol, UK

Carsten Grimm

General Practitioner; Clinical Lead, Alcohol Treatment Service, Locala CIC Kirklees; RCGP Clinical Lead Alcohol Certificate (job share), RCGP Clinical Commissioning Champion, Kirklees, UK

Dan Harris

Consultant in Emergency Medicine, Kingston Hospital NHS Trust, Kingston upon Thames, Surrey, UK

James S. Huntley

Consultant Orthopaedic Surgeon and Honorary Clinical Associate Professor, School of Medicine, University of Glasgow, Glasgow, UK

Yasmin Ismail

Specialist Registrar in Cardiology, Bristol Heart Institute, Bristol, UK

Paul Jordan

KTP Research Associate, Violence and Society Research Group, Cardiff University School of Dentistry, Cardiff, UK

Nitin Kumar

Cardiology Speciality Registrar, Bristol Heart Institute, Bristol, UK

Anne McCune

Consultant Hepatologist, Department of Hepatology, Bristol Royal Infirmary, University Hospitals Bristol NHS Foundation Trust, Bristol, UK

Peter McGovern

F2 Doctor – Severn Deanery, Queens University Belfast, Belfast, UK

Zulfiquar Mirza

Consultant A&E Medicine, West Middlesex University Hospital, Isleworth, Middlesex, UK

Kieran J. Moriarty

Consultant Gastroenterologist, Alcohol Service Lead, British Society of Gastroenterology, Bolton NHS Foundation Trust, Bolton, UK

Alex Paton

Retired consultant physician, Oxfordshire, UK

Jarrod Richards

North Bristol NHS Trust, Southmead Hospital, Bristol, UK

John B. Saunders

Professor and Consultant Physician in Addiction Medicine and Internal Medicine, Disciplines of Addiction Medicine and Psychiatry, Sydney Medical School, University of Sydney, NSW; and Centre for Youth Substance Abuse Research, Faculty of Health Sciences, University of Queensland, Brisbane, QLD, Australia

Jonathan Shepherd

Vice Dean, Professor of Oral and Maxillofacial Surgery, Cardiff University School of Dentistry, Cardiff, UK

Julian Strange

Consultant Cardiologist, Bristol Heart Institute, Bristol, UK

Nicola Taylor
Clinical Teaching Fellow, Honorary Clinical Lecturer, University of Bristol, Bristol, UK

Robin Touquet
Emeritus Professor of Emergency Medicine, Imperial College London, London, UK

Sian Veysey
Consultant in Emergency Medicine, Bristol Royal Infirmary, Bristol, UK

Sarah L. Williams
Senior health information officer, Cancer Research UK, London, UK

Preface to fifth edition

It is now more than 10 years since the last edition of the *ABC of Alcohol* was published and I was honoured to be asked to take over the editorial reigns for this new publication from Alex Paton and Robin Touquet, both of whom have enjoyed very successful and illustrious medical careers whilst maintaining a passion and boundless enthusiasm for informing and educating on alcohol-related illnesses.

The remit and spirit of the book remains strongly the same however and both Alex and Robin's wise words continue to influence this present edition. All three of us remain committed to educating new generations of medical and nursing students, hospital and primary care trainees and allied health practitioners on the harms associated with alcohol misuse. The new edition should also appeal to the experienced alcohol nurse specialist and perhaps those relatively new to the alcohol field, such as social workers and commissioners.

Sadly, the effects of alcohol misuse pervades every aspect of society and the fact alcohol is now the biggest single global risk factor of a man dying before the age of 60 is quite staggering. The recent *NCEPOD* report (*Measuring the Units 2013*) is a sobering and troubling account of the quality of care provided to patients who died of alcohol-related liver disease in the United Kingdom. As a liver specialist, I am perhaps allowed a little indulgence in highlighting this report but do so not lightly as the central theme is one of repeated missed opportunities and avoidable failings around screening and recognition of alcohol harm on the 'shop floor'. Disappointingly in less than half of admitted patients was an adequate alcohol history recorded, or a risk assessment of dependence or withdrawal undertaken. As a matter of routine, all patients presenting to hospital services should be routinely screened for alcohol misuse and all clinical staff should be competent in undertaking a simple assessment of dependence and withdrawal. Sadly, many healthcare professionals continue to neglect this important task, sometimes because they do not think it is part of their role, but more often than not because they lack the necessary skills and confidence to do so. This new edition of the *ABC of Alcohol* is designed in part to refocus on this unmet training need.

The majority of the chapters in this edition have been extensively revised and refreshed but there are also 10 new informative chapters as well. The text, although concise, can in no way be considered lightweight and am sure will remain an invaluable companion for all those working alongside people with alcohol-related problems whilst appealing to both the experienced and novice practitioner alike.

Special thanks must go to the leading clinical specialists and academics who have contributed to the book, responding admirably to my vision and delivering far more than I imagined possible from the outset. I am indebted also to the staff of the publishers Wiley who guided me throughout this editorial journey and were wholeheartedly supportive of my request for an expanded edition, for which I am eternally grateful.

Anne McCune
February 2015

Preface to the fourth edition

It is 10 years since the last edition of *ABC of Alcohol* was published, and problems from misuse of alcohol have not gone away; indeed, they are statistically more frequent than they were then. An epidemic of binge drinking, a sharp rise in drinking by women, who are particularly vulnerable to physical damage, and increasing violence associated with alcohol are current causes of concern. Given the number of calories in alcoholic drinks, it may not be too fanciful to suggest that alcohol contributes to the present epidemic of obesity. Like most of the population, we enjoy a drink, but having witnessed the many harms caused by overindulgence, we have tried to produce an introduction to alcohol and its effects that will not only inform health professionals but may be of use to involved lay people and governments wanting evidence to back up action.

When *ABC of Alcohol* was first published, the objective was to encourage doctors to regard alcohol misuse as a legitimate part of professional practice. Unfortunately, that aim has not been realised fully: in some quarters, the feeling is still that doctors should not get involved. This is largely because of lack of knowledge about how misuse of alcohol affects society and people and thus a lack of confidence in tackling misuse. *ABC of Alcohol* is designed to remedy this and to show that sympathetic management of people with problems, especially if detected early, can be a rewarding experience.

Every medical school should cover prevention and management of alcohol misuse, teaching opportunities abound in every hospital department and in general practice. Existing chapters of *ABC of Alcohol* have been revised extensively, and important sections have been added on the impact of alcohol on accident and emergency departments and most types of surgical practice, as well as the potential dangers of alcohol's interaction with drugs – legal and illegal. Alcohol misuse is indeed every doctor's business.

Finally, we have received encouraging comments in the past about the value of *ABC of Alcohol* from health and social professionals in all disciplines. As there are now some 500 voluntary alcohol agencies in England and Wales that deal with alcohol problems, which are more often social than medical, we have tried where possible to broaden the 'doctor–patient' model to encompass alcohol workers and their clients. We believe that the future success of alcohol services depends on much closer cooperation between doctors and workers in the alcohol field; the latter should be able to make their expertise available to primary care trusts and hospitals.

Special thanks are due to Sally Carter for her close involvement and constructive help and to Samuel Groom for technological support in the preparation of this new edition.

Alex Paton
Robin Touquet

CHAPTER 1

Alcohol use: Consumption and costs

Peter McGovern and Eric Appleby

OVERVIEW

- The changing face of alcohol consumption around the world.
- Global alcohol morbidity and mortality.
- The growing burden and impact of alcohol misuse in the developing world.
- The rising health costs of alcohol at home and abroad.

Alcohol misuse is an issue that expands beyond its physical and psychological consequences. Overconsumption of, and addiction to alcohol, is a global health challenge. The social consequences of alcohol transcend class and its impact at the individual and population levels are of equal importance. At home it is a burden on the NHS budget (Figure 1.1) and abroad an issue that stifles development in resource-poor countries. It is through understanding the nature of excessive consumption that health professionals can act as advocates for the best use of resources at home and abroad.

Patterns of consumption

Although the United Kingdom over the past century has never been more than a moderate consumer in terms of the total amount of alcohol drunk per capita, it is nevertheless considered to have one of the more problematic relationships with alcohol, as a result of the drinking patterns and style that have developed. For the first half of the 20th century, the United Kingdom was relatively abstemious, but the decades after the Second World War saw a rapid increase, with per capita consumption almost doubling. This rise was highest within northern regions of the United Kingdom and was a divergence from the downward trend in southern European consumption. More recently the United Kingdom has reason to be positive in terms of alcohol consumption. Since 2008, there has been a downward trend in the proportion of adults drinking. In 1998, 75% of men and 59% of women had consumed alcohol in the week prior to a department of health interview. In 2011 this proportion dropped to 66% (men) and 54% (women). Over the past decade, there has been a 16% decline in the number of children of

school age admitting to regular alcohol consumption. Attitudes are also changing, with fewer young people (9% between 2003 and 2010) agreeing that it was acceptable for a person of school age to get drunk. Unfortunately this shift has yet to translate into a reduction in accident and emergency (A&E) attendances in this age group.

Baby boomer boozers

The cohort of problem drinkers in the United Kingdom however is changing rapidly. Costly healthcare impacts of the binge drinking culture of the 1990's were traditionally associated with 16 to 24 year olds. This demographic have now been surpassed by 55 to 74 year olds, costing £825.6 million in hospital admissions per year, 10 times that of their younger counterparts. This group of middle aged, and often middle-class drinkers, consistently drink above recommended limits and have the greatest complex care needs. Despite rising consumption within this age group (often parents), there has been a parallel decrease in alcohol consumption among young people. The cultural phenomenon of binge drinking remains a pervasive force for young people but is less likely in children with stronger school bonds that are bought alcohol by their parents, rather than their own expendable income (Bellis et al., 2007).

Alcohol and low- and middle-income countries

A large proportion of global alcohol consumption (24.8%) is home-made, produced illegally or sold outside of normal governmental controls. This unrecorded alcohol is much more prevalent in low- and middle-income countries where unregulated production often outweighs regulated brewers. In the eastern Mediterranean region and South East Asia, it amounts to more than 50% of consumption (WHO, 2014). Home-made spirits make up a particularly high proportion of consumption in India. The alcohol consumption rates of early economic development can worsen despite a shift to commercial alcohol production. A review by Riley and Marshall of middle-income countries showed that with economic development, the shift to industrial beverages can lead to more sustained drinking patterns within the population. Thus, alcohol is increasingly being identified as a health challenge that is part of a wider epidemiological shift to a non-communicable disease burden in resource-poor settings.

ABC of Alcohol, Fifth Edition. Edited by Anne McCune.
© 2015 John Wiley & Sons, Ltd. Published 2015 by John Wiley & Sons, Ltd.

Alcohol-related healthcare costs in Manchester were an estimated £39.1 m, equating to £95 per adult

£9.3 m	£25.1 m	£4.7 m
Cost of A&E (accident & emergency) attendances	Cost of inpatient admissions	Cost of outpatient attendances

Cost of alcohol-related inpatient admissions by cause

£9.4 m	£15.8 m
Admissions wholly attributable to alcohol	Admissions partly attributable to alcohol

Cost of alcohol-related inpatient admissions by gender

£16.7 m	£8.4 m
Male inpatient admissions cost	Female inpatient admissions cost

Cost of alcohol-related inpatient admissions by age

£1 m	£9.9 m	£9.8 m	£4.5 m
16–24 year olds	25–54 year olds	55–74 year olds	75+ year olds

The inpatient admissions and A&E attendances data in this map is for 2010/11. Estimates for outpatient attendances are based on benchmarks from the Birmingham Heavy Drinkers Project (1997 to 2004), The General Lifestyle Survey (2009) and the number of high risk drinkers taken from Local Alcohol Profiles (LAPE) (2005) estimates. 2010–11 costs were applied to estimate outpatient attendance costs.

Figure 1.1 From the alcohol harm map 2013: City of Manchester. Source: Alcohol Concern (2013). Reproduced by permission of Alcohol Concern.

Currently the highest level of alcohol consumption is found in the high-income Western world (Figure 1.2), but this is partly due to a higher level of abstention across Africa and South East Asia. This hides the fact that regions with high abstention rates in the developing world and low average alcohol intake per capita often have the highest consumption per drinker. Any future reduction in abstention rates worldwide could result in a large increase in the global burden of disease from alcohol.

Morbidity and mortality

That the effects of long-term heavy drinking can be serious and even fatal is generally well known. Less well known is the range of medical conditions to which alcohol contributes (Figure 1.3) and the relatively low levels of consumption at which the risk of harm begins to be important. The relationship between alcohol and health is complex. Alcohol-*related disease* has a direct dose–response relation: the greater the amount drunk, the more the harm done. This applies to liver cirrhosis, hypertension, and haemorrhagic stroke. Alcohol-*attributable disease* results from a series of factors that can be 'related to levels and patterns of consumption but also other factors such as culture, regulation and beverage quality' (WHO, 2011). These are deaths that would not have happened without the presence of alcohol. In cardiovascular disease a modest beneficial effect had been reported with moderate amounts of alcohol; however, recent research suggests that any benefit had

been overestimated and the so-called protective effect is losing favour among experts.

In 2012, 3.3 million deaths globally were attributable to alcohol (WHO, 2014), which amounts to 5.9% of global deaths in the year. This is greater than the proportion of deaths from HIV/AIDS, violence and tuberculosis combined. The incidence of alcohol-related mortality is highest among men (7.6% total deaths). This is believed to be due to higher levels of associated violence, injury, and cardiovascular disease. In the same year, 139 million disability-adjusted life years (DALYs) were attributed to alcohol consumption across the world, which is 5.1% of the global burden of disease. Alcohol is the third leading cause of disability in high-income countries after smoking and hypertension. Robust data have been notoriously difficult to collect due to doctors' reluctance to certify alcohol as a cause of death and difficulty defining the contribution of alcohol. In the United Kingdom, alcohol accounts for 10% of the burden of disease as measured by DALYs. Fifteen thousand deaths a year in England are caused by alcohol (3% of total deaths) with only 21% of these deaths due to alcohol-related cirrhosis.

On a global scale, greater economic wealth results in a larger alcohol-attributable burden in keeping with the associated higher consumption in these areas. However the new 'Global Status Report on Alcohol and Health 2014' from the WHO suggests that this relationship may be more complex, with a trend developing in low-income countries, with traditionally lower consumption, having a higher alcohol-attributable burden of disease per litre of alcohol

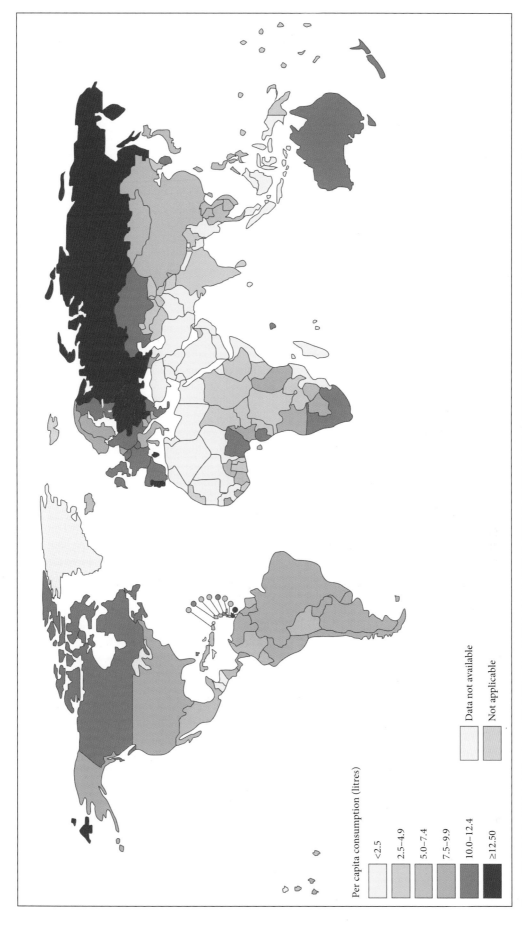

Figure 1.2 Total alcohol per capita consumption (15+ years; in litres of pure alcohol), 2010. Source: WHO (2014). Reproduced with permission from the World Health Organization.

Per capita consumption (litres)

<2.5

2.5–4.9

5.0–7.4

7.5–9.9

10.0–12.4

≥12.50

Data not available

Not applicable

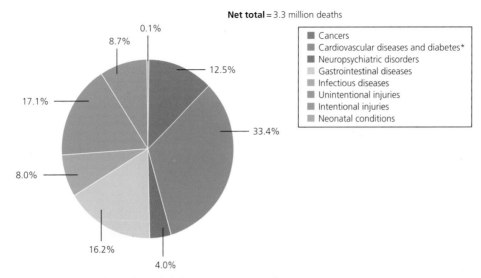

*Including beneficial effects of low risk drinking patterns on some diseases.

Figure 1.3 Distribution of alcohol-attributable deaths, as a percentage of all alcohol-attributable deaths by broad disease category, 2012. Source: WHO (2014). Reproduced with permission from the World Health Organization.

consumed (WHO, 2014). This is thought to be in keeping with more risky patterns of drinking. Worryingly, middle-income countries expanding economically, such as India and China, have relatively high and increasing alcohol-related consumption and mortality (Figure 1.4). The highest alcohol-related mortality is in the Russian Federation and neighbouring countries where every fifth death among men is attributable to alcohol. In parts of Siberia this figure rises to more than one in two male deaths (Zaridze, 2009). In Russia, surrogate alcohols (not designed for drinking) feature highly as a cause for alcohol-related harm and surgical spirits and perfumes are both popular and particularly harmful. They are often twice as potent as vodka and with specific health risks, such as blindness and act as an important black market commodity. Since the dissolution of the Soviet state the biggest shift in drinking pattern has been in the consumption of beer (only classified as an alcoholic drink in 2013). Foreign breweries entered the Russian market in 1995 and beer consumption has increased from 15 l per year (per capita) to 81 l. This increase in consumption is unequalled by any other nation.

Burdens and costs

Unfortunately the recent shift in UK attitudes to drinking has not resulted in a lower health expenditure on alcohol. Alcohol-related hospital admissions have rocketed by 40% since 2003. A total of 198,900 admissions in 2010–2011 had alcohol as the primary diagnosis (Figure 1.5) and 1,168,300 admissions were to some degree attributable to alcohol, leaving the cost of alcohol-related harm to the NHS at £3.5 billion per year (2009–2010 costs) (Figure 1.6). The full economic impact of alcohol misuse has a wider scope than just healthcare costs, and the obvious loss to society due to premature deaths. Perhaps the most insidious and costly aspect of alcohol misuse is lost productivity, costing the UK £7.3 billion a year. Secondary costs resulting from social care, drink driving, and other alcohol-related crimes place the overall

estimate of cost to society at £25.1 billion in the United Kingdom alone (Department of Health, 2007).

The cost to the individual is devastating; in England the average years of life lost for men and women dying from alcohol-attributable conditions was 20 and 15 years, respectively (Department of Health, 2005). Although the association between alcohol and mental health problems is complex, links are indisputable. People who have a pre-existing mental health problem are more likely to drink hazardously than those without, and people who drink hazardously are more likely to develop a mental health problem than those who do not.

In resource-poor settings, the higher burden of alcohol-related disease and injury per litre of alcohol consumed is in part explained by lower socioeconomic status, poorer diet, and deprivation in general. Alcohol misuse in low- and middle-income countries has also been shown to have a causal relationship with infectious disease such as tuberculosis and pneumonia, as alcohol depresses the immune system leaving drinkers more susceptible to these endemic infections associated with poverty.

In primary care there has been a drive over the past decade to identify problem drinkers. 'Identification and brief advice' interventions (IBAs), where patients answer screening questions and are then given advice on the risks of their consumption as well as advice on how to cut down are common practice. IBAs have proven benefit in reducing alcohol consumption in primary care settings, and these positive effects can last up to 48 months after the consultation. This approach has been combined with wider access to alcohol liaison services in hospitals and to some extent in the community.

The interaction between the health service and alcohol misuse is by no means confined to the hospital ward or GP surgery. Anyone familiar with emergency departments, particularly on a weekend evening, will know that doctors, nurses and increasingly security staff spend considerable time not just treating patients but controlling the behaviour of those who are extremely intoxicated and have received an injury or been assaulted. Similarly, ambulance

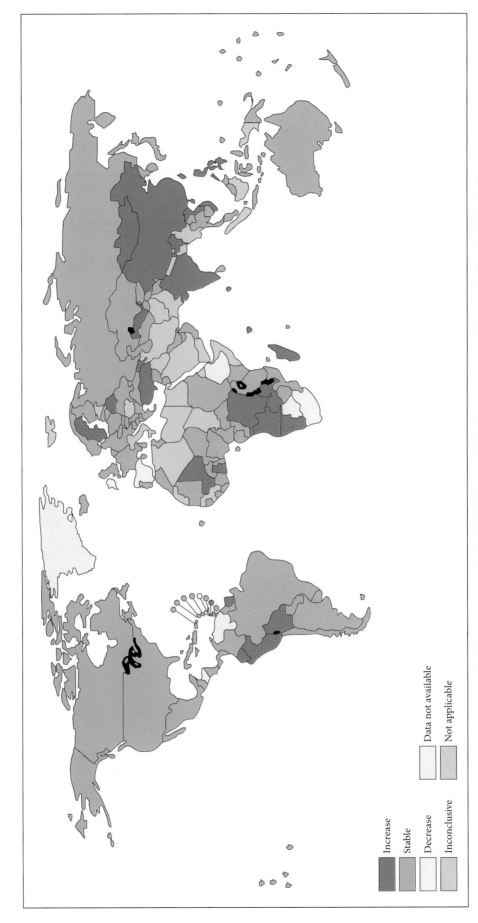

Figure 1.4 Five-year change in recorded alcohol per capita (15+ years) consumption, 2006–2010. Source: WHO (2014). Reproduced with permission from the World Health Organization.

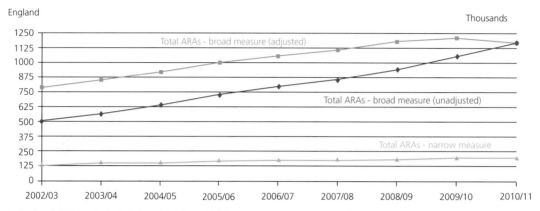

Figure 1.5 Alcohol-related NHS hospital admissions (ARAs) 2002/2003 to 2010/2011. Source: Health and Social Care Information Centre (2012).

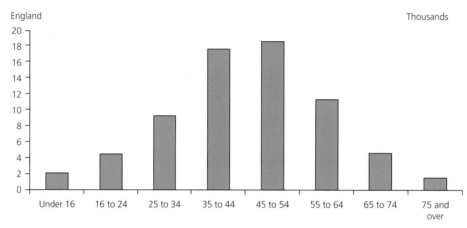

Figure 1.6 Number of hospital admissions where there was a primary diagnosis of a disease or condition wholly attributable to alcohol, by age, 2010/2011. Source: Health and Social Care Information Centre (2012).

paramedics estimate that most of their work at these times involves dealing with the aftermath of drinking.

Public opinion and governmental policy has been centred on public order issues and anti-social behaviour associated with alcohol misuse. This focus risks inattention and lack of investment in the insidious and growing health costs of alcohol.

Further reading

Alcohol Concern. *Alcohol harm map.* 2013. http://www.alcoholconcern.org.uk/campaign/alcohol-harm-map (accessed 18 September 2014).

Bellis MA, Hughes K, Morleo M, Tocque K, Hughes S, Allen T, et al. Predictors of risky alcohol consumption in schoolchildren and their implications for preventing alcohol-related harm. *Substance Abuse Treatment, Prevention, and Policy* 2007;2(15):1–10.

Centre for Excellence and Outcomes in Children and Young People's Services. *Reducing alcohol consumption by young people and so improve their health, safety and wellbeing.* London: Centre for Excellence and Outcomes in Children and Young People's Services, 2010.

House of Commons – Health Committee. *Government's alcohol strategy: third report of session 2012–2013,* Volume I, HC 132 Incorporating HC 1928-i, Session 2010–12. London: House of Commons – Health Committee, 2012.

The Association of Public Health Observatories. *Indications of public health in the English regions: alcohol.* York: The Association of Public Health Observatories, 2007.

The British Psychological Society and The Royal College of Psychiatrists. *Alcohol use disorders: diagnosis, assessment and management of harmful drinking and alcohol dependence* (National Clinical Practice Guideline 115). Leicester: The British Psychological Society, and London: The Royal College of Psychiatrists, 2011.

The Health and Social Care Information Centre & North West Public Health Observatory. *Hospital episode statistics.* Leeds: The Health and Social Care Information Centre & North West Public Health Observatory, 2012.

The NHS Information Centre for Health and Social Care. *Statistics on alcohol: England, 2012.* Leeds: The NHS Information Centre for Health and Social Care, 2012.

Riley L, Marshall M, eds. *Alcohol and public health in eight developing countries.* Geneva: World Health Organisation, 1999.

Walker S. Russia's alcohol problem. *British Medical Journal* 2011;342:d5240.

World Health Organization (WHO). *Global status report on alcohol and health – 2014.* Geneva: World Health Organization, 2014. http://apps.who.int/iris/bitstream/10665/112736/1/9789240692763_eng.pdf?ua=1 (accessed 18 September 2014).

Zaridze D. Alcohol and cause-specific mortality in Russia. A retrospective case-control study of 48,557 deaths. *Lancet* 2009;373:2201–14.

CHAPTER 2

Alcohol use: Society and politics

Peter McGovern and Eric Appleby

> **OVERVIEW**
>
> • The social impacts of alcohol misuse.
> • Perspectives on the role of public policy in alcohol misuse.
> • Was the 2003 licensing act a success?
> • The future of UK alcohol policy.

Excessive alcohol consumption has wider implications for a society than just its costly health impact. Debate in recent years around the role of alcohol in society has increasingly centred on its social consequences. Alcohol misuse has a role in violent crime, road deaths and family breakups. This generates a culture of insecurity and fear even among those that have not yet suffered directly. Politically the misuse of alcohol has become synonymous with visible antisocial, often violent behaviour, and this in turn has been the focus of governmental alcohol policy. In the 2012 Crime Survey, 32% of British people experienced this behaviour at least once a week. This desire to quell alcohol-related disorderly behaviour in public spaces may serve political expediency but will do little to solve the hidden epidemic of alcohol-fuelled abuse and violence that occurs in the home which can pervade an individual's or family's private life.

Crime and disorder

It is widely acknowledged that alcohol is a significant risk factor for both perpetrating and being a victim of violent crime. The 2012 Crime Survey for England and Wales noted that there were over 1 million violent alcohol-related crimes in the past year. In 2010, although 50% of all victims of violent crime believed that their attacker was under the influence of alcohol, the majority of crimes will never be reported to the police. One Home Office survey found that only half of people considered themselves a victim of crime and one-third felt that alcohol related crime was 'something that just happens'. Perhaps this nonchalance signifies the normalisation and acceptance of assault associated with the excess consumption of alcohol.

Domestic violence and rape

There is no evidence of a direct causal relationship between domestic abuse and alcohol consumption (Galvani, 2004) – perpetrators can be abusive even when sober. However, drinking is known to increase the frequency and seriousness of incidents. A 2010 study by Gilchrist found that 73% of documented perpetrators of domestic violence had been drinking at the time of the attack. The American Medical Association estimated 75% of partners of alcoholics have been threatened and 45% assaulted. Sadly the victims of domestic abuse also drink more, most likely because alcohol is used as a coping strategy. Similarly sexual assaults often take place when one or both parties have been drinking. More than half of those convicted of rape had been drinking at the time of the offense.

On the road

In 2011, there were 280 deaths on UK roads, 1290 serious injuries and 10,000 casualties related to drink-and-drive incidents. A UK campaign over the past 30 years to curb drink-driving culture has been widely regarded as a success, and the casualties have dropped dramatically over the past three decades. Despite this success, one in six of all road deaths are due to alcohol and 80,000 people a year in the United Kingdom are caught above the legal limit (Figure 2.1). The worst offenders are male, who have nine out of every ten of convictions for dangerous driving under the influence of alcohol. Younger drivers 17–24 have the highest level of drink-drive crashes per distance travelled.

The evidence base for reduction of the current legal blood alcohol level in the United Kingdom (currently 80 mg/100 ml) is strengthening. Most drivers will be impaired at blood alcohol levels above 50 mg/100 ml and are six times more likely to be involved in a fatal accident. In European terms, the United Kingdom now stands with just Malta as the only other country to tolerate levels above this (Figure 2.2) after Ireland reduced its legal limit to 50 mg/100 ml in 2011. It is estimated that a reduction of the legal limit would save 65 lives per year and prevent 230 serious injuries in the United Kingdom. In Northern Ireland, ministers have discussed going a

---

ABC of Alcohol, Fifth Edition. Edited by Anne McCune.
© 2015 John Wiley & Sons, Ltd. Published 2015 by John Wiley & Sons, Ltd.

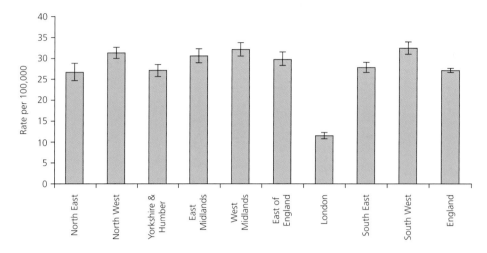

Note: Adjusted for under-reporting

Figure 2.1 Rate of casualties from road accidents involving illegal levels of alcohol by region. Source: Association of Public Health Observatories (2007).

step further than 50 mg/100 ml and place a 20 mg/100 ml limit on younger drivers and those that drive as a profession.

Children and families

If the impact of drink driving is an obvious marker of alcohol misuse, the effect of heavy drinking on families and social networks is much more subtle. One or more problematic drinkers in a family can lead to the breakdown of relationships and the family unit. A third of petitions for divorce cite excessive drinking by a partner as a contributory factor. Alcohol is also a risk factor for the neglect, and in some cases abuse, of children. A total of 40% of child protection cases and 74% of child mistreatment cases in the United Kingdom are alcohol related. Parents who drink heavily may have an impact on their children's mental well-being, educational attainment, and ability to develop normal friendships.

The politics and policy of alcohol

Can public policy curb our alcohol problem?

The first documented public policy intervention on alcohol was during the Xia dynasty in China 2070 BC. This took the form of prohibition, later popularised in 20th-century America and supported by the Quaker movement in the United Kingdom. Prohibition in America resulted in a black market of alcohol, a surge in organised crime and the rise of the speakeasy (illicit bars and nightclubs) (Figure 2.3). This global temperance movement is regarded by some as an example of heavy-handed state interference.

Modern Western governments have shifted away from a prohibitive stance but maintain a variety of approaches toward alcohol regulation and policy. These range from liberal licensing laws in the United Kingdom to the strict government monopoly of the 'System Bolaget' in Sweden. The overall global direction of policy is crystallised in the World Health Organisation's 2011 10-point global strategy to reduce the harmful use of alcohol:

1 Leadership, awareness and commitment
2 Health services' response
3 Community action
4 Drink-driving policies and countermeasures
5 Availability of alcohol
6 Marketing of alcoholic beverages
7 Pricing policies
8 Reducing the negative consequences of drinking and alcohol intoxication
9 Reducing the public health impact of illicit alcohol and informally produced alcohol
10 Monitoring and surveillance

Behind the often heavy rhetoric of alcohol policy is a pragmatic acknowledgement that the alcohol industry is an important part of the global economy. In the United Kingdom, the alcoholic drinks industry pays £15 billion per year in excise duty alone, employs 650,000 people and supports a further 1.1 million jobs in the wider economy (Alcohol Industry Joint Submission-Budget 2009). Policy on alcohol needs to be based on, and directed at, a wider societal benefit rather than just an economic gain. Babor points out in his 2003 paper that 'policy has been incremental, deliberate and accepting of adults drinking in moderation'. Preventative rather than prohibitive policy has generally had three strands: attitude change, health education and beverage availability.

Cafe culture – a dream not realised

The 2003 Licensing Act was designed to revolutionise the way in which the UK population consumed alcohol. The act extended the hours in which licensed premises could trade, ending the regimen of 'permitted hours'. This was hoped to reduce the number of people being disgorged onto the streets at a common (and, arguably, early) closing time. Government claimed it would help increase the diversity of evening and late night venues, and aid the development of a Parisian cafe culture often associated with more moderated drinking habits. The first review of the act in 2008 showed a mixed picture. There was a small fall in serious violent crime but a limited impact on crime overall and worryingly evidence that crime in the early hours of the morning is increasing. The British public also still readily identify alcohol as a leading cause of anti-social behaviour (Figure 2.4). There has yet to be a discernible change in diversity of

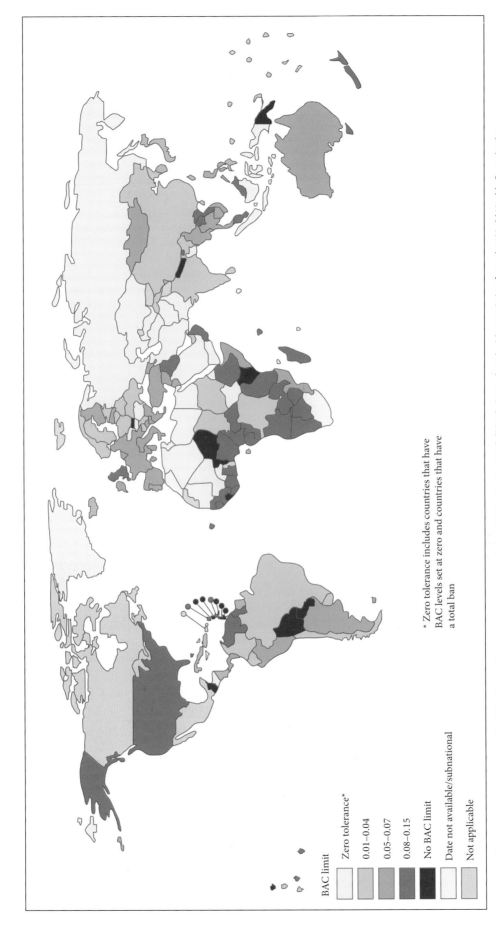

BAC limit

Zero tolerance*

0.01–0.04

0.05–0.07

0.08–0.15

No BAC limit

Date not available/subnational

Not applicable

* Zero tolerance includes countries that have
BAC levels set at zero and countries that have
a total ban

Figure 2.2 Blood alcohol concentration (BAC) limits for drivers in the general population, 2012. Source: WHO (2014). Reproduced with permission from the World Health Organization.

evening and late night venues holding a license and perhaps the biggest failing, on average across regions no clear improvements on dispersal from premises. Enforcement of the act has also been a concern. Although it is an offence under the act to serve alcohol to a drunk person in 2010, there were only three related convictions.

Figure 2.3 American prohibition poster 1920 (source unknown).

Minimum pricing and the multi-buy

Until now in the United Kingdom, price regulation of alcohol has mainly been achieved by taxation alone; however, there is growing evidence for the benefits of a minimum price set for alcohol alongside regulation prohibiting selling of multi-buy options where alcohol is discounted based on purchase of larger quantities. In 2012, the government made clear its desire to pursue this policy; however as yet, it has not come to fruition. A minimum price would likely be set at between 40p and 50p per unit of alcohol. University of Sheffield research estimates that a 50p unit, alongside bans on multi-buy options would reduce consumption by 7.8% as well as reducing hospital admissions by 13% at full effect. Although minimum pricing of 50p was set to be introduced in Scotland it has faced a long legal battle, waged by the whiskey industry, resulting in the case being referred to the European court of Justice in April 2014. Opposition in Westminster, to a lower minimum price of 45p resulted in the shelving of the policy in 2013 and cast doubt on any eventual implementation in England and Wales, leaving the government with a very limited strategy on alcohol.

Proponents of the policy say that this is an intervention targeted at the misuse of alcohol and hits the heaviest drinkers, while having a minimal effect on moderate consumers. Those opposed fear that this 'sin tax' is regressive and discriminates against poorer consumers already hit by a general rise in the cost of living, while leaving drinks consumed by the rich untouched (Snowdon, 2012). Minimum pricing is estimated to have a proportionately lesser effect on crime (2% reduction at 50p) because the young adult male population, most associated with alcohol related crime, consumes the majority of their alcohol on licensed premises.

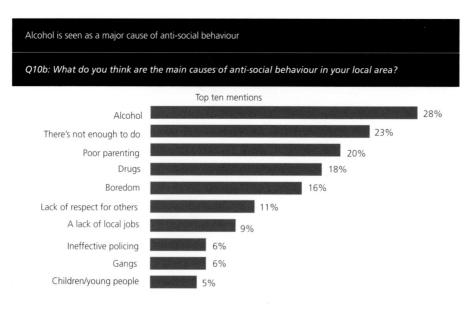

Base: 9.311 individuals in England and Wales recorded as having called the police to report anti-social behaviour in September 2011. Fieldwork dates: 9 February–22 March 2012.

Figure 2.4 Alcohol is seen as a major cause of antisocial behaviour. Source: HMIC (2012).

'Oh demon alcohol'

In 1971, The Kinks sang about what a shame it was to become 'a slave to demon alcohol'. In the four decades since, the United Kingdom has yet to devise radical policy that is fit to grapple with the growing health and societal costs of alcohol misuse. The biggest challenge remains balancing the economic costs and benefits of reform alongside pressure from a powerful and growing alcohol industry. The Prime Minister's 2012 Alcohol Strategy makes it clear that 'The responsibility of being in government isn't always about doing the popular thing (but) about doing the right thing.' To reduce the annual bill of £25.1 billion and limit the damage alcohol misuse causes individuals and communities throughout the United Kingdom, it surely has become time to act.

Further reading

Alcohol Industry Joint Submission-Budget. A submission on behalf of five trade associations representing the UK alcoholic drinks sector, 2009.

Babor TF, Caetano R, Casswell S, Edwards G, Giesbrecht N, Graham K, et al. *Alcohol: no ordinary commodity*. Oxford: Oxford University Press, 2003.

Bertholet N, Daeppen JB, Wietlisbach V, Fleming M, Burnand B. Reduction of alcohol consumption by brief alcohol interventions in primary care: systematic review and meta-analysis. *Archives of Internal Medicine* 2005; 165(9):986–95.

Department for Culture, Media and Sport. *First review of the 2003 Licensing Act*. London: Department for Culture, Media and Sport, 2007.

Galvani S. Responsible disinhibition: alcohol, men and violence to women. *Addiction, Research and Theory* 2004;12(4):357–371.

Galvani S. *Grasping the nettle: alcohol and domestic violence*. London: Alcohol Concern, 2010.

Gilchrist G. The association between intimate partner violence, alcohol and depression in family practice. *BMC Family Practice* 2010;11:72.

Her Majesty's Inspectorate of Constabulary (HMIC). *A step in the right direction. The policing of antisocial behaviour*. Edinburgh: HMIC, 2012. http://www.hmic.gov.uk/media/a-step-in-the-right-direction-the-policing-of-anti-social-behaviour.pdf (last accessed July 2014).

House of Commons – Health Committee. *Government's alcohol strategy: third report of session 2012–2013*, Volume I. London: House of Commons – Health Committee, 2012.

McMurran M. *Alcohol-related violence: prevention and treatment*. Chichester: Wiley-Blackwell, 2013.

Meng Y, Hill-McManus D, Brennan A. *Model-based appraisal of alcohol minimum pricing and off-licensed trade discount bans in Scotland using the Sheffield alcohol policy model*. Sheffield: University of Sheffield, January 2012.

NHS Information Centre for Health and Social Care. *Statistics on alcohol: England, 2012*. Leeds: The NHS Information Centre for Health and Social Care, 2012.

Scally G. Crunch time for the government on alcohol pricing in England. *BMJ* 2013;346:f1784.

Snowdon C. *The wages of sin taxes*. London: The Adam Smith Institute, 2012.

The Association of Public Health Observatories. *Indications of public health in the English regions: alcohol*. York: The Association of Public Health Observatories, 2007.

World Health Organization. *Global status report on alcohol and health – 2014*. Geneva: World Health Organization, 2014. http://apps.who.int/iris/bitstream/10665/112736/1/9789240692763_eng.pdf?ua=1 (accessed 18 September 2014).

CHAPTER 3

Alcohol in the body

Alex Paton and Anne McCune

OVERVIEW

- Alcohol is a small, water-soluble molecule and is absorbed from the stomach and small intestine.
- Alcohol is distributed throughout water in the body, so that most tissues are exposed to the same concentration as the blood.
- Women have higher blood and tissue alcohol levels than men of the same weight as their body water (volume of distribution) is smaller.
- More than 90% of alcohol is metabolised and eliminated in the liver.
- Alcohol is a sedative and mild anaesthetic.
- Even at low blood alcohol concentration, fine motor tasks, coordination, and decision-making are impaired. At 80 mg/100 ml (17.4 mmol/l) – the current legal limit for driving in the United Kingdom – the risk of road accident more than doubles.

Alcohol (ethanol) is a drug, and health professionals should know something of its physiological and pathological effects and its handling by the body. It is a small, water-soluble molecule that is relatively slowly absorbed from the stomach, more rapidly absorbed from the small intestine, and freely distributed throughout the body. Rate of absorption depends on a number of factors: it is quickest, for example, when alcohol is drunk on an empty stomach and the concentration of alcohol is 20–30% (Figure 3.1).

Thus, sherry, with an alcohol concentration of about 20% increases the levels of alcohol in blood more rapidly than beer (3–8%), while spirits (40%) delay gastric emptying and inhibit absorption. Drinks aerated with carbon dioxide – for example, whisky and soda and champagne – get into the system quicker.

Food, and particularly carbohydrates, retards absorption: blood concentrations may not reach a quarter of those achieved on an empty stomach. The pleasurable effects of alcohol are best achieved with a meal or when alcohol is drunk diluted in the case of spirits.

Alcoholic drinks are a major source of calories: for example, six pints of beer contain about 500 kcal and half a litre of whisky contains 1650 kcal. The daily energy requirement for a moderately active man is 3000 kcal, and for a woman it is 2200 kcal. Alcohol is distributed throughout the water in the body so that most tissues – such as the heart, brain, and muscles – are exposed to the same concentration of alcohol as the blood (Figure 3.2). The exception is the liver, where exposure is greater because blood is received direct from the stomach and small bowel via the portal vein. Alcohol diffuses rather slowly, except into organs with a rich blood supply such as the brain and lungs. Very little alcohol enters fat because of the latter's poor solubility, so blood and tissue concentrations are higher in women, who have more subcutaneous fat and a smaller blood volume, than in men, even when the amount of alcohol consumed is adjusted for body weight. Women also may have lower levels of alcohol dehydrogenases in the stomach than men, so that less alcohol is metabolised before absorption. Alcohol enters the fetus readily through the placenta and is eliminated by maternal metabolism. Blood alcohol concentration varies according to sex, size and body build, phase of the menstrual cycle (it is highest premenstrually and at ovulation), previous exposure to alcohol, type of drink, whether alcohol is taken with food or drugs such as cimetidine (which inhibits gastric alcohol dehydrogenase) and antihistamines, phenothiazines and metoclopramide (which enhance gastric emptying, thus increasing absorption).

Metabolism of alcohol

More than 90% of alcohol is eliminated by the liver; 2–5% is excreted unchanged in urine, sweat, or breath. The first step in metabolism is oxidation by alcohol dehydrogenases (ADH), of which at least four isoenzymes exist, to acetaldehyde in the presence of cofactors (see Figure 3.3). In healthy people, nearly all of the acetaldehyde, a highly reactive and toxic substance, is oxidised rapidly by aldehyde dehydrogenases (ALDHs) to harmless acetate. Several isoenzymes of ALDH exist, one of which is missing in about 50% of Japanese people and possibly other south Asian people (but unusually in Caucasians).

Unpleasant symptoms of headache, nausea, flushing and tachycardia are experienced by people who lack ALDHs and who drink; this is believed to be because of accumulation of acetaldehyde. Under normal circumstances, acetate is oxidised in liver and peripheral tissues to carbon dioxide and water.

ABC of Alcohol, Fifth Edition. Edited by Anne McCune.
© 2015 John Wiley & Sons, Ltd. Published 2015 by John Wiley & Sons, Ltd.

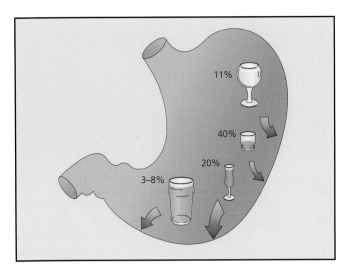

Figure 3.1 Rate of absorption of alcohol is quickest on an empty stomach, and the concentration of alcohol is between 20 and 30%.

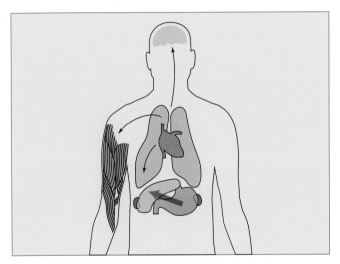

Figure 3.2 Alcohol is distributed throughout the body water so that most tissues, such as heart, brain, and muscles, are exposed to the same concentration as is in the blood.

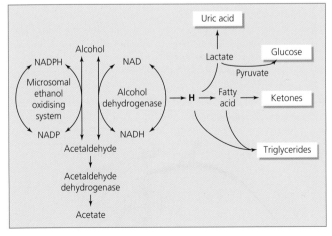

Figure 3.3 Metabolism of ethanol. Source: Data from Lieber (1978).

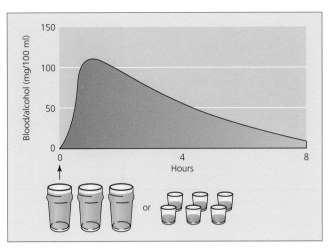

Figure 3.4 Concentrations of alcohol in the blood after six units of alcohol (in this illustration, three pints of beer or three double whiskies).

On an empty stomach, blood alcohol concentration peaks about 1 h after consumption, depending on the amount drunk; it then declines in a more or less linear manner for the next 4 h (Figure 3.4). Alcohol is removed from the blood at a rate of about 15 mg/100 ml/h, but this varies in different people, on different drinking occasions, and with the amount of alcohol drunk. At a blood alcohol concentration of 20 mg/100 ml, the curve flattens out, but detectable levels are present for several hours after three pints of beer or three double whiskies in healthy people; enough alcohol to impair normal functioning could be present the morning after an evening session of drinking. Alcohol consumption by heavy drinkers represents a considerable metabolic load: for example, half a bottle of whisky is equivalent in molar terms to 500 g aspirin or 1.2 kg tetracycline.

Two mechanisms dispose of excess alcohol in heavy drinkers and account for 'tolerance' in established drinkers. Firstly, normal metabolism increases, as shown by high blood levels of acetate. Secondly, the microsomal ethanol oxidising system is brought into play; this is dependent on P450 cytochrome, normally responsible for drug metabolism, and other cofactors. This is called 'enzyme induction' and is produced by other drugs that are metabolised by the liver, and by smoking.

The two mechanisms lead to a redox state, in which free hydrogen ions, which have to be disposed of by a number of alternative pathways, build up. Some of the resultant metabolic aberrations can have clinical consequences: hepatic gluconeogenesis is inhibited, the citric acid cycle is reduced, and oxidation of fatty acids is impaired. Glucose production is thus reduced, with the risk of hypoglycaemia, overproduction of lactic acid blocks uric acid excretion by the kidneys, and accumulated fatty acids are converted into ketones and lipids (see Figure 3.3).

Behavioural effects

Alcohol is a sedative and mild anaesthetic that is believed to activate the pleasure or reward centres in the brain by triggering release of neurotransmitters such as dopamine and serotonin. It produces a sense of well-being, relaxation, disinhibition, and

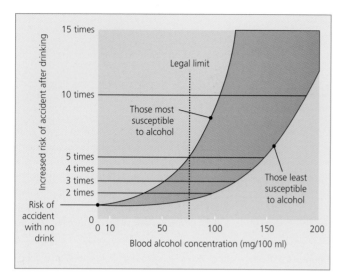

Figure 3.5 Effect of alcohol on behaviour.

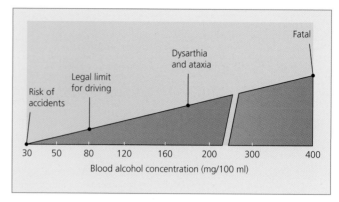

Figure 3.6 Risks associated with concentrations of alcohol in the blood.

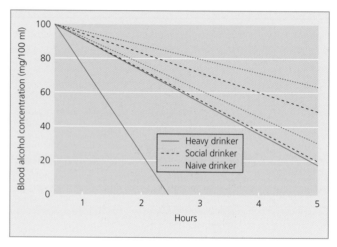

Figure 3.7 Rate of decrease of concentrations of alcohol in the blood in heavy, social, and naive drinkers.

euphoria. These are accompanied by physiological changes such as flushing, sweating, tachycardia and increases in blood pressure, probably because of stimulation of the hypothalamus and increased release of sympathomimetic amines and pituitary-adrenal hormones. The kidneys excrete more urine, not only because of the fluid drunk, but also because of the osmotic effect of alcohol and inhibition of secretion of antidiuretic hormone (ADH).

Increasing consumption leads to a state of **intoxication**, which depends on the amount drunk and previous experience of drinking. Even at a low blood alcohol concentration of around 30 mg/100 ml (6.5 mmol/l), the risk of accidental injury is higher than in the absence of alcohol, although individual experience and complexity of task have to be taken into account (Figure 3.5). In a simulated driving test, for example, bus drivers with a blood alcohol concentration of 50 mg/100 ml (10.9 mmol/l) thought they could drive through obstacles that were too narrow for their vehicles. At 80 mg/100 ml (17.4 mmol/l)—the current legal limit for driving in this country—the risk of a road accident more than doubles; and at 160 mg/100 ml (34.7 mmol/l), it increases more than 10-fold (Figures 3.6 and 3.7).

People become garrulous, elated, and aggressive at levels greater than 100 mg/100 ml (21.7 mmol/l) and then may stop drinking as drowsiness supervenes. After-effects ('hangover') include insomnia, nocturia, tiredness, nausea, and headache. If drinking continues, slurred speech and unsteadiness are likely at around 200 mg/100 ml (43.4 mmol/l), and loss of consciousness may result (Figure 3.6). Concentrations greater than 400 mg/100 ml (86.8 mmol/l) commonly are fatal as a result of ventricular fibrillation, respiratory failure, or inhalation of vomit (this is particularly likely when drugs have been taken in addition to alcohol) (Figure 3.7).

Further reading

Lewis KO. Back calculation of blood alcohol concentration. *BMJ* 1987;295: 800–1.

Lieber CS. Pathogenesis and early diagnosis of alcoholic liver injury. *N Engl J Med* 1978;298:888–93.

Lieber CS, Salaspuro MP. Alcoholic liver disease. In: Millward-Sadler CHM, Wright R, Arthur MJP, eds. *Wright's liver and biliary disease*, 3rd edn. London: Saunders, 1992:899–964.

Paton A. The body and its health. In: Cooper DB, ed. *Alcohol use*. Oxford: Radcliffe, 2000:25–38.

Transport and Road Research Laboratory. *The facts about drinking and driving*. Crowthorne: Berkshire, 1983.

CHAPTER 4

Definitions

Alex Paton

OVERVIEW

- The alcohol content of various alcoholic beverages varies widely.
- In the United Kingdom, one unit is equal to approximately 8 g of absolute alcohol per 10 ml, as is found in half a pint (285 ml) of average strength beer, a glass of wine (125 ml), a small glass of sherry (50 ml) or a 'single' of spirits (25 ml).
- There is no universal standardisation of alcohol units – the alcohol content of a standard drink varies considerably across different countries.
- No such thing exists as a completely safe level of drinking.
- The UK Government sensible drinking message recommends that.
  - men should not regularly drink more than three to four units a day;
  - women should not regularly drink more than two to three units a day; and
  - after an episode of heavy drinking, it is advisable to refrain from drinking for 48 h.
- In the United Kingdom, 23% of men and 18% of women had an estimated weekly consumption of more than sensible levels.

Confused thinking about the use and misuse of alcohol arises from myths that have grown up around drink (Table 4.1), disagreement over defining what is healthy drinking and what is harmful, and the belief that any criticism of overindulgence is antialcohol, a threat to personal pleasure, and nobody else's business.

In general, people are embarrassed about discussing their drinking, so health professionals need to acquire 'the knowledge' (like taxi drivers) by reading a simple guide that is the map of alcohol in order to be confident in dealing dispassionately and subtly with problems that are more common than even health workers realise.

Alcohol

The name is derived from the Arabic *al-kuhl*, literally meaning 'the kohl', the antimony powder used to brighten the eyes; it seems to have been adopted in the Middle Ages to describe the 'essence' of distillation, while today 'alcohol' in everyday speech indicates intoxicating drinks. Technically though, alcohol refers to a large group of chemicals made up of carbon, hydrogen, and oxygen atoms in the form of a single hydroxyl (OH) group and varying numbers of methyl (CH_2) groups. The simplest are water-soluble liquids with only a few carbon atoms, those with perhaps half a dozen or more carbons are oily substances, and the most complex, with up to 20 carbon atoms, are waxes (Table 4.2).

Strictly speaking, the alcohol we drink is ethyl alcohol or **ethanol** (a term favoured by North American workers); it has the chemical formula C_2H_5OH. In this chapter, the term 'alcohol' will be used in the popular sense, denoting a drink containing ethyl alcohol. Such drinks are produced by two processes:

1 **fermentation** by yeast of crushed fruits such as grape wines, or grains such as barley for beer
2 **distillation**, in which alcoholic drinks are evaporated to produce spirits.

Alcohol content

For scientific purposes, the amount of alcohol in a drink is best measured in grams (g) of absolute alcohol; this allows comparison across countries. It is unhelpful to talk about 'number of drinks', because volume of drink and quantity of alcohol in individual beers, wines, and spirits vary (Figures 4.1, 4.2 and 4.3). Some countries have tried to get around the problem by defining a 'standard drink' that in theory can be understood by everyone.

In the United Kingdom, one unit is equal to approximately 8 g of absolute alcohol per 10 ml, as is found in half a pint (285 ml) of average strength beer, a glass of wine (125 ml), a small glass of sherry (50 ml) or a 'single' of spirits (25 ml) (Figure 4.3).

The formula to calculate units in different types of drink is % alcohol by volume × volume/100 × 10. When an alcohol worker enquires about a person's drinking, it is worth checking details of the amounts, as pubs and restaurants serve drinks that are larger than these standards – and so do people pouring drinks at home.

ABC of Alcohol, Fifth Edition. Edited by Anne McCune.
© 2015 John Wiley & Sons, Ltd. Published 2015 by John Wiley & Sons, Ltd.

Table 4.1 Myths of alcohol

Myth	Reality
No one, especially heavy drinkers, tells the truth about their drinking. Health workers and their clients and patients are uncomfortable about discussing alcohol. Treatment of alcoholics is a hopeless business.	Do you know how much you drank last week, or in the pub last Saturday? It is an excuse for letting untrained health workers, especially doctors, off the hook. Most heavy drinkers are not 'alcoholics', and two-thirds will accept advice from a health professional to cut down.

Table 4.2 Different alcohols

Chemical name	Molecular formula	Common name	Comment
Methyl alcohol	CH_3OH	Methanol, meths	Can cause blindness
Ethyl alcohol	C_2H_5OH	**Ethanol**	The alcohol we drink
Amyl alcohol	$C_5H_{11}OH$		Oily
Cetyl alcohol	$C_{16}H_{35}OH$		Waxy, spermaceti
Melissyl alcohol	$C_{20}H_{41}OH$		Beeswax

Figure 4.1 Drinks equivalent to one unit of alcohol.

Figure 4.2 Number of glasses per bottle of different drinks.

Although the United Kingdom favours 8 g as the standard drink, the standard in other countries varies from 6 g in Ireland, to 10 g in Australasia, 12 g in the United States, and as much as 20 g in Japan. Three 'drinks' a day in Japan would be well into hazardous levels in the United Kingdom. The alcohol content of individual beers varies from 3 to 8%, of wines from 10 to 20% and of spirits from 40 to 60%. Strong lagers may contain four units per 330 ml can (equal to two pints of beer) and alcopops mostly contain 4–5.5% alcohol, while some designer drinks enjoyed by the young contain 8–20% alcohol; the alcohol in many of these is disguised by the fruit flavour.

Sensible drinking

No such thing exists as a completely safe level of drinking; only teetotallers run no risk. A few particularly sensitive people – women more often than men – find that they are made ill by small quantities of alcohol; this may be a true hypersensitivity or perhaps because of an inborn defect of an enzyme such as acetaldehyde dehydrogenase.

Blood pressure rises with each unit of alcohol, even with social drinking, although this probably is physiological and harmless. More alarming is the modest rise in relative risk of breast cancer in women drinking as few as seven units a week (Chapter 14); one suggestion is that this may be connected with women drinking under the age of 25 years. Naive (inexperienced) drinkers may become intoxicated and damage themselves or others with relatively small amounts of alcohol.

> Social drinking can therefore be defined as drinking within sensible levels.

At the end of the 1980s, the then Health Education Council and a consensus of the medical Royal Colleges established a sensible (low risk) level of 21 units a week for men and 14 units a week for women (Figure 4.4). The government in the United Kingdom later refined these figures by recommending a **daily** intake of not more than four units for men and three units for women, with 2 alcohol-free days a week, in order to avoid people drinking large amounts on one or more occasion even though remaining within weekly limits.

Alcohol misuse

Somewhere under 15% of men and 20% of women in the United Kingdom do not drink alcohol at all. Government statistics in 2013 detail 23% of men and 18% of women had an estimated weekly consumption of more than sensible levels These people are best described as **misusing** (not abusing) alcohol; no longer is it acceptable to call such people 'alcoholics' or to label misuse as 'alcoholism'. The first term is stigmatising and the second implies the existence of a disease called alcoholism. Although the latter still may be a popular concept in the United States, the consensus in the United Kingdom is that a spectrum exists from no drinking to dependency, and that people are capable of passing from one stage to another in either direction in the course of their lives. Very rarely, even dependent drinkers have been known to return to 'comfortable' drinking. Scottish experts recently suggested that the phrase 'the problems some people have with alcohol' is less judgmental than 'misusing alcohol'.

> Alcohol misuse is a convenient shorthand to indicate repeated, excessive consumption of alcohol that can lead to problem drinking – 85% of which involves social, economic, moral, or psychological difficulties and 15% physical damage or dependence (addiction) (Box 4.1)

Despite claims for and against different types of drink, what matters is not what is drunk but how much **ethanol**, although factors such as constitution, sex, social background, occupation, diet and, above all,

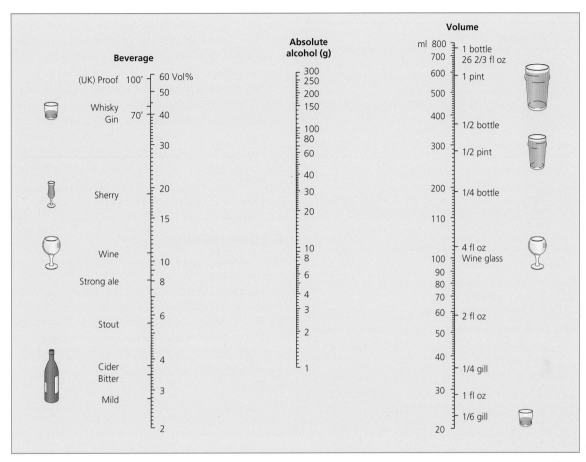

Figure 4.3 Calculating the amount of absolute alcohol in a drink. Source: Adapted from Mellor (1970). Reproduced by permission of BMJ Publishing Group.

Box 4.1 **Features of alcohol dependence**

- Drinking more than 10 units daily
- Tolerance to alcohol: blood alcohol levels greater than 150 mg/100 ml without drunkenness
- Repeated withdrawal symptoms; morning shakes relieved by alcohol
- Repertoire narrowed by drink
- Compulsion to drink in spite of problems
- Abnormal laboratory tests

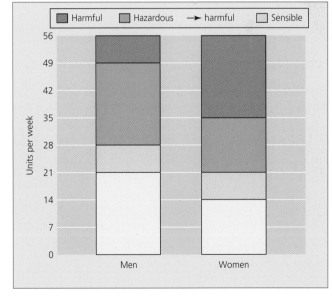

Figure 4.4 Number of units of alcohol per week considered sensible, hazardous to harmful, and harmful.

reasons for drinking must be taken into account. In general, the younger a person starts drinking regularly, the more likely they will have problems and the earlier they will arise, and, in general, women are more sensitive than men. Generalisation about how much and for how long any one person has to drink before trouble starts is not possible. Two examples make this clear. Firstly, people aged 18–24 years are notorious for their capacity to drink, yet most will moderate their drinking in later years, largely because of lifestyle pressures, without coming to harm. Secondly, some people can drink heavily all their lives and still function successfully. Heavy drinking may be used as a catch all for several varieties of drinking more than sensible levels:

- Binge drinking
- Hazardous drinking
- Harmful drinking

To the definitions in Table 4.3 should be added **social harm**, which is perhaps the most important danger of alcohol misuse, to emphasise that it is not just the drinker who suffers – family, friends

Table 4.3 Types of drinking

Type	Definition
Sensible	Women three units a day, and men four units a day with 2 alcohol-free days, or women 14 units, and men 21 units a week
Social	As above with occasional drinking over sensible moderate levels
Naive	Infrequent drinker, sensitive to overindulgence
Heavy	Persistent drinking above sensible levels
Hazardous	*Risk* of harm at levels around six units for women and eight units for men a day (WHO)
Binge drinking	Double sensible levels or more on a single occasion
Harmful	*Presence* of social or physical harm or problems problem caused at levels around six units for women and eight units a day for men (WHO)
Dependent	Addiction to alcohol

and even strangers also are affected. An average of six people are said to be affected by a problem drinker.

The **dependent (addicted drinker)** has a high daily intake of alcohol and is totally unable to stop. Physical features of shakes, sweating and nausea combine with psychological symptoms of compulsion, craving and anxiety to keep the drinking going, so that it overrides all other activities. A drink first thing in the morning to relieve the shakes is characteristic; if alcohol cannot be obtained, withdrawal symptoms, including delirium tremens, are likely.

Skid row drinker is the term used for people who have been taken over by alcohol to the extent that he (less often she) is down and out, lives rough and begs or steals to finance the habit. The name is derived from a sloping area of Seattle where logs used to be rolled into Puget Sound.

The amounts of alcohol that are potentially harmful are impossible to predict because of individual variation in sensitivity, but regarding continued consumption of 35 units a week (5 units a day) by men and 28 units a week (4 units a day) by women as risky is reasonable. The World Health Organization gives eight or more units a day for men and six or more units a day for women as the usual level associated with all types of heavy drinking, but this does not mean that lesser amounts are safe.

Further reading

Mellor CS. Nomogram for calculating mass of alcohol in different beverages. *BMJ* 1970;3(5724):703.

Morgan MY, Ritson EB. *Alcohol and health. A guide for health-care professionals.* London: Medical Council on Alcohol, 2010.

Saunders JB, Aasland OG, Amundsen A, Grant M. Alcohol consumption and related problems among primary care patients: WHO collaborative project on early detection of persons with harmful alcohol consumption – I. *Addiction* 1993;88:349–62.

CHAPTER 5

The nature of alcohol use d

John B. Saunders

OVERVIEW

- Alcohol use and misuse exist as a spectrum, and people often move between categories during life.
- In young people, the most injurious pattern is binge drinking, which is typically part of a pattern of hazardous alcohol consumption.
- Developing dependence on alcohol can occur in anyone, but some people are particularly susceptible to this.
- Alcohol dependence is a neurobiological syndrome of disregulated consumption, which comprises a 'driving force' to continue drinking – despite the consequences.
- Alcohol has a unique capacity among psychoactive substances to cause harm; the spectrum is vast and encompasses physical illness and trauma, brain damage, psychiatric disorders, and social, occupational and legal problems.

Alcoholic drinks are widely enjoyed in Western societies, and most people drink alcohol in a way that is unlikely to cause significant problems. However, the potential for harm is considerable, and this reflects alcohol's intoxicating properties, its intrinsic tissue toxicity (to most organs and body systems including the brain) and the fact that it is an addictive substance and can cause the neurobiological syndrome of alcohol dependence.

The spectrum of alcohol use and alcohol use disorders

Alcohol use and misuse exist as a spectrum (Figure 5.1). In any society this ranges from (1) abstinence from alcohol (for personal, family or religious reasons, or because of previous harm) to (2) moderate-level and low-risk consumption (typically the majority in Western countries), (3) hazardous or 'risky' consumption, (4) harmful consumption, and through to (5) alcohol dependence. The proportion of people in each category varies from country to country and from region to region; in India, some other Asian countries, and in many African countries consumption is low, and in Islamic countries it tends to be minimal. The proportion within

a country also changes over the years, depending on prevailing consumption.

In most individuals, alcohol consumption changes during the life course from the teen years onwards. Drinking tends to be heaviest in young people, particularly during that modern-day phenomenon of 'extended adolescence', when binge drinking is a common experience. However, only a minority of people develop more protracted alcohol use disorders such as harmful use or alcohol dependence.

The importance of drinking in young people is that as a socially infectious behaviour, it can spread and may result in large cohorts adopting hazardous patterns of consumption. With time, they may demonstrate a trajectory of increasing consumption, increasing problems, alcohol dependence and multiple physical, mental and social sequelae.

Understanding alcohol use disorders: The three-dimensional approach

Alcohol and its disorders are best understood using a tri-dimensional construct. The three dimensions are as follows:

1 *Intake* of alcohol – comprising the amount per session, frequency of drinking, variability or pattern of drinking (e.g. weekend bingeing), and duration of consumption;
2 *Dependence* on alcohol – the 'driving force' to drink;
3 *Consequences* of use, which may be physical, neuropsychiatric, and/or social.

Understanding this construct helps us navigate around the various problematic types of alcohol use.

Definitions and criteria of alcohol use disorders

The term 'alcohol use disorders' denotes the central (or 'core') syndromes of misuse of alcohol. Low-risk or moderate alcohol consumption – typically below four units (one standard unit is 8 g of alcohol) of alcohol per day for men and below three units per day for women – is within the spectrum of normality in Western societies, and will not be discussed further (note that this does not

---

ABC of Alcohol, Fifth Edition. Edited by Anne McCune.
© 2015 John Wiley & Sons, Ltd. Published 2015 by John Wiley & Sons, Ltd.

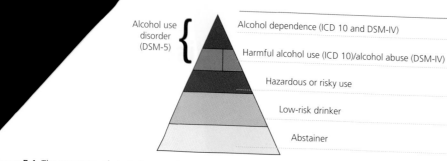

Figure 5.1 The spectrum of alcohol use and misuse.

apply in certain cultures, where any amount of alcohol is frowned upon or forbidden).

Alcohol intoxication

Alcohol intoxication (ICD 10 code: F10.0) is a *disturbance of consciousness, cognition and/or behaviour that follows recent consumption of alcohol,* and typically in large quantities. The features reflect the known effects of alcohol. The condition needs to be clinically significant (potentially requiring medical attention) and is typically time limited.

Hazardous or 'risky' alcohol consumption

At the lower end of the spectrum of alcohol use disorders, where there is a repetitive pattern of use, is hazardous alcohol consumption or 'risky' consumption. This means *a level or pattern of consumption which poses the risk of harmful consequences* in the future if consumption remains unchecked. Hazardous alcohol consumption is not listed in the ICD 10 'F' codes, but it is a term used by many national authorities.

Harmful alcohol use

Harmful alcohol use is a diagnostic term in ICD 10, where it is coded as F10.1. It represents *a repetitive pattern of alcohol use which is actually causing physical or psychological harm* to that person. It does not infer that the person has dependence on alcohol; indeed, if a person has experienced harm from alcohol and fulfils the criteria for alcohol dependence, the latter diagnosis takes precedence over harmful use.

Alcohol dependence

Alcohol dependence (ICD 10 code: F10.2) is a neurobiological syndrome in which there is a *chronic disregulation of alcohol consumption, with an internal driving force to continue drinking.* This arises after changes have occurred to key neurocircuits in the mid- and lower forebrains; these changes may well be permanent. As a result of this, alcohol consumption is driven by an internal 'force' which becomes ever more powerful such that consumption becomes increasingly stereotyped or 'fixed', responding less to external circumstances and more to internal urges and (often) subconscious triggers. The diagnostic criteria, adapted from ICD 10, are listed in Table 5.1.

For the diagnosis of alcohol dependence to be made, three or more of these central criteria need to occur together (i.e. they

Table 5.1 Diagnostic criteria for alcohol dependence

1. A strong desire or craving to drink alcohol
2. Impaired control over alcohol consumption – in relation to when it is consumed, how much is consumed, and the ease or otherwise in ceasing consumption
3. Salience of alcohol, meaning that it takes a higher priority in the person's life than other activities
4. Increased tolerance, such that more is required to obtain the desired effect
5. Withdrawal symptoms, which occur on cessation or reduction in alcohol consumption or the prevention of such withdrawal symptoms by repeated consumption of alcohol
6. Continued use of alcohol despite knowledge or experience of the harmful consequences

Source: Adapted from ICD 10.

should 'cluster') and repeatedly so over a period of 12 months or more (or continuously for at least 1 month).

Alcohol withdrawal syndrome

The alcohol withdrawal syndrome (F10.3) is a common feature of alcohol dependence, specifically when consumption is interrupted or the person attempts to reduce consumption. It is a syndrome of motor, sensory and autonomic hyperactivity, which tends to run a course of 4–5 days, although may persist for a further week.

Practical implications of the diagnoses

Alcohol dependence is an important diagnosis to make as it identifies patients who are at risk of a withdrawal syndrome (e.g. after hospitalisation). In addition, it is an indication for an alcohol pharmacotherapy such as naltrexone. Patients with alcohol dependence are typically advised on a goal of abstinence from alcohol, especially if they experience recurrent withdrawal symptoms, whereas moderated, low-level consumption would generally be advised in the long term where the person has hazardous or harmful drinking.

DSM-5 alcohol use disorder

In the United States and in the mental health field in many countries worldwide, the American Psychiatric Association's *Diagnostic and Statistical Manual (DSM)* holds sway. The latest version, *DSM-5,* published in 2013, aggregates alcohol dependence and what was termed alcohol abuse (essentially social consequences of repeated drinking) into a unitary condition 'alcohol use disorder'. The concept is a much broader one than alcohol dependence and is diagnosed by the presence of only 2 or more of 11 criteria (mostly the previous dependence and abuse criteria combined). The nearest in the ICD system (as illustrated in Figure 5.1) to this concept would be a combination of alcohol dependence and harmful alcohol use and a proportion of hazardous drinkers. Indications are that the prevalence of alcohol use disorder is higher than alcohol dependence and abuse combined. It is arguably less useful clinically because it does not readily distinguish between patients who are at risk of withdrawal, or require an abstinence goal, or are appropriate for pharmacotherapy treatment, from those who are not.

A note about 'alcoholism'

The diagnostic term 'alcoholism' is an old one, and dates back nearly 200 years. It is still commonly employed but is variably defined and is no longer included as a diagnostic entity in the ICD or DSM systems. In many ways the concept of alcoholism is like an expanded version of alcohol dependence but including 'denial' (of the extent or impact of alcohol use on the person) as a central feature, and having a progressive course. In some definitions it encompasses various of the physical and neuropsychiatric complications. The term 'alcohol dependence' excludes consequences of use.

The neurobiology of alcohol dependence

Developments in neurobiological knowledge help explain why alcohol consumption tends to become increasingly stereotyped with the passage of time and why dependence develops.

With repeated alcohol consumption, there is progressive re-setting of key neurocircuits which subserve reward, excitation, salience and behavioural control. They course from the ventral tegmental area of the midbrain, to the nucleus accumbens of the lower forebrain and have connections to and from the prefrontal gyrus and the cingulate gyrus. The changes that occur can be regarded as adaptive mechanisms to repeated consumption of alcohol which causes perturbation of these circuits. These adaptive changes result in alterations in neurotransmission and abnormal levels of key transmitters such as dopamine, glutamate and gamma-aminobutyric acid (GABA). These changes (particularly affecting dopamine levels) in turn induce neuroplastic changes in nerve fibres and synapses leading to what might be described as a 're-wiring' of these neurocircuits and generation of the 'driving force' of alcohol dependence.

The key neurocircuits which are affected are as follows:
- *The reward system.* The mesolimbic reward circuitry is down-regulated because of repeated exposure to alcohol, with diminution of response to natural rewards and development of a persistent anhedonic and amotivational state.
- *The alertness neurocircuitry.* This is a balance of GABA-mediated inhibitory neurotransmission and glutamate-mediated excitatory

transmission. Repeated consumption of alcohol results in a state of relative hyperexcitation manifest by (i) elevated responsiveness to alcohol-related triggers and (ii) heightened tension and perception of stress.
- *Behavioural control circuits.* These run to and from the prefrontal gyrus of the frontal lobe and serve to dampen down more primitive behavioural responses and try to bring behaviour under greater cognitive control.
- *Salience.* This is subserved by iterative neurotransmission from the reward systems to and from the cingulate gyrus. These circuits are altered in a way that leads to a change in priorities in the individual between alcohol-focused activities and other interests, enjoyments and responsibilities.

In summary, these neurobiological changes initiate a driving force to consume alcohol that is no longer primarily dependent on the context of drinking or on the psychological mechanisms that favour drinking alcohol or not doing so. The neurobiological changes result in alcohol consumption becoming more stereotyped and responding more to internal physiological mechanisms than the external environment.

Causes and influences on the development of alcohol use disorders

Historically, the essential features of alcohol use disorders were often conflated with predisposing and underlying factors (see Table 5.2). Thus, many viewed them as primarily of biological cause, or alternatively not so but simply developing due to prevailing norms of drinking.

One now recognises that they are discrete disorders but with numerous predisposing factors. The latter are extremely heterogeneous and include (i) genetic influences, (ii) adverse experiences in earlier life, (iii) underlying or comorbid psychiatric disorders, and environmental influences such as (iv) the availability and cost of alcohol, (v) its legal status and (vi) the degree to which it is sanctioned in a particular society and for a particular age–sex group.

In clinical practice, one tends to see three groups of patients.
1 Alcohol consumption begins in the mid-to-late teens as an enjoyable social activity. Consumption varies as time goes by and is influenced by peer group, occupation, disposable income, prevailing cost of alcohol, social events and special occasions. Due to repeated consumption and influenced by several behavioural mechanisms, an unhealthy pattern of consumption develops. This is called hazardous use or, when problems arise, harmful use. Eventually and often after many years have elapsed, drinking becomes a more stereotyped behaviour, and the other features of alcohol dependence emerge. Physical disorders are commonly experienced.
2 On a background of a family history of alcohol dependence (or 'alcoholism'), an individual finds that alcohol has an effect which is different to that experienced by others. Sometimes alcohol is a disappointing experience, and the person finds he/she has to drink more to get the effect that others are experiencing. In other cases, the person rapidly becomes intoxicated. These reactions tend to accelerate consumption and/or cause the person to rapidly descend into harmful drinking and alcohol dependence. Most of the familial predisposition is of genetic origin.

Table 5.2 Facts and fallacies about alcohol use disorders

Assumptions	Some facts
Moral weakness or character flaw	A popular theory in Victorian times and still a prevalent view among many in the community. No support for this as a primary explanation. Impaired control over alcohol consumption, as seen in alcohol dependence, and behaviours uncharacteristic of the person previously often construed as character flaws.
Underlying personality disorder	Alcohol use disorders were once classified with the personality disorders (e.g. in *DSM-II*, published in 1968). Personality disorder underlies some cases but no evidence for their being a unifying cause.
Self-inflicted condition	Although alcohol consumption is a voluntary chosen activity initially, behavioural mechanisms (often in combination with underlying disorders/experiences) combined with neurobiological changes make alcohol consumption increasingly a disorder of regulation and predominately in the subconscious.
Environmental influences predominate	Environmental influences are undoubtedly important at a population level. Recognised factors include the costs of alcoholic drinks in relation to disposable income, availability (e.g. number and location of sales outlets), legal drinking age, presence of random breath testing and promotional campaigns. However, these factors are much less helpful in identifying why particular individuals develop alcohol use disorders and others, exposed to the same influences, do not.
Behavioural mechanisms all important	Elements of classical conditioning, operant conditioning and social learning therapy all contribute to the development of repetitive alcohol consumption and thereby to hazardous consumption and then harmful consumption. However, neurobiological mechanisms then re-set key neurocircuits governing reward, the stress response, incentive and salience, and behavioural control. These constitute the 'driving force' of dependence and become 'hard wired', leading to a chronic syndrome of stereotyped consumption, not readily reversible to 'normal' drinking.
What's the trigger?	There is an assumption that if and when a relapse occurs, there is always an identifiable trigger. Certainly, some triggers have been identified, for example negative emotional states and peer influence. However, many trigger factors operate at the subconscious level and in a timeframe less than that required to recognise the trigger.

Evidence for genetic factors

Biometrical genetic studies
- Studies of adopted children show that those born to alcohol-dependent biological parents are four times more likely to develop an alcohol use disorder themselves, irrespective of the adoptive home.
- Twin studies show substantially greater concordance for alcohol dependence among monozygotic (identical) twins compared with dizygotic (fraternal) ones.

Genome studies
- Some 40 genes are known to influence some aspect of the handling or effects of alcohol, of which around half seem to impact on the neurocircuitry of alcohol dependence.
- Some genetic variants are ***protective*** against the development of alcohol dependence – such as aldehyde dehydrogenase (ALDH) deficiency.

Table 5.3 Examples of underlying conditions and experiences

- **Abuse** – physical, sexual and (severe) emotional
- **Trauma** – military (combat and non-combat), in civilian forces (police, ambulance and fire brigade officers)
- Being **in a gang** in childhood
- **Personality** structure – impulsiveness, antisocial traits and borderline personality disorder
- **Psychiatric disorders** – depression (various forms – but relatively weak association), anxiety (various forms: social anxiety fairly strong, others relatively weak), post-traumatic stress disorder, bipolar disorder and schizophrenia (potent effect but relatively uncommon because of low prevalence)
- **Physical illness** – chronic pain and disability
- **Loss and grief** – usually a loved one
- **Loss of role** – redundancy, unemployment and unplanned retirement
- **Occupation** – alcohol production and sales, catering and hospitality, construction work and other manual labour and finance industry

3 Alcohol consumption may be a response to adverse circumstances, bad experiences or underlying disorders. Many predisposing factors have been identified from longitudinal studies, including various forms of abuse and trauma, certain psychiatric disorders, physical illness and impairments, and grief. It should not be thought that there is necessarily a cause-and-effect relationship between underlying factors as reported by patients, and the pathway by which a putative underlying influence has its effect may be complex. Table 5.3 lists some of the individual predisposing and non-genetic family influences.

Persons with the alcohol dependence syndrome therefore tend to experience a persistent drive to drink alcohol despite the circumstances, and despite the harms, and do so in a way that their consumption becomes resistant to attempts at voluntary control and more responsive to changes in the person's internal milieu than their external environment. Alcohol consumption becomes increasingly self-perpetuating and harms occur, which may initially tend to limit consumption but may subsequently reinforce it (Figure 5.2).

The consequences of alcohol use disorders

There are countless physical, psychological and social consequences of alcohol use disorders. Table 5.4 lists some of them.

Certain physical disorders tend to occur with a repeated binge pattern of drinking (the person would be described as having harmful alcohol consumption). Examples include acute gastritis, and accidents, assaults and injuries. Others characteristically occur after a longstanding pattern of daily (or near daily) alcohol consumption, as is typical of alcohol dependence. However, the

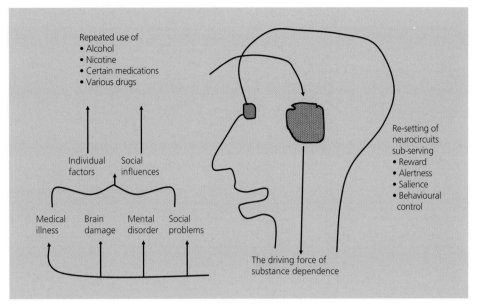

Figure 5.2 Building up our understanding: the vicious circle of addiction.

Table 5.4 Consequences of alcohol misuse

Physical disorders	Neuropsychiatric and mental disorders	Social problems
Liver disease (fatty liver, alcoholic hepatitis, alcoholic cirrhosis)	Confusional state	Relationship breakup
Gastro-oesophageal reflux	Delirium	Loss of employment
Peptic ulcer	Memory impairment	Social isolation
Oropharayngeal cancer	Executive dysfunction	Financial problems
Hypertension	Visual impairment	Driving under the influence charges
Arrhythmias	Anxiety disorders	Victim of assault
Cardiomyopathy	Mood disorders	Perpetuation of assault
Pancreatitis (acute, recurrent, chronic)	Psychosis	Intoxicated behaviours
Myopathy (acute, chronic)		Public nuisance charges
Peripheral neuropathy Cerebellar disease		Family dysfunction

severity of the disorder is not always closely related to the severity of the dependence syndrome. In many cases the dependence is quite subtle; there may be no overt withdrawal symptoms and often the clue is that despite evidence of physical disease, consumption continues. Why would it unless there was dependence?

In ICD 10 these physical complications are listed in the respective chapter for the particular organ or body system. For example, alcoholic cirrhosis is coded as K70.3 and alcoholic cardiomyopathy as I42.6.

Mental and cognitive consequences of repetitive alcohol consumption are grouped as follows and are found in the 'F' codes:

- Alcohol-induced amnestic syndrome (memory loss for recent events): F10.6.

- Alcohol-induced psychotic disorder: F10.5.
- Other alcohol-induced neurocognitive syndromes (including frontal lobe damage, executive dysfunction): F10.7.

Relationship between alcohol use disorders and consumption

Although there is a strong correlation between the presence of an alcohol use disorder and measures of alcohol consumption, consumption itself is not a necessary criterion for the diagnosis in any of the international diagnostic systems. However, in clinical practice, the assessment of consumption is a key part of the assessment.

Conclusions

Alcohol use disorders need to be defined in each patient where alcohol is considered problematic. There are clear advantages in doing so, in terms of understanding, for example, why a patient with cirrhosis of the liver continues to drink excessively (they have the driving force of alcohol dependence, but it may be subtle), whether a patient needs to be placed on an alcohol withdrawal rating scale after hospital admission, or what is the most medically appropriate goal for a particular patient (abstinence from alcohol or moderated consumption). In this way, treatment can be based on explicit diagnoses and optimised.

Further reading

Koob GF, Volkow ND. Neurocircuitry of addiction. *Neuropsychopharmacology* 2010;35:217–38.

Marshall EJ, Humphreys K, Ball DM. *The treatment of drinking problems: a guide for the helping professions*, 5th edn. New York: Cambridge University Press, 2010.

Saunders JB, Latt NC. Diagnosis and classification of substance use disorders. In: Johnson BA, ed. *Addiction medicine: science and practice*. New York: Springer, 2011:95–113.

Saunders JB, Conigrave KM, Latt NC, Nutt DJ, Marshall EJ, Ling W, et al. *Addiction medicine*, 2nd edn. Oxford: Oxford University Press, to be published in 2015.

Wodak AD, Saunders JB, Ewusi-Mensah I, Davis M, Williams R. Severity of alcohol dependence in patients with alcoholic liver disease. *British Medical Journal* 1983;287:1420–2.

CHAPTER 6

The detection of alcohol use disorders

John B. Saunders

OVERVIEW

- Alcohol use and alcohol use disorders are most conveniently assessed by direct enquiry of the patient.
- The Alcohol Use Disorders Identification Test (AUDIT) and similar questionnaires are valuable aids to screening and early detection.
- Early detection avoids over-investigation and inappropriate treatment, and also provides a convenient opportunity for a brief therapeutic intervention.
- The alert clinician can identify cutaneous stigmata of alcohol.
- Biological markers are helpful when abnormal, but too much should not be expected of them.
- To identify excessive alcohol consumption as a cause or contributory factor to mental health disorders – such as depression, social and other forms of anxiety – and to provide the basis for advice to patients for modification of alcohol consumption.
- To alert patients with injuries and other forms of trauma to its link with their alcohol consumption.
- To provide personal feedback so that patients can modify their alcohol intake as part of a personal health improvement plan.

Alcohol is a risk factor for many human disorders and personal and family problems. More than that, the effects of excessive alcohol consumption can interfere with medical treatment and can cause unexpected problems during a patient's hospital stay. It is widely accepted that enquiry should be made of a patient's alcohol intake, just as enquiry about cigarette smoking is understood as a universal component of the medical history. However, there continue to be difficulties in assessing alcohol consumption and the disorders related to it. What follows is a practical guide as to how to best achieve this in different clinical settings.

Rationale for enquiring about alcohol use

- Contributes to an accurate diagnosis of an alcohol-related disorder, with clarification of the initial differential.
- Avoidance of unnecessary and potentially hazardous investigations of the presenting condition.
- Avoidance of unnecessary and ineffective treatments (e.g. if hypertension is alcohol-related, modification of alcohol consumption may be sufficient in itself to normalise the blood pressure).
- Given that excess alcohol is a recognised cause of (or contributory factor to) multiple physical disorders (e.g. peptic ulceration, liver disease and various forms of cancer), detection of such use at an early stage allows the patient to be given advice and strategies to reduce or cease consumption.

Alcohol consumption was historically regarded as part of the personal world of the patient and not particularly the subject for medical enquiry unless it was overtly harmful. Given the mass of evidence indicating its major role as a health risk factor – globally it causes 4% of all deaths and nearly 5% of healthy years of life lost – there has grown an expectation that systematic enquiry will be undertaken. Indeed, it has been argued in several medicolegal cases that a medical practitioner is negligent in not enquiring when the patient subsequently suffers harm as a result of their alcohol intake.

Making the enquiry

There are three domains for enquiry about alcohol use as follows:
1 *Intake* of alcohol, for example the level and frequency of use
2 *Dependence* on alcohol – the 'driving force' to drink
3 *Consequences* of use – physical, neuropsychiatric and social

Assessment

1 Questions should first be posed to quantify aspects of alcohol consumption.
2 A key issue is whether the patient has alcohol dependence. This has significant implications for treatment goals and approaches. Patients with dependence are at risk of withdrawal; and for them, a goal of abstinence from alcohol is recommended.

ABC of Alcohol, Fifth Edition. Edited by Anne McCune.
© 2015 John Wiley & Sons, Ltd. Published 2015 by John Wiley & Sons, Ltd.

Intake

- **Type of alcohol** typically consumed and its concentration (v/v%) (Chapter 4).
- **Amount** consumed per session of drinking or per drinking day.
- **Frequency** of drinking (number of days per week or per month).
- **Variability and pattern** of drinking – is alcohol consumption a regular occurrence or a weekend activity or confined to special occasions?
- **Cumulative consumption** over a week or month.
- **Duration** of alcohol consumption – it may be important to identify the duration of various levels of consumption in the person's history.
- **Last occasion** alcohol was consumed – of particular relevance if diagnosis of alcohol intoxication or alcohol withdrawal is being considered.

Dependence – the 'driving force'

- The patient feels an **urge to drink** (sometimes termed a 'craving' or 'compulsion') alcohol – in general, or after a period of not drinking, or when triggered by an alcohol-related cue such as a pub or negative emotion.
- **Impaired control** over consumption, such that drinking occurs at inappropriate times or occasions, and/or that the person drinks more than they had intended or so that they are incapable of self-protection.
- **Alcohol becomes a central feature** of the person's life, and other activities, interests and personal responsibilities are relegated to the periphery.
- **Increased tolerance** to alcohol such that more is required to achieve the desired effect.
- **Withdrawal symptoms** occur on cessation or reduction in drinking, usually in a few hours (the patient's attempts to reduce alcohol consumption are rendered futile because of withdrawal symptoms), or he/she continues drinking to prevent or alleviate withdrawal symptoms.
- **Continued drinking despite harm.**

All these features of dependence (some might use the term 'addiction') to alcohol reflect an internal driving force to consume alcohol. This reflects the re-setting of key neurocircuits governing reward, alertness, behavioural control and salience (Chapter 5). According to the International Classification of Diseases, Tenth Revision (ICD 10), three of these six central criteria occurring repeatedly over 12 months (or continuously for 1 month) are required for the diagnosis. The features need to be clustered and the disorder is, therefore, syndromal.

3 Questions are then posed about the problems or harms from alcohol. These embrace several domains, including physical health consequences, mental health problems and a range of social problems.

Commonly the problems described by a patient occur across the three domains listed earlier. In addition, patients may have multiple non-specific physical symptoms, and multiple presentations to the general practice, clinic or hospital.

Consequences		
Physical harm	**Neuropsychiatric harm**	**Social harm**
Reflux oesophagitis	Confusion	Argumentativeness
Nausea and vomiting	Blackouts	Abusive and aggressive behaviour
Epigastric pain	Memory disturbance	Financial problems
Bowel disturbance	Ataxia	Lack of follow through in work
Jaundice	Peripheral neuropathy	Generally impaired work performance
Right hypochondrial pain	Abnormalities of gait	Breakdown of relationships
Muscle weakness	Lowering of mood	Excessive time spent outside the home
Cardiac failure	Anxiety, fear and panic	Predisposition to other forms of substance use
Recurrent chest infections	Hallucinations	Predisposition to gambling
Laryngitis	Disorganisation in personal or work life	Unreliability
Recurrent headache	Bad decision-making	
Accidents and injuries	Visual disturbance	
Risk of sexually transmitted diseases		

Detection in practice

In most cases an alcohol use disorder will be identified through relevant questions that are posed during the interview. At what point in the assessment this takes place will depend on whether the patient gives any leads to a possible alcohol-related condition – in which case enquiry will be made then. If there is no mention of alcohol in the interview, questions about it are often conveniently asked immediately after questions on tobacco (cigarette) smoking, as this is an issue that raises comparatively few sensitivities.

A comprehensive assessment of alcohol use and potential-associated problems would logically include enquiry of all the domains listed earlier. Although this would be undertaken in specialist alcohol problems practice, with further exploration of the details of the patient's experiences, in other areas of clinical practice a briefer approach is needed. This is where screening questionnaires are valuable. These instruments can be administered during the interview, or can be self-administered while the patient is in the waiting room, *or some of their component questions can be employed in the interview.*

The AUDIT

The most widely used general alcohol screening instrument is the AUDIT, which is structured around the three domains of intake, dependence and consequences. Figure 6.1 illustrates the AUDIT questionnaire, which has 10 questions. The first three questions are

Alcohol Use Disorders Identification Test (AUDIT)

Please circle the answer that is correct for you.

1. How often do you have a drink containing alcohol?

| Never | Monthly or less | Two or four times a month | Two or three times per week | Four or more times a week |

2. How many drinks containing alcohol do you have on a typical day when you are drinking?

| 1 or 2 | 3 or 4 | 5 or 6 | 7 or 9 | 10 or more |

3. How often do you have six or more drinks on one occasion?

| Never | Less than monthly | Monthly | Two or three times per week | Four or more times a week |

4. How often during the last year have you found that you were not able to stop drinking once you had started?

| Never | Less than monthly | Monthly | Two or three times per week | Four or more times a week |

5. How often during the last year have you failed to do what was normally expected from you because of drinking?

| Never | Less than monthly | Monthly | Two or three times per week | Four or more times a week |

6. How often during the last year have you needed a first drink in the morning to get yourself going after a heavy drinking session?

| Never | Less than monthly | Monthly | Two or three times per week | Four or more times a week |

7. How often during the last year have you had a feeling or guilt or remorse after drinking?

| Never | Less than monthly | Monthly | Two or three times per week | Four or more times a week |

8. How often during the last year have you been unable to remember what happened the night before because you had been drinking?

| Never | Less than monthly | Monthly | Two or three times per week | Four or more times a week |

9. Have you or someone else been injured as a result of your drinking?

| No | Yes, but not in the last year | Yes, during the last year |

10. Has a relative or friend, or a doctor or other health worker, been concerned about your drinking or suggested you cut down?

| No | Yes, but not in the last year | Yes, during the last year |

Figure 6.1 The AUDIT questionnaire.

measures of intake, Questions 4–6 explore possible dependence, and Questions 7–10 enquire about problems.

There are fixed-choice responses to each of the AUDIT questions, and the responses for Questions 1–8 score 0, 1, 2, 3 and 4 (from left to right). Questions 9 and 10 have three choices, which score 0, 2 and 4, respectively. The total potential score ranges from 0 to 40.

As a self-completion questionnaire, the AUDIT can be provided to the patient by reception staff (sometimes with additional questions on cigarette smoking or current medication), so that the completed questionnaire is available to the doctor (or other clinician) at the beginning of the consultation. The AUDIT questions can be read out in the consultation, although this does take a few minutes.

Interpreting the AUDIT

When the full 10-item AUDIT is used as a screening questionnaire (with a score range of 0–40), a score of 8 or more indicates a presumptive alcohol use disorder (including hazardous alcohol consumption). In that case, it is appropriate to repeat or expand on some of the questions for which there is a positive response and confirm

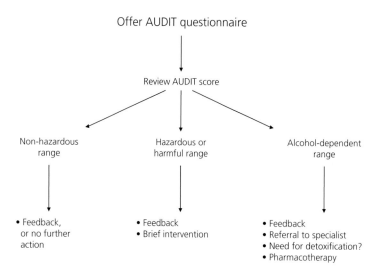

Figure 6.2 Decision tree based on the AUDIT score.

the diagnosis of an alcohol use disorder. The stage is then set for feedback to be offered to the patient and for advice to be given on reducing alcohol consumption or to explore possible needs for treatment. A score of 13 or more should alert the practitioner to the possibility of alcohol dependence (15+ is more definite) and in particular the answers to Questions 4–6 should be scrutinised and expanded upon in order to confirm or exclude this diagnosis.

Figure 6.2 illustrates a decision tree which shows the recommended responses according to the overall AUDIT score.

The broader value of the AUDIT

Although the AUDIT was developed primarily as a screening instrument, it has other purposes. For example, it can provide information about the three individual domains of intake, dependence and problems (consequences). Each domain can be scored separately, and, essentially, a score of 4 or more on each domain indicates (Q 1–3) hazardous alcohol consumption, (Q 4–6) alcohol dependence and (Q 7–10) alcohol-related problems respectively.

This in turn can lead to further exploration of a broader set of experiences in that area, and targeted advice and treatment. More generally, as all the AUDIT questions have high face validity, the instrument can be used for the purposes of brief assessment, with each positive response potentially acting as a platform for further enquiry and patient-specific advice.

Briefer questionnaires

For many screening and early detection purposes it is sufficient to ask Questions 1–3 alone. This simplified version is termed the AUDIT-C, and in identifying hazardous alcohol consumption, it performs as well as the full AUDIT. Scores exceeding 4 for men and 3 for women are taken to indicate hazardous alcohol

consumption and a rationale for providing a brief alcohol intervention.

Single item derivations of the AUDIT are also employed when time is at a premium and particularly when the practitioner wants to incorporate a question about alcohol within a broader enquiry as part of the consultation. Asking Question 3 alone ('How often over the past 12 months have you had six or more drinks on one occasion?'), and using a score of 2 as the threshold, allows one to detect approximately two-thirds of patients with alcohol use disorders. Question 3 forms the first step in a two-stage brief screening instrument – the FAST questionnaire, another popular instrument.

The **Paddington alcohol test (PAT)** was developed by Touquet and colleagues to screen for problematic alcohol use in emergency departments and other acute care settings (see Figure 6.3). It has been shown to be comparable with the AUDIT in these settings and takes less time to administer, a key consideration in these pressured environments.

A comment about the CAGE

The **CAGE** is a four-item questionnaire. It is an older screening instrument which was developed for the detection of alcoholism and before the modern understanding that there is a spectrum of alcohol use and misuse. It does not therefore purport to screen for hazardous alcohol consumption or the broader range of alcohol use disorders. The four questions of the CAGE are as follows:

1. Do you feel the need to cut down on your alcohol consumption?
2. Have people annoyed you by commenting on your alcohol consumption?
3. Do you feel guilty about your alcohol consumption?
4. Do you have a first drink in the morning to get yourself going?

It will be apparent that some of these questions explore advanced stage alcohol dependence although Questions 1 and 2 may illicit affirmative responses from people with less severe alcohol use disorders.

PADDINGTON ALCOHOL TEST 2009

'make the connection'

A. <u>PAT</u> for <u>TOP 10</u> presentations – circle as necessary.

B. _Clinical Signs_ of alcohol use

C. _BAC_ (PTO)

1. FALL (incl. trip) **2. COLLAPSE** (incl. fits) **3. HEAD INJURY** **4. ASSAULT**

5. ACCIDENT **6. UNWELL** **7. GASTRO-INTESTINAL** **8. CARDIAC** (t.chest pain)

9. PSYCHIATRIC (incl. **DSH & OD**) please state **10. REPEAT ATTENDER** _Other_ (please state)

EARLY IDENTIFICATION TO REDUCE RE-ATTENDANCE

Only proceed after dealing with patients 'agenda' i.e, patient's reason for attendance.
"We <u>routinely</u> ask all patients having...(above presentation)...**do you drink alcohol?"**

1	**Do you drink alcohol?**	**YES** (go to #2) **NO** (end)

2	**What is the most you will drink in any one day?**	(UK alcohol units)

Use the following guide to **estimate** total daily units,
(Standard pub units in brackets; home measures often three times the amount)

Beer/lager/cider	Pints (2) [ ]	Cans (1,5) [ ]	Litre bottles (4,5) [ ]
Strong beer/lager/cider	Pints (5) [ ]	Cans (4) [ ]	Litre bottles (10) [ ]
Wine	Glasses (1,5) [ ]	750 ml bottles (9) [ ]	**Alcopops**
Fortified wine (Sherry, Port, Martini)	Glasses (1) [ ]	750 ml bottles (12) [ ]	330 ml bottles (1,5) [ ]
Spirits (Gin, Vodka, Whisky etc)	Singles (1) [ ]	750 ml bottles (30) [ ]	

If more than <u>twice</u> daily limits (8 units/day for men, 6 units/day for women) **PAT +ve**   (Continue to Q3 for all)

3	**How often do you drink?**	

Every day
——— **times per week**   May be dependent, consider thiamine (? Nutrition) & chlordiazepoxide (?CIWA).
Advise against daily drinking.

Less than weekly   (Continue to next question)

4	**Do you feel your attendance at A&E is related to alcohol**	**YES** (PAT+ve) **NO**

If PAT +ve give feedback e.g, **"Can we advise that your drinking is harming your health"**.
"It is recommended that you do not regularly drink more than 4 units/day for men or 3 units/day for women".

5	**We would like to offer you further advice. Would you be willing to see our alcohol nurse specialist (ANS)?**	**YES** **NO**

If "Yes" to Q5 give ANS appointment card and leaflet and make appointment in diary @ 9am to 10 am.
Other appointment times available, please speak to ANS or ask patient to contact (phone number on app. card).
Give alcohol advice leaflet ("Units and You") to all PAT +ve patients, especially if they decline ANS appointment.

Please note here if patient admitted to ward ....

Referrer's Signature   **Name Stamp**   **Date:**   <u>PTO</u>

THANK YOU

ANS OUTCOME:

Figure 6.3 The Paddington alcohol test (PAT).

Embracing modern technologies

Questionnaires such as the AUDIT and the AUDIT-C have been adapted for electronic presentation through laptops, tablets and similar instruments and smart phones, and enable self-assessment of alcohol use and receiving appropriate advice without the need for a consultation. Many patients prefer this approach to a face-to-face enquiry. Increasingly people have access to websites providing screening, and the AUDIT, and other instruments are available through these sites. The provision of advice on alcohol use has a high degree of acceptability, especially among younger generations, and it is being adopted as one of the main public health approaches to reduce alcohol-related harm at a population level.

The difficult patient

Although enquiry about alcohol use is regarded by most people as an unremarkable and legitimate part of a medical history, some patients are sensitive about their consumption, some understate their consumption (sometimes seriously) and some can respond in a hostile manner, which is off-putting to the clinician. In these circumstances, face-to-face questions may be preferred, and the following tips can be helpful in reducing the patient's concern and enhancing their cooperation and accuracy of response:

Specialised questionnaires

Many questionnaires are available to assess aspects of alcohol use disorders, psychiatric comorbidity, to provide a template for a comprehensive clinical assessment or to conduct a complete interview. Most are research instruments and require an investment of time that does not exist in clinical practice. Two groups of instruments that are suitable for everyday use are as follows:

- questionnaires to assess alcohol dependence (e.g. the Severity of Alcohol Dependence Questionnaire (SADQ));
- alcohol withdrawal scales such as the Clinical Institute Withdrawal Assessment for Alcohol, Revised (CIWA-Ar), and the Alcohol Withdrawal Scale (AWS).

Physical examination

There are many findings on physical examination which reflect the pathophysiological effects of alcohol, and point to an alcohol use disorder (Table 6.1).

Table 6.1 Physical examination findings

Cutaneous stigmata and related signs	Physical examination findings	Mental-state examination findings
Erythematous face Facial puffiness	Alcohol on breath Cutaneous signs of chronic liver disease	Anxiety and agitation Poor eye contact
Cushingoid appearance (accentuation of above signs)	Tremor	Memory disturbance – especially short-term memory
Telangiectasia – esp. at angle of jaw and zygomatic area	Truncal obesity (especially in men)	Signs of frontal lobe impairment
Conjunctival injection Coating of the tongue Furrowing of the tongue	Hepatomegaly Hypertension Signs of cardiac failure (potential cardiomyopathy)	Concreteness of thinking Poor abstraction ability Impaired insight and judgement
Skin overgrowth – nose (rhinophyma) and chin particularly	Cerebellar signs (especially truncal ataxia)	Impaired decision-making
Bilateral parotid enlargement	Peripheral neuropathy	Reduced performance on word generation
Dupuytren's contracture	Proximal myopathy	

Laboratory tests

Many abnormalities of common laboratory tests are evident in patients with alcohol use disorders. This again reflects the numerous pathophysiological effects of alcohol. The more common biological markers are listed in Table 6.2.

The biological markers of alcohol are useful in alerting to the presence of an alcohol use disorder when this was not suspected. The probability of an abnormal result in relation to daily alcohol intake is depicted in Figure 6.4.

They are also valuable in providing physiological (and therefore 'objective') measures of alcohol exposure. They can help considerably in monitoring a patient's response to treatment and providing positive feedback when levels reduce and/or normalise or backing up concern expressed when levels remain elevated.

As screening and early detection tests, the biological markers of alcohol have not quite lived up to the original expectations. This largely reflects their relative lack of sensitivity, compared with questionnaires that directly enquire about alcohol intake. Biological markers are more sensitive in patients who have alcohol dependence or chronic disease, but even so they detect only 50–60% of patients at best, and their sensitivity may be only 20–30% in a broader clinical population of patients with alcohol use disorders. Physiological markers also are affected by many other pathological processes; for example, there are numerous causes of macrocytosis or liver function test abnormalities other than alcohol, and so their specificity may be only 20–40%, depending on the population studied.

A generally sensitive alcohol biomarker is carbohydrate-deficient transferrin (CDT). This has a sensitivity of 50–70% depending on the assay method and the clinical population. Its outstanding feature is a specificity for alcohol use disorders of 95%. The few causes of a raised CDT apart from alcohol, such as pregnancy and some other forms of chronic liver disease are easily identified. Rare inherited causes of abnormal CDT levels are described, but these barely enter into consideration in routine clinical practice.

Alcohol as its own marker

Measuring a patient's blood alcohol concentration (BAC), or detecting alcohol in other body fluids is a direct and (almost) unequivocal way of identifying alcohol consumption, including consumption at excessive levels. Detecting alcohol consumption in this way and the interpretation of the person's alcohol intake depends crucially on the time of the last drink. After drinking, blood alcohol concentration declines (due to metabolism) at an average rate of 15 mg/100 ml/h. Hence, if a person has a BAC of 50

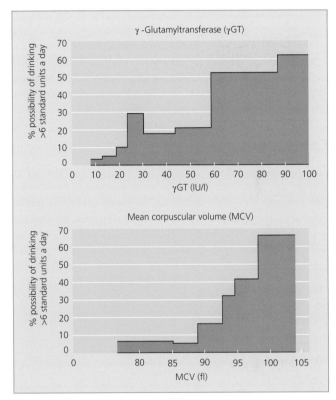

Figure 6.4 Laboratory markers of alcohol misuse.

Table 6.2 Biological markers of alcohol

Alcohol concentration in body fluids	Haematological markers	Liver function tests	Other physiological markers	Metabolites of alcohol
Whole blood or serum alcohol concentration	Mean cell volume (MCV), on full blood count	Raised gamma-glutamyltransferase (GGT)	Carbohydrate-deficient transferrin (CDT)	Raised ethyl acetate
Urinary alcohol concentration	Macrocytic blood picture	Aspartate aminotransferase (AST) or alanine aminotransferase (ALT)	Raised HDL cholesterol	Raised urinary salsolninol
Breath alcohol concentration	Low platelet count	An AST : ALT ratio of 2 : 1 or more		Raised ethyl glucuronide
Salivary alcohol concentration				Raised urinary 5-hydroxy tryptofol and
Sweat patch test				Raised 5-HTOL: 5-HIAAA ratio
Continuous electronic measures of alcohol concentration				

mg/100 ml and has not had any alcohol for 4 h, one can calculate that shortly after their last drink, their BAC would have been around 100 mg/100 ml, and they could have consumed six to eight drinks in the previous couple of hours. If their last drink was 24 hours before, their peak alcohol concentration could have been 300–400 mg/100 ml.

BACs are therefore very useful 'present state' markers of alcohol exposure. They can point to alcohol's involvement in accidents and injuries and are used legally and forensically for this purpose. Note that alcohol-containing swabs should not be used to clean the skin before venepuncture. If a person has a high BAC and is unimpaired, that is good evidence of tolerance and, potentially, alcohol dependence. BACs are not, however, helpful in gauging a person's usual alcohol intake, and their risk of alcohol-related disease.

Breath alcohol analysis is a convenient way of detecting alcohol in the body. Breath concentrations have a relatively fixed relationship with the BAC (the ratio is ~1 : 2200). Time must be allowed for any remaining alcohol in the mouth to be eliminated.

Conclusions

Detecting alcohol use disorders requires the same skill set as other areas of clinical practice – asking relevant questions in a courteous, empathic and non-judgemental way. Screening questionnaires are helpful; for identification alone, the simpler the better, but they are also helpful as a framework for further enquiry and for providing feedback to the patient. Cutaneous stigmata and other physical examination findings are under-recognised and underutilised.

Biological markers provide additional information, especially when abnormal, but better ones are needed and to conclude on the basis of a blood test that a patient has no alcohol use disorder is an act of folly.

Further reading

Bush K, Kivlahan DR, McDonell MB, Fihn SD, Bradley KA. The AUDIT alcohol consumption questions (AUDIT-C): an effective brief screening test for problem drinking. *Archives of Internal Medicine* 1998;158:1789–95.

Hodgson R, Alwyn T, John B, Thom B, Smith A. The FAST alcohol screening test. *Alcohol and Alcoholism* 2002;37:61–6.

Kaner EFS, Dickinson HO, Beyer F, Pienaar E, Schlesinger C, Campbell F, et al. The effectiveness of brief alcohol interventions in primary care settings: a systematic review. *Drug and Alcohol Review* 2009;28:301–23.

National Institute for Health and Care Excellence (NICE). *Alcohol use disorders: diagnosis, assessment and management of harmful drinking and alcohol dependence* (NICE Clinical Guidelines No. 115). London: NICE, February 2011.

Saunders JB, Aasland OG, Babor TF, de la Fuente JR, Grant M. Development of the Alcohol Use Disorders Identification Test (AUDIT): WHO collaborative project on early detection of persons with harmful alcohol consumption II. *Addiction* 1993;88:791–804.

Smith SG, Touquet R, Wright S, Das Gupta N. Detection of alcohol misusing patients in accident and emergency departments: the Paddington Alcohol Test (PAT). *Journal of Accident and Emergency Medicine* 1996;13:308–12.

Sullivan JT, Sykora K, Schneiderman J, Naranjo CA, Sellers EM. Assessment of alcohol withdrawal: the revised Clinical Institute Withdrawal Assessment for Alcohol Scale (CIWA-Ar). *British Journal of Addiction* 1989;84:1353–7.

Wolff K, Marshall EJ. Biological markers of alcohol use. *Psychiatry* 2006;5:437–8.

CHAPTER 7

Medical problems

Alex Paton

OVERVIEW

- Persistent drinking at hazardous and harmful levels can result in damage to almost every organ or system of the body and may be associated with the development of a wide range of chronic diseases affecting most of the body including liver cirrhosis, neurological damage, pancreatitis, cardiomyopathy, intra-uterine growth retardation and foetal alcohol syndrome.

- Hazardous and harmful drinking are commonly encountered among hospital attendees; approximately 20% of patients admitted to hospital for illnesses unrelated to alcohol are drinking at potentially hazardous levels.

- Women contemplating pregnancy should avoid alcohol during conception and in the first trimester. If women chose to drink, they should limit themselves to one to two units once or twice a week and should not get drunk.

Before medical problems are discussed, it is worth emphasising that **more than 80% of the harm done by heavy drinking is socio-economic rather than physical and that severe physical damage is uncommon and often irreversible**. Alcohol misuse is as common as diabetes, and it has replaced syphilis as the great mimic of disease. Its protean symptoms are compounded by the reluctance of drinkers, relatives and health professionals to face up to there being a problem. In addition, as most organs in the body can be affected, the medical approach is that of the doctor looking for signs of gross disease. To concentrate on these is unhelpful and deceptive, because their absence gives a false sense of security. They will not be discussed in detail here; instead, we need to highlight the many non-specific symptoms, which are often vague, multiple and psychosomatic and do not always fit into a recognisable diagnostic pattern.

A few heavy drinkers are referred to doctors because of their drinking and a few are picked up at health checks because of an enlarged liver or abnormal blood test, but most problem drinkers are missed because a drinking history is not obtained or because the importance of symptoms is not appreciated. Surveys show that around 20% of patients in medical wards drink too much, but most are unrecognised; similar findings almost certainly apply to other hospital departments and general practice.

Spotting the problem drinker

The brash, jocular, over familiar manner of the problem drinker, inappropriate to a consultation, may sometimes provide a clue, as might shifty answers to preliminary questions, as denial is common. Symptoms should be regarded sympathetically and not brushed aside, and it is important not to jump to conclusions and lose the person's confidence.

Certain features in the history may provide other evidence (Box 7.1). Sometimes the spouse is the person who attends because of problems with family and children, but they are likely to be reluctant to reveal the true cause.

Family history may reveal risk factors such as alcohol misuse, teetotalism, depression, a broken home and being last in a large family. Drug taking, heavy cigarette smoking, marital disharmony and drinking by the spouse may be features of a dysfunctional family.

People of Irish and Scottish descent seem to drink more than the English and to be more prone to physical damage. Other Europeans may have problems because they are socially accustomed to larger amounts of alcohol. The taboo against drinking among Muslim men is breaking down, and, as a result, they seem to be sensitive to damage but because of the stigma are reluctant to seek help.

Signs

If present, certain signs may be useful pointers: a bloated, plethoric face with telangiectases (Figure 7.1a), bloodshot conjunctivae, acne rosacea, smell of stale alcohol (sometimes disguised by peppermint or aftershave lotion) and raw, red gums that bleed easily. About a third of problem drinkers have a facial appearance that resembles that of Cushing's syndrome. The skin is warm and moist, with a fast bounding pulse and tremor of nicotine-stained fingers,

---

ABC of Alcohol, Fifth Edition. Edited by Anne McCune.
© 2015 John Wiley & Sons, Ltd. Published 2015 by John Wiley & Sons, Ltd.

Figure 7.2 Obesity, infertility and poorly understood hormonal and metabolic changes may not always be recognised as the result of overindulgence. Source: Reproduced with permission from Pressdram Ltd, London. © Pressdram Limited 2014.

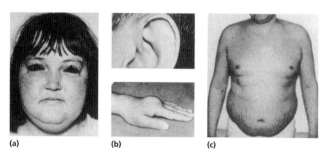

Figure 7.1 Certain signs may be useful pointers. These include **(a)** a bloated, plethoric face, **(b)** gouty tophi on hands and ears, and **(c)** obesity with a pot belly and gynaecomastia.

sometimes designated a pseudothyrotoxic state. Other signs to look for are palmar erythema, bilateral Dupuytren's contractures, parotid swelling (rare) and gouty tophi on ears or hands (Figure 7.1b). Abdominal obesity is common and is sometimes associated with gynaecomastia and abdominal striae (Figure 7.1c). Bruising and scarring indicate old injuries.

Morbidity

Intoxication, for example from bingeing, can be associated with serious metabolic disturbance (alcoholic ketoacidosis), cardiac arrhythmias, nerve palsies, stroke and respiratory failure.

The best-known physical complication, used as a marker for alcohol damage, is cirrhosis of the liver (Box 7.2), although fewer than 10% of heavy drinkers are affected. Numbers have been rising steadily, especially in women, which reflects the increase in misuse over the past 20 years. Other organs that are particularly sensitive have not been studied in such detail, but that constant exposure of the gastrointestinal tract to alcohol might lead to oesophagitis; gastritis; cancers of the mouth, oesophagus, and larynx (with heavy smoking); diarrhoea; and pancreatitis – one of the most unpleasant and painful consequences of misuse – is understandable.

Next in importance is the cardiovascular system, where hypertension and irregularities of cardiac rhythm are relatively frequent. Atrial fibrillation has been called 'holiday heart' in the United States, because it occurs especially during weekend and holiday drinking among relatively naive drinkers.

Ventricular arrhythmias are a likely cause of sudden death in intoxicated people. Alcohol can also precipitate heart muscle disease – cardiomyopathy – which used to be confined to men but is now being diagnosed increasingly in women.

Brain damage from alcohol misuse may be associated with strokes at a young age, cerebral atrophy, subdural haematoma, dementias and Wernicke–Korsakoff syndrome, in which an acute confusional state can be improved dramatically by injection of thiamine (see Chapter 8); otherwise, progressive loss of memory for recent events occurs. Hallucinatory and amnesic states (blackouts and fugues), alcoholic psychosis, alcohol and drug overdose (often a lethal combination), depression, and suicide are well recognised.

Inadequate nutrition can result in beri beri from lack of thiamine, scurvy from deficiency of vitamin C and macrocytic anaemia because of lack of folic acid. Heavy drinking depresses immunity, with a consequent risk of serious infections. Obesity, infertility and poorly understood hormonal and metabolic changes may not always be recognised as the result of overindulgence (Figure 7.2).

Women in particular can suffer from menstrual disturbances and miscarriage, and if drinking is particularly heavy and continuous, fetal growth may be delayed and the child may subsequently suffer behavioural and cognitive impairment. Fortunately, the complete fetal alcohol syndrome is extremely rare, affecting babies of only 1% of mothers who drink really heavily. The usual advice given to women contemplating pregnancy in Britain is that they should avoid alcohol during conception and in the first trimester. If women chose to drink, they should limit themselves to one to two units once or twice a week and should not get drunk. There is uncertainty about how much alcohol is safe to drink in pregnancy; but if a low level is consumed, there is no evidence of harm to an unborn baby.

Box 7.2 **Conditions associated with heavy drinking. See also Figure 7.3**

Conditions associated with heavy drinking

Gut and liver
- Morning anorexia
- Indigestion
- Heartburn
- Vomiting
- Bleeding
- Jaundice
- Oesophagitis
- Gastritis
- Mallory Weiss syndrome
- Aero-digestive cancers
- Diverticulitis
- Pancreatitis
- Hepatitis/cirrhosis/ liver cancer

Gynaecological
- Irregular periods
- Premenstrual tension
- Infertility
- Miscarriage
- 'Small for date' babies
- Fetal alcohol effects
- Fetal alcohol syndrome
- Breast cancer

Chest and heart
- Palpitations
- Chest pain; can mimic angina
- Bronchitis
- 'Asthma'
- Arrhythmias
- Hypertension
- Lobar pneumonia
- Tuberculosis
- Fractured ribs
- Heart failure from beri beri

Hormones and metabolism
- Weight gain or weight loss
- 'Sugar'
- Impotence
- Infertility
- Obesity
- Hyperglycaemia or hypoglycaemia (binge drinking)
- Pseudo-Cushing's syndrome
- Malnutrition – deficiencies of thiamine, vitamin C (scurvy), folic acid
- Alcoholic ketoacidosis (binge drinking)

Nervous system
- Tremor
- Sweating
- Flushing
- Insomnia
- Headache
- Blackouts
- Fits
- Confusion
- Inability to concentrate
- Problems with memory
- Anxiety or depression
- Hallucinations

Renal
- Loin pain
- 'Blood in urine'
- Pelvi-ureteric obstruction
- Chronic nephritis
- Myoglobinuria from rhabdomyolysis

Skin, muscles, nerves and bones
- Bruises, scars
- Flushing
- Acne rosacea
- Psoriasis

- Weakness of thighs
- Myopathy
- Burning legs
- Peripheral neuropathy
- Saturday night palsy (binge drinking)
- Rhabdomyolysis (binge drinking)
- Dupuytren's contracture

- Backache
- Osteoporosis
- Rheumatism
- Gout
- Repeated injuries
- Fractures

Immune system
- Defective immunity
- Infections including AIDS

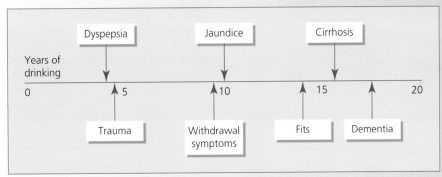

Figure 7.3 Pattern of complications during a heavy drinker's life.

"That's the trouble with us alcoholics. We're a dying breed"

Figure 7.4 Around 33,000 deaths a year in England and Wales are attributed to alcohol misuse. Source: Reproduced with permission from Pressdram Ltd, London. © Pressdram Limited 2014.

Mortality

Around 33,000 deaths a year in England and Wales are attributed to alcohol misuse. Lack of awareness among doctors and reluctance to include alcohol on death certificates mean that this figure is likely to be an underestimate; for example, the death rate from cirrhosis may be up to five times the official figure (Figure 7.4). Furthermore, numbers are weighted heavily towards men, although women increasingly are affected and are more vulnerable.

Deaths are customarily divided into those **specifically related** to alcohol, namely intoxication and binge drinking, fatal accidents and violence, suicide and organ damage known to be alcohol related, and those **associated** with alcohol excess, such as certain cancers, coronary heart disease and stroke and some neuropsychiatric conditions. Death rates for the former have doubled in the past 20 years in both sexes. Drinking in amounts that cause biochemical changes is associated with twice the mortality of the general population.

Is moderate drinking good for the heart?

A great deal of interest has been aroused by epidemiological evidence that moderate drinking is associated with a reduction in deaths from coronary heart disease (Figure 7.5). If the relative risk for non-drinkers is taken as 1, the relative risk may be as low as 0.5 in people who drink moderately and then rise again to exceed 1 in those who drink heavily – the U-shaped or J-shaped curve.

This so-called 'protective' effect can be produced by as little as one to two units of alcohol two or three times a week, and seems to be because of alcohol rather than any particular type of drink. A possible reason is that alcohol reduces clotting and increases

Figure 7.5 … and take the brewery's commendation with a pinch of salt.

protective lipoproteins, although those who champion red wine point to the presence of antioxidants that may help combat oxygen free radicals produced during breakdown of alcohol.

All kinds of deaths related to alcohol tend to be premature, occurring most often between the ages of 40 and 60 years

Much epidemiological evidence for a 'protective' effect is based on studies of white, middle-class, middle-aged men, and alcohol is unlikely to be a universal panacea against coronary heart disease. Women and young drinkers, in whom heart disease is rare, are underrepresented, as are heavy drinkers who may be expected to die prematurely from alcohol-related damage. The benefit seems to be in older men and postmenopausal women. Calls to drink large quantities of, say, red wine 'to protect the heart' should be resisted firmly, because excessive consumption not only **causes** heart attacks but also damages other organs.

To equate the number of lives that *might* be saved by alcohol against those killed is to miss the point that alcohol in excess is *always* potentially dangerous

Further reading

Day C. Who gets alcoholic liver disease: nature or nurture? *Journal of the Royal College of Physicians of London* 2000;34:557–62.

Edwards G, Peters TJ, eds. *Alcohol and alcohol problems.* Edinburgh: Churchill Livingstone, 1994.

Kemm J. Alcohol and breast cancer. *Alcoholism* 1998;17:1–2.

Royal College of Physicians. *A great and growing evil. The medical consequences of alcohol abuse.* London: Tavistock, 1987.

CHAPTER 8

Problems in the Emergency Department – and their solutions

Zulfiquar Mirza and Robin Touquet

OVERVIEW

- The emergency department treats a vast number of patients with alcohol-related conditions.
- It is an ideal environment to identify problems.
- Intervention can make a big difference.
- Referral to an alcohol nurse specialist can reduce re-attendance.
- Alcohol can mask serious underlying pathology.

Emergency departments (EDs) throughout the United Kingdom are all too familiar to patients presenting with alcohol-related problems, and also to those waiting alongside who are entirely sober. Last year, there were approximately 1 million hospital admissions relating to alcohol (Figure 8.1). The total cost to the United Kingdom, in crime, public disorder and health is approximately £20 billion and to the NHS £3 billion. The cost in human life, domestic violence and suffering is incalculable.

Role of the emergency department

The ED not only treats a vast number of patients with alcohol-related problems, but is an excellent opportunity to potentially **prevent** further unscheduled alcohol-related re-attendance (Figure 8.2). This is a 'teachable moment' when the patient is most susceptible to listening to health care professionals (doctor, nurse or alcohol health worker) and realising that they may be drinking excessively, thereby making the alcohol connection for their ED attendance. In this way, the patient is encouraged to 'contemplate change' (i.e. reduce their drinking) as most find attending the ED both unwelcome and intrusive. EDs are extremely busy places with the added pressures of the 4 hour target, so early identification of such patients is a challenge though not insurmountable with in-house alcohol nurse specialists (ANSs)/alcohol health workers (AHWs) providing supportive brief intervention, education, audit and feedback (anagram 'BEAF'). Junior doctors now often rotate jobs every 4 months, so this is of necessity a rolling process.

The role of the ED doctor begins with recognising that the patient has an alcohol-related attendance, treating the acute potentially life-threatening emergency or more minor problem, followed by referral for assessment by an ANS, who can provide invaluable expert help. The ANS may subsequently refer the patient onto a community alcohol service.

Detection in the ED

There is ample evidence to suggest that detection in the ED with early identification together with brief advice (BA) is highly effective. In fact, two systematic reviews have concluded this strategy can reduce alcohol consumption as well as harm. The most focused and commonly used means of detection in the ED is the Paddington alcohol test (PAT) – an evolving educative clinical tool, the latest edition being PAT 2009 (Box 8.1 – see also Chapter 6, Figure 6.3).

This is designed to be brief and pragmatic for use where time is at a premium. The 'Top Ten' presenting conditions in the ED with the highest association with alcohol misuse are listed as an aide memoire: fall, collapse, head injury, assault, accident, feeling unwell, non-specific gastrointestinal, psychiatric and cardiac symptoms, with repeat attendance. These cover approximately 60% of all ED attendances and so reap the most fruitful harvest of misusers for the time spent applying the questionnaire, especially asking, 'Do you feel your current attendance is related to alcohol?' Selective, focused identification reveals a crop of patients who by being led to have insight to cause and effect – drinking and attendance at the ED – the greater the chance of a positive response and the less the likelihood of re-attending.

This early identification and the giving of BA (only 1–2 min by a doctor or nurse) who has managed the patient, having attended to their clinical presenting problem first, are accompanied by the offer of referral to a dedicated AHW for the longer (20–30 min) and more structured BI. The benefits of this approach have been demonstrated by a randomised trial, which found that for every two referrals to the AHW, there was one less re-attendance during the next 12 months. If patients are offered an appointment with the AHW for the same day, almost two-thirds attend; when the gap is

---

ABC of Alcohol, Fifth Edition. Edited by Anne McCune.
© 2015 John Wiley & Sons, Ltd. Published 2015 by John Wiley & Sons, Ltd.

2 days, the figure drops to 28%. The half-life of the 'teachable moment' is therefore less than 48 h. PAT was recently identified as the most commonly (40.5%) used tests in a cross-sectional survey of 187 English EDs.

Another well-recognised screening tool, which can be utilised easily in the ED, is the four-question FAST. A shortened version of the 'gold standard' 12 question alcohol use disorders identification test (AUDIT) (too long itself for ED usage) questionnaire is AUDIT C, which is a series of 3 quick questions which can be used to identify early potential dependence as well as harmful and hazardous

drinkers. Lastly, there is the modified Single-Alcohol Screening Questionnaire (SASQ) as used in the multi-centre SIPS study (Screening and Intervention for Problem drinkerS).

SIPS provides further evidence that the presence of an 'alcohol champion' is associated with successful early identification and delivery of brief advice, provided there is ANS/AHW support (http://www.sips.iop.kcl.ac.uk/).

Clinical presentation and resuscitation

The Advanced Life Support (ALS) mantra of Airway, Breathing and Circulation (ABC) still applies to the initial management of the patient presenting to the ED Resuscitation Room or to Majors.

Figure 8.1 Patient with Colles' fracture holding his own bottle of 'thunderbird'.

> Box 8.1 **PAT 2009 clinical assessment of alcohol misuse (see Touquet and Brown, 2009)**
>
> PAT (2009) is a clinical and therapeutic tool to '**make the connection**' between ED attendance and drinking. PAT was specifically developed to make best use of the '**OPPORTUNISTIC TEACHABLE MOMENT**'.
>
> Any ED doctor or nurse can follow PAT to give **brief advice** (BA) taking less than 2 min for most patients.
>
> **Firstly** – Gain the patient's confidence: Deal with the patient's reason for attending **first,** so they are in a receptive frame of mind for receiving BA (1–2 min).
>
> Then afterwards, apply PAT for '**THE TOP 10'** presentations or when signs of alcohol use.
>
> PAT takes less than a minute for most patients who drink.
>
> **BA** is followed by the offer of a **brief intervention** (BI) from the ANS.
>
> **BI** is a specialist session lasting more than 20 min given by an ANS/AHW – NOT by routine clinical ED staff.
>
> **This reduces the likelihood of re-attendance at the ED.**

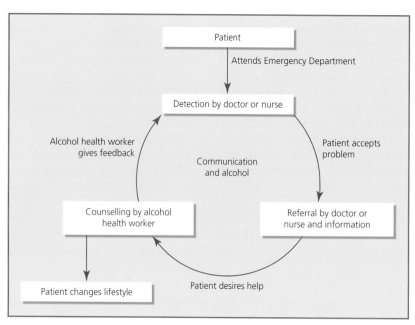

Figure 8.2 Cycle of detection, referral and counselling.

Excluding hypo or hyperglycaemia is an immediate priority – as both may be associated with alcohol misuse and a cause of diminished consciousness or 'collapse'.

Airway

Head injury is common in alcohol misusers attending the ED (see Chapter 14). Airway problems can arise due to a depressed level of consciousness followed by the loss of their gag reflex leaving them unable to maintain their airway. This is further exacerbated by the CNS depressant effect of the alcohol and may be further compounded by other drugs, illicit or not, the patient may have taken simultaneously. The patient may require high flow oxygen or may need a definitive airway, especially if their Glasgow coma score (GCS) is 8 or less.

Breathing

Breathing problems due to excess alcohol can be due to aspiration pneumonia or in extremis respiratory arrest. In this situation, full UK Resuscitation ALS guidelines apply. An extremely helpful though often forgotten indicator of respiratory compromise is the respiratory rate (normal 12–20 breaths/min), combined with oxygen saturation monitoring, remembering the possible problem of carbon dioxide retention and respiratory or metabolic acidosis.

Circulation

Circulatory collapse manifesting with tachycardia, hypotension, increased capillary refill time, pallor and sweating, and cold peripheries may be due to otherwise unrecognised liver cirrhosis and bleeding gastro-oesophageal varices. It is important to recognise that any suspected upper GI bleeding is as likely to be non-variceal bleeding as bleeding due to varices. Timely endoscopy is thus important for this group of patients. No examination of blood loss is complete without doing a rectal examination and looking for clinical stigmata of liver disease (Chapter 11). Shock with warm peripheries may be due to septic shock as dependent drinkers, as well as those with cirrhosis, are more likely to develop infections.

The immediate management would include two large bore cannulae in the antecubital fossae, drawing blood for a full blood count, clotting, liver function tests, creatinine and electrolytes, glucose, amylase, and a group and save (minimum) or cross match as well as a base line blood alcohol concentration (BAC). Patients with an initial BAC of more than 100 mg/100 ml who start to withdraw are more likely to develop signs of delirium tremens (DTs) which warrants early detection and prevention. In addition, the environment of the ED resuscitation room (RR) is frenetic; patients are usually obtunded and management consequently is standardized ('ABCDE' as taught in ATLS). BACs should be requested (see Box 8.3) at the outset. The BAC may be low – less than 50 mg/100 ml – which excludes alcohol as a possible cause of unconsciousness. Knowing the BAC helps clinical judgement and decisions. When high, the level must also be flagged up later for the ANS/AHW when the patient has left the RR, remembering that, for the tolerant drinker, levels of up to 600 mg/100 ml are possible (demonstrating the vital need for BI).

However, BAC requests sent to the laboratory will take an hour for a result. An 'alcostick' (Figure 8.3 – to work like a glucostick) that gives an immediate trolley-side result for clinical management would be an extremely useful tool. If giving IV (or IM) B vitamins (pabrinex) for chronic alcohol misuse with malnutrition ensure a BAC is requested (or test by 'alcostick') first.

Withdrawal symptoms

Patients with alcohol problems can present with a myriad of symptoms, including confusion, agitation, anxiety, sweating, nausea, vomiting, tremor, tachycardia, hallucination and fits. Benzodiazepines are the drugs of choice (NICE CG 100) for the management of withdrawal symptoms. The dependent drinker risks developing Wernicke's encephalopathy from a combination of chronic alcohol misuse and poor diet leading to thiamine deficiency. This is relatively common and potentially lethal – reversible if treated early – but often not recognised or even considered early on. The common signs of confusion, ataxia and varying levels of impaired consciousness are difficult or impossible to differentiate from drunkenness, and the characteristic eye signs of nystagmus and ophthalmoplegia are present in only 25% of patients (see neurology

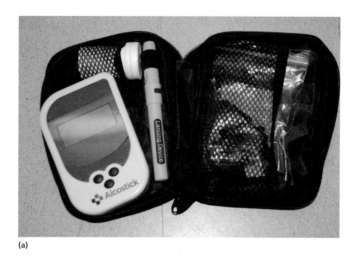

(a)

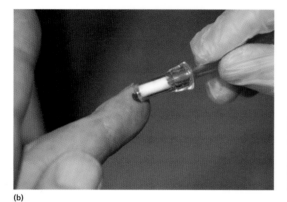

(b)

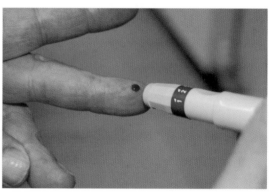

(c)

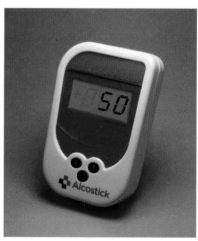

Figure 8.3 (a) Alcostick pack. **(b)** Finger-prick (for [alcohol] as per Glucostick. **(c)** One minute [alcohol] – as per [glucose]. (manufactured by 'SureScreenScientifics', Derby).

chapter 14). Therefore if in doubt, parenteral B complex vitamins should be administered while the patient is still drunk. Oral treatment is ineffective even if such patients were compliant because absorption is poor. The only available intravenous (iv) treatment which includes thiamine (B_1), riboflavin (B_2), pyridoxine (B_6), ascorbic acid and nicotinamide is Pabrinex®. Two pairs of vials of Pabrinex® 1 and 2 diluted in 100 ml crystalloid solution should be given IV over 30 min (anaphylaxis is then rare). Intramuscular

Pabrinex® includes benzyl alcohol as a local anaesthetic and can be used in patients lacking venous access.

Drunk patients can be very stressful for inexperienced ED medical and nursing staff to manage. If clinically trained ANSs are available on the 'shop floor' (who often have prescribing skills), then they can not only improve the standards of care for such challenging patients but by relieving colleagues' stress can stimulate mutual respect to facilitate education over alcohol management issues generally.

Alcohol and trauma

Falls

Head injury is a common reason for drunk patients to present to the ED. This can be caused by falling whilst walking due to an unsteady gait or falling from a height.

These can be a challenge to manage as the depressed level of consciousness may not necessarily be due the alcohol itself, but due to an underlying intracranial bleed (subdural haematoma).

Domestic violence

Patients with alcohol-related problems may be the perpetrators or victims of domestic violence and the ED physician must maintain a high index of suspicion.

Road traffic accidents

Alcohol is well known to play a significant role. Road traffic accidents (RTAs) often lead to multiple injuries and can be caused by drink driving or when an inebriated pedestrian is struck by an oncoming vehicle. This will necessitate a full trauma work up as per the Advanced Trauma Life Support guidelines. Being drunk makes clearing the cervical spine impossible clinically and may therefore necessitate a CT scan of both the brain and the cervical spine.

Alcohol and multi-disciplinary team working in the ED

Patients with alcohol-related problems often have co-existent psychiatric illness. Their attendance to the ED gives an ideal opportunity to involve psychiatry colleagues and undertake joint assessments with the ANS/AHW. The Royal College of Physicians recommended that all acute hospitals use the latter to counsel such patients. The ANS/AHW is an ideal resource to not only educate and support these patients but also to make best use of the 'teachable moment'. The ANS/AHW can be instrumental in ensuring a smooth transition of these patients into the community services.

The development of the cadre of ANSs/AHWs, based preferably in the ED itself or elsewhere in every acute hospital is perhaps the biggest single advance in the management of alcohol misusing patients in the ED this new millennium.

Further reading

Crawford MJ, Patton R, Touquet R, Drummond C, Byford S, Barrett B, et al. Screening and referral for brief intervention of alcohol-misusing patients in an emergency department: a pragmatic randomized controlled trial. *Lancet* 2004;364:1334–9.

Kaner EF, Dickinson HO, Beyer F, Pienaar E, Schlesinger C, Campbell F, et al. The effectiveness of brief alcohol interventions in primary care settings: a systematic review. *Drug and Alcohol Review* 2009;28:301–23.

Nilsen P, Baird J, Mello MJ, Nirenberg T, Woolard R, Bendtsen P, et al. A systematic review of emergency care brief alcohol interventions for injury patients. *Journal of Substance Abuse Treatment* 2008;35:184–201.

Thomson AL, Cook CCH, Touquet R, Henry JA. Royal College of Physicians report on alcohol: guidelines for managing Wernicke's encephalopathy in the A and E department. *Alcohol & Alcoholism* 2002;37:513–21.

Touquet R, Brown A. PAT (2009) – revisions to the Paddington Alcohol Test for early identification of alcohol misuse and brief advice to reduce emergency department re-attendance. *Alcohol & Alcoholism* 2009a;44:284–6. Open access http://alcalc.oxfordjournals.org/cgi/reprint/agp016?ijkey=HImeNE O7f6izT0F&keytype=ref (accessed 18 September 2014).

Touquet R, Brown A. Pragmatic implementation of brief interventions. In: Cherpitel CJ, Borges G, Giesbrecht N, Hungerford D, Peden M, Poznyak V, et al., eds. *Alcohol and injuries*. Geneva: World Health Organization, 2009b: Chap 12.4. http://www.who.int/substance_abuse/msbalcinuries.pdf (accessed 18 September 2014).

Touquet R, Csipke E, Holloway P, Brown A, Patel T, Seddon AJ, et al. Resuscitation room blood alcohol concentrations: one-year cohort study. *Emergency Medicine Journal* 2008;25:752–6. OPEN ACCESS. http://emj. bmj.com/cgi/content/short/25/11/752?keytype=ref&ijkey=ObfG2ppgeG5 Gwwr (accessed 18 September 2014).

Williams S, Brown A, Patton R, Crawford MJ, Touquet R. The half life of the 'teachable moment' for alcohol misusing patients in the Emergency Department. *Drug and Alcohol Dependence* 2005;77:205–8.

CHAPTER 9

Alcohol and the young person

William Christian, Sian Veysey and Anne Frampton

OVERVIEW

- The number of young people who drink appears to be falling.
- However, for those who do drink the amount of alcohol consumed is rising in part due to an increase in binge drinking.
- Parental influence on young people can be both positive and negative with most childrens' first exposure to alcohol being in the home.
- A knowledge of local safeguarding procedures is essential for clinicians who come into contact with children, young people or their parents where alcohol misuse is suspected.

Epidemiology of alcohol and the young person

The reasons why children drink are multifactorial (Table 9.1). Many children's first ever experience of alcohol is within the home, and up to three-quarters cite their parents as the primary influence on whether they drink alcohol or not. It has been suggested that the amount of alcohol that young people see as 'normal' is increasing. In the United Kingdom, this observation goes hand in hand with an increase in adults drinking at home.

The mean weekly alcohol consumption for young people aged 11–15 years has increased significantly over the past two decades (see Table 9.2). Some of this increase appears to be due to a greater tendency to binge drink amongst older children.

However, the overall number of young people under the age of 15 years who drink alcohol appears to be falling. In 2010, a survey of secondary school children in England, commissioned by the NHS Information Centre, reported that only 45% of 11–15-year-olds had tried alcohol once in their lives compared with 61% in 2003 and 51% in 2009.

Compared with the rest of Europe, 15–16-years-olds in the United Kingdom are more likely to have drunk alcohol in the previous 30 days (65% compared with a European average of 57%) and to have binge drunk (52% vs a European average of 32% drinking five or more drinks on one occasion in the previous 30 days).

Alcohol policy and young people

The government outlined its alcohol strategy in 2012. This aimed to reduce alcohol consumption amongst young people by tackling some of the causes of increased drinking in the young outlined in Table 9.1.

Interventions included increasing the minimum unit price for alcohol, increasing the powers given to local agencies working with young people who do drink, providing clear information to young people about the risks of alcohol consumption and working with the advertising industry to reduce the attractiveness to young people of alcohol in advertisements.

Some of the other policies covering young people and alcohol are outlined in Table 9.3.

Alcohol and pregnancy

The relationship between alcohol intake during pregnancy and its effect on the unborn child and subsequent childhood development is complicated and not fully understood. Although there is some evidence supporting a dose-related effect, there does not appear to be a minimum threshold or clear differences between regular and binge drinking during pregnancy. What is known is that alcohol consumption at any stage during pregnancy can lead to a range of associated cognitive, behavioural and physical problems in the foetus, collectively known as the 'foetal alcohol spectrum disorders' (FASD), which, at their most severe, form the clinical diagnosis of foetal alcohol syndrome. Four criteria are required for a diagnosis of foetal alcohol syndrome. These are as follows:

1 pre- and/or post-natal growth deficiency,
2 central nervous system dysfunction,
3 physical dysmorphism (see Figure 9.1) and
4 evidence of maternal antenatal alcohol consumption.

Because of the known risks of alcohol intake during pregnancy, it is important that pregnant women have an alcohol screen antenatally. In addition to providing an opportunity for counselling and closer surveillance postnatally, this also allows for identification of problems that may be associated with alcohol use such as tobacco/recreational drug use and increased risk of domestic violence.

Early drinking and the young brain

The effects of alcohol exposure *in utero* on the developing brain and the consequent potential outcomes are shown in Table 9.4. However, as maturation of brain development is not complete until after adolescence, excessive consumption of alcohol by young people themselves can also cause neurological problems in both the short term (depression, poor concentration and decreased reaction times) and long term (reduction in verbal and non-verbal memory and ability to learn). This correlates with MRI studies demonstrating a 10% reduction in hippocampal volume and disruption of neural transmission in the hippocampus and cortex of adolescents who drink excessively.

Parental influence on young people's drinking

Parental influences can be both positive and negative. Relevant factors include how the parents themselves drink and their associated attitudes to alcohol. They also include their actual parenting methods, for example enforcing rules and boundaries and having an open dialogue between members of the family.

Whilst most children's first experience of alcohol is in the home, it would appear that significantly less young people see the adults in their lives as providing a *positive* role model of responsible drinking.

Table 9.1 Common factors influencing alcohol intake in children

Children may drink more if there is

- a lack of family support or parental supervision
- a family history of problematic alcohol use
- increased access by the young person to expendable income
- increased access to cheap alcohol
- exposure to appealing advertising material
- increased peer expectations of alcohol consumption

Table 9.2 Mean weekly units of alcohol consumed by young people aged 11–15 years (1990–2009 data)

Gender	1990	1992	1994	1996	1998	2000	2001	2002	2003	2004	2005	2006	2007	2007[a]	2008[a]	2009[a]
						1990–2007									**2007–2009**	
Boys	5.7	7.0	7.4	9.7	11.3	11.7	10.6	11.5	10.5	11.3	11.5	12.3	9.6	13.1	16.0	11.9
Girls	4.7	4.7	5.4	7.0	8.4	9.1	8.9	9.6	8.5	10.2	9.5	10.5	8.8	12.4	13.1	11.3
Total	5.3	6.0	6.4	8.4	9.9	10.4	9.8	10.6	9.5	10.7	10.5	11.4	9.2	12.7	14.6	11.6

Source: The Information Centre for Health and Social Care. Smoking, drinking and drug use among young people in England in 2009. © http://www.hscic.gov.uk.
[a]The method of calculating units of alcohol changed in 2006, making direct comparisons with data published before this time is difficult.

Table 9.3 Policies, Young people and alcohol

The *Youth Alcohol Action Plan* (Department for Children Schools and Families, 2008)	Three main strategies – (i) working with police and the courts to stop underage drinking, (ii) providing health information for parents and young people about how consumption of alcohol can affect children and young people and (iii) working with the alcohol industry to reduce the sale of alcohol to under-18s and to promote alcohol in a more responsible way
Every Child Matters – Change for Children (2004); *Every Child Matters: Change for Children Young People and Drugs (2005)*	Aims for every child to have the support they need to be healthy; stay safe; enjoy and achieve; make a positive contribution; and achieve economic well-being. Places the emphasis on multi-agency working. Part of the focus is on reduction of harm from alcohol and drugs which was updated in 2005
Safe. Sensible. Social. The Next Steps in the National Alcohol Strategy (2007)	Includes strategy to deal with underage drinking through measures such as promoting guidance, education and awareness to young people, stopping underage sales and working with local businesses

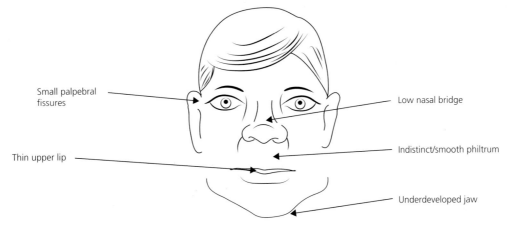

Figure 9.1 Facial features associated with foetal alcohol spectrum disorder.

Small palpebral fissures

Thin upper lip

Low nasal bridge

Indistinct/smooth philtrum

Underdeveloped jaw

Table 9.4 Effect of alcohol on the central nervous system structure and function

Area of brain affected	Anatomical/MRI findings	Example of behavioural deficit
Parietal lobe	Reduced size; increased reduction in white matter compared to grey matter	Reduced visual–spatial awareness
Frontal lobe	Reduced tissue density	Behavioural problems, lack of inhibition, reduced executive functions such as ability to plan and organise
Cerebellum	Reduction in cerebellar volume – in particular, the cerebellar vermis	Impaired balance and co-ordination
Corpus callosum	Partial or complete agenesis	Impaired verbal learning, impaired attention
Basal ganglia	Reduced growth – particularly in the caudate nucleus	Impaired motor control, longer reaction times, impaired visual–spatial ability and Impaired ability to switch between tasks
Hippocampus	Reduced size	Impaired spatial learning and memory tasks

Parental alcohol misuse

Some studies estimate that parental alcohol misuse affects over a million children in England alone.

Direct disclosure of an alcohol problem at home is not common, although some children do try to ask for help, e.g. Childline calls.

Apart from directly affecting a young person's drinking behaviour, parental alcohol problems clearly have marked effects on a child's family life.

Day-to-day life can become more chaotic and unpredictable, with less routine, more uncertainty and blurring of family roles and responsibilities. Communication often breaks down, both within the family unit and outside it. Possibly because of shame or guilt, social isolation of all or part of the family can occur, including the child.

The end results of parental drinking include behavioural, psychological and physical effects, which can manifest from antisocial or emotional problems to a range of issues with schooling.

It is important to be aware that the outcomes of drinking (chaos and conflict for example) are as harmful as the actual drinking itself.

One recognised strategy to reduce harm to children whose parents have an alcohol problem is to build coping mechanisms and 'resilience' within children and young people. Some of these appear to be intrinsic to the child, and others could be modified.

Domestic violence

Whilst there is a clear link between domestic violence and alcohol (up to a third of domestic violence is alcohol related), it is unclear whether either is causative. It is possible that alcohol may be a cause or at least cited as an excuse for domestic violence. With one in four women and one in seven men encountering domestic violence at some point in their lives, this has an important consequence for the children that reside within those relationships.

Safeguarding children and child protection

The effects of alcohol on a child's well-being are extensive and complex. The link between alcohol and child abuse of all kinds is well recognised, with literature reports of up to a quarter of child abuse cases having alcohol playing a part.

The effects of parental alcohol problems on their parenting capacity may be as simple as not picking up from school or organising meals, through to emotional detachment or instability. The outcome however, can be a lack of ability to 'care' through to neglect, violence, cruelty or sexual abuse.

Sharing information between education, health and social care agencies on potential risk to children from their own or family alcohol use is well documented to be a fundamental part of protecting children. Possibly because of the wide acceptance of alcohol within our society, reporting the issues relating to alcohol may be overlooked, especially if compared to other substance misuse reporting.

It is essential that local Child Protection procedures are in place to ensure that the impact on children and young people from adverse alcohol behaviour is reduced. Is also important for clinicians to consider there may be child protection issues when a parent admitted with alcohol use disorder and be aware of local policies for sharing this information.

Risk behaviours and personal safety

Because the physical effects of alcohol are more marked, the other outcomes are more pronounced also. Young people may be less able to manage the emotional effects or lack the experience necessary to handle altered judgements, behaviours and perceptions.

Overall, this means that the behaviours that come from drinking or getting drunk can leave young people open to greater risks over and above just physical effects.

There are well recognised risks associated with young people who drink alcohol, above the level seen in those who do not. This applies especially within the teenage population (Table 9.5).

Education and schooling

Alcohol education is now in the National Curriculum for 11–16-year-olds, and much supporting information is available via the Internet and other media, including advice from the Department for Children, Schools and Families. Associated recommendations have also placed emphasis on parental and community education and information.

The aim is to support young people to learn positive alcohol behaviours for life by giving them the tools to make safe and informed decisions. The behaviours learnt as children become set into young adulthood.

Table 9.5 Risks associated with alcohol in young people

Physical	Victims of assault including robbery
	Accidental injury
	Direct medical effects including hangovers, blackouts and vomiting
	Other substance use
Sexual	Unsafe sex
	Sexually transmitted infections
	Unplanned pregnancy
	Sexual assault
Police	Driving effects – licence removal/fines
	Drunkenness/antisocial behaviour
	Criminal record
	Effects on employment/job prospects

An associated approach has focussed on delaying the age at which children begin to drink regularly rather than attempting to stop them drinking altogether. The younger the age of a regular drinker, the more likely they are to suffer the longer term effects of alcohol.

While there has been a reduction in the overall number of young people drinking in the United Kingdom in recent years (compared to a sharp increase prior to that), it remains unproven whether this is a direct effect of education and information programmes.

However, it is clear that young people themselves welcome information about alcohol, drugs and tobacco.

Assessment and referral of children and young people identified as having an alcohol problem

When alcohol misuse in a young person is identified, any assessment undertaken should take into consideration the duration and severity of the alcohol misuse, associated health and social problems and the potential need for assisted withdrawal. The goal of any intervention in young people who are identified as misusing alcohol is abstinence in almost all circumstances.

Strategies used will depend on the individual circumstances but include the following:

- Referral to the child and adolescent mental health services (CAMHS);
- Cognitive behavioural therapy;

Table 9.6 Advice from the Chief Medical Officer

1. Children and their parents and carers are advised that an alcohol-free childhood is the healthiest and best option. However, if children drink alcohol, it should not be until at least the age of 15 years.
2. If young people aged 15–17 years consume alcohol, it should always be with the guidance of a parent or carer or in a supervised environment.
3. Parents and young people should be aware that drinking, even at of age 15 years or older, can be hazardous to health and that not drinking is the healthiest option for young people. If 15–17-year-olds do consume alcohol, they should do so infrequently and certainly on no more than 1 day a week. Young people aged 15–17 years should never exceed recommended adult daily limits and on days when they drink, consumption should usually be below such levels.
4. The importance of parental influences on children's alcohol use should be communicated to parents, carers and professionals. Parents and carers require advice on how to respond to alcohol use and misuse by children
5. Support services must be available for children and young people who have alcohol-related problems and their parents

- Family therapy;
- In patient care for those who need assisted withdrawal. This may include the use of withdrawal medication under the direction of a specialist.

Advice from the chief medical officer

Advice from the Chief Medical Officer is summarised in Table 9.6.

Further reading

Centre for Excellence and Outcomes in Children and Young People's Services (C4EO). *Reducing alcohol consumption by young people and so improving their health, safety and wellbeing.* March 2011. http://archive.c4eo.org.uk/themes/youth/alcoholconsumption/ (accessed 05/02/2015).

HM Government Home Office. *The Government's alcohol strategy.* 2012. https://www.gov.uk/government/uploads/system/uploads/attachment_data/file/224075/alcohol-strategy.pdf) does work (accessed 05/02/2015).

National Centre for Social Research/National Foundation for Educational Research, 2010. *Smoking, drinking and drug use among young people in England in 2013.* http://www.hscic.gov.uk/catalogue/PUB14579 (accessed 05/02/2015).

The European School Survey Project on Alcohol and Other Drugs 2011. http://www.espad.org/ (accessed 18 September 2014).

CHAPTER 10

Alcohol and the older person

Jarrod Richards and Rachel Bradley

OVERVIEW

- Elderly alcohol use is common, increasing and under-recognised.
- Presentation is not always typical.
- Screening tools can be useful with a comprehensive history.
- Alcohol is associated with falls and cognitive problems.
- Older people can do well with treatment.

Epidemiology

There is currently both a rising trend in problem drinking and in the proportion of elderly people. Alcohol problems are under-diagnosed in the elderly; and with alcohol intake increasing amongst the younger population, we are likely to see a cohort of people ageing from a population of heavier drinkers. As with many other conditions, the elderly have rarely been included in alcohol research, though this is changing. In a recent survey of non-institutionalised Americans older than 65 years of age, 13% of men and 8% of women reported at-risk alcohol use, and more than 14% of men and 3% of women reported binge drinking. Of elderly patients who present to hospital emergency departments, the prevalence of alcohol dependency may be as high as 15%. The definitions for alcohol misuse and the UK government guidelines for alcohol intake are based on evidence relating to a younger population, and may not be appropriate for older people as their handling of alcohol is impaired. This is due to a lower ratio of body fat to water, generally poorer health, reduced hepatic blood flow and less efficient hepatic metabolism. This results in a higher blood alcohol level for a given amount of alcohol which will be less well tolerated by the older person and lead to more significant effects, particularly on the brain.

There may be an impact of retirement on drinking patterns, and it is generally assumed that retirement can bring an increased risk of alcoholism. Retirement may change a social network and cause stress due to financial or societal role changes (Box 10.1). Associations between retirement and alcohol intake are not direct or consistent. Older alcohol drinkers are more likely to drink alone at home, which is more difficult to recognise and monitor. They may be self-medicating other physical or mental health problems. The majority of older alcohol misusers have had chronic alcohol problems throughout their lives. Others start drinking later in life, with habits that are more likely to have resulted from stressful life events. These drinkers tend to have better outcomes.

Presentation and screening in older people

As with a number of illnesses, older, frailer patients often present their alcohol problems with frailty syndromes such as memory problems, falls, incontinence or functional limitation and vulnerability (Figure 10.1). These are lacking the specific signs and symptoms that a younger patient may display (Box 10.2). This limits recognition. Older patients already take a larger amount of medications, increasing the risk of pharmacological interactions between them and alcohol.

Older patients have a greater reluctance to admit to alcohol abuse, often due to stigma or shame. There may be a lack of understanding or awareness by healthcare practitioners. Ageism remains prevalent in attitudes towards alcohol use, with carers often reluctant to recognise the gravity of a problem, as it is 'all they have left'. A detailed alcohol history remains important and must be attenuated to consider the lower levels of alcohol required to cause health problems (Box 10.3).

Historically there has been an underestimating of problem drinking in older people, particularly as screening tools were validated using younger patients. The commonly used CAGE questionnaire (Chapter 6) relies on symptoms of dependence seen less in the elderly; so though it retains specificity, it becomes insufficiently sensitive. The Michigan alcohol screening test (MAST) was adapted to the MAST-G questionnaire or (short) SMAST-G for use in the elderly. These tests are sensitive in elderly populations, but have a limited applicability as they are validated in a US as opposed to a UK population, and have a reduced sensitivity in an inpatient and medical outpatient population. It is scored out of 10, with a score of 2 or more indicating a degree of problem. They are also

---

ABC of Alcohol, Fifth Edition. Edited by Anne McCune.
© 2015 John Wiley & Sons, Ltd. Published 2015 by John Wiley & Sons, Ltd.

Figure 10.1 Older, frailer patients with alcohol problems often present to hospital with frailty syndromes © Jarrod Richards.

Box 10.1 **Reasons why older people may drink:**

- Habitual
- Boredom
- Anxiety
- Depression
- Insomnia
- Grief
- Loneliness
- Ill health
- Pain

Box 10.2 **Frailty syndromes that alcoholism may acutely present with:**

- Falls, injuries and fractures
- Immobility
- Functional decline
- Delirium and confusion
- Incontinence
- Hypothermia

more time-consuming to complete than the CAGE questionnaire. The AUDIT tool and its variations were also initially designed for use in younger adults to screen for hazardous alcohol use before alcohol related damage occurred, making it particularly useful in primary care. Due to the limited validity and acceptability of these screening tools, they should always be used in careful conjunction with a thorough clinical assessment (Chapter 6).

Box 10.3 **Important chronic presentations of alcohol use in the elderly:**

- Cognitive decline
- Depression
- Malnutrition
- Bone marrow suppression, macrocytosis
- Heart disease (AF, cardiomyopathy, hypertension)
- Stroke
- Adverse drug reactions
- Liver disease (fatty liver, cirrhosis)
- Self-neglect
- Social isolation

Figure 10.2 Alcohol as a falls risk factor will not be as obvious as this Source: Reproduced with permission from Mike Cannings/BMinc. © Mike Cannings, Creative Director, BMinc.

Falls (Figure 10.2)

High alcohol use increases the frequency of falls. Frequent, unexplained falls and recurrent injuries are a common way in which an older alcohol abuser may present to a healthcare service. Bruising, rib fractures or facial trauma should act as a prompt to screen for alcohol misuse. Chronic alcohol use impairs balance and can result in incoordination and postural instability. Direct effects of peripheral neuropathy and myopathy can also contribute to falls (see Chapter 13). Alcohol may also potentiate the effect of other sedatives or anticoagulants increasing the risk of a fall, bleeding after a fall or even a spontaneous bleeding such as subdural haemorrhage.

A high alcohol intake is associated with an increase in fragility fractures, such as hip, wrist and vertebral fractures, and impaired fracture healing. Alcohol is a cause of secondary osteoporosis, and may have a direct toxic effect on bone metabolism, though its direct mechanism is unclear, and likely to be multifactorial. Alcohol-related liver disease also leads to impaired vitamin D metabolism which impacts on bone health. Excess alcohol use is frequently accompanied by malnutrition, low weight, immobility and smoking as confounders for osteoporosis. A high index of suspicion is required regarding falls in the older alcohol user. Prompt referral to a falls service for multidisciplinary assessment is indicated. Here, other falls risk factors can be identified and addressed. Physiotherapy and occupational therapy can reduce risk of falls, along with other interventions such as cataract surgery or chiropody. Calcium and vitamin D supplementation along with bone protection therapy should be considered. This should be in parallel with the support of alcohol cessation.

Cognition

Chronic alcohol use can result in cerebral atrophy in many brain areas independent of Wernicke's encephalopathy or Korsakoff's psychosis (Chapter 13). There is an epidemiological association between chronic alcohol use and cognitive impairment, though a neuropathological process is yet to be definitively identified.

Alcohol problems are often uncovered in the memory clinic. Alcohol use should be screened for in patients presenting with memory problems, and advice to cut down or stop alcohol should be given as many will recover. There is probably an overlap of other dementias in many alcohol users, so the role of dementia medication is not yet clear. It is important to reassess cognition after a period of abstinence as alcohol abuse remains a potentially reversible cause of pseudodementia.

Delirium is common, and also a presentation of an alcohol use disorder in the elderly, and should be considered in any delirious patient as part of a comprehensive assessment (Box 10.4). Wernicke's encephalopathy is under-recognised in the elderly, as it is often mistaken for dementia or other causes of delirium (Box 10.4). Clinicians should have a low threshold for treating Wernicke's encephalopathy, treating confused patients with intravenous thiamine (Chapter 13). Acute intoxication, delirium and underlying dementia can result in circumstances where assessment and approach to someone's capacity to decide on drinking, medical treatment, or deciding to live in dangerous circumstances can be incredibly challenging. Many of these states are reversible, so care must be taken in deciding on a lack of capacity without view to reassessment.

Box 10.4 **Characteristics of delirium:**

- Abrupt onset
- Fluctuating course
- Clouding of consciousness
- Reduced attention
- Disorientation
- Hallucinations
- Behaviour changes

Box 10.5 **Approach to managing alcohol problems**

- Ask
- Assess
- Advise
- Assist
- Arrange

Managing alcohol in the elderly

Ageism remains prevalent, and can manifest as therapeutic nihilism. Referral for treatment should not be limited because of age, though significant barriers do exist such as co-morbid health conditions and cognitive impairment. A holistic approach should be taken with a comprehensive history to establish an underlying cause, with a detailed enquiry into the psychological and social consequences (Box 10.5). In tailored groups, interventions for alcohol misuse in the elderly do work, so it is important to remain positive.

Safe drinking limits for the elderly remain a controversial area. A significant proportion of alcohol-related liver disease presents over the age of 60 years, with mortality outcomes significantly worse in this group. Similar approaches are required in the elderly as in the young. Though it is of limited availability, age-specific services can give added benefit. Older patients may disengage from the more boisterous support groups in areas of a town they may fear going to.

Alcohol withdrawal symptoms can be more protracted in the elderly, and confusion is a predominant feature of withdrawal in the elderly. In the very old or frail, withdrawal is best managed in an in-patient setting, ideally electively in a specialised addiction unit. Excessive sedation with benzodiazepines should be avoided, and lower doses of drugs such as benzodiazepines should be used. A shorter acting benzodiazepine such as oxazepam could be considered (Chapters 11 and 17). Relapse prevention medications, such as disulfram, may be tolerated less well than in a younger patient. Older patients with liver disease and encephalopathy may have intolerable difficulty with diarrhoea when prescribed lactulose because of frailty and immobility.

Key recommendations have been made in the joint working party document 'Our invisible addicts' which should be taken into consideration for future policy, such as safe drinking limits for the elderly. Future work in alcohol misuse in the elderly will hopefully include a better understanding of the scale of the problem, research into new age-appropriate interventions, and individuals and institutions prioritising the training of staff and developing of specific services.

Further reading

Berks J, McCormick R. Screening for alcohol misuse in elderly primary care patients: a systematic literature review. *International Psychogeriatrics* 2008;20:1090–103.
Blazer DG, Wu L-T. The epidemiology of at-risk and binge drinking among middle-aged and elderly community adults: national survey on drug use and health. *The American Journal of Psychiatry* 2009;166:1162–9.

Blondell R. Alcohol abuse and self-neglect in the elderly. *Journal of Elder Abuse & Neglect* 2000;11:55–75.

Blow F. *Michigan Alcoholism Screening Test – Geriatric Version (MAST-G).* Ann Arbor: University of Michigan Alcohol Research Center, 1991.

Dar K. Alcohol use disorders in elderly people: fact or fiction? *Advances in Psychiatric Treatment* 2006;12:173–81.

Our invisible addicts. First report of the Older Persons' Substance Misuse Working Group of the Royal College of Psychiatrists (College Report CR165). June 2011. http://www.rcpsych.ac.uk/files/pdfversion/cr165.pdf (accessed 18 September 2014).

CHAPTER 11

Alcohol and the liver

Anne McCune

OVERVIEW

- Liver disease is the fifth commonest cause of death in the United Kingdom, and alcohol is the main cause of liver disease in the United Kingdom and Europe. The prevalence of alcohol-related liver disease (ALD) has risen sharply in the United Kingdom over the past few years.

- ALD disease is preventable. Screening for alcohol misuse should be universal in healthcare settings.

- Binge drinking is more prevalent in Northern and Eastern European countries, especially in younger people. The effect of this pattern of drinking on ALD disease risk is still not precisely known.

- Alcoholic hepatitis (AH) is an acute form of ALD with a high mortality. Severe AH requires hospitalisation and specialist care, including assessment for liver biopsy and nutritional support. Consensus guidelines currently recommend the use of corticosteroids.

- With abstinence the majority of patients with decompensated ALD improve and do not require liver transplantation.

- Patients with ALD cirrhosis should be considered for transplantation if their liver disease has failed to recover sufficiently after around 3 months of abstinence.

Introduction

Harmful drinkers (men drinking more than 50 units/week and women more than 35 units/week) have a substantially increased risk of organ damage, including liver disease, and alcohol ranks third (behind smoking and high blood pressure) as a cause of premature death in Europe. Liver disease is now the fifth most common cause of death in the United Kingdom, and the majority of liver deaths are alcohol related. A close correlation exists between population alcohol consumption and liver disease mortality. Deaths from ALD have risen sharply (Figure 11.1) – in stark contrast to lung, heart disease, cancer and stroke where rates have fallen. Of concern too is that the United Kingdom is one of the few developed nations with an upward trend in mortality (Figure 11.2), especially

as alcohol-related liver cirrhosis is a disease of the relatively young with most deaths occurring below the age of 60 years.

Pattern of drinking and risk of liver disease

Alcohol is metabolised in the liver (mainly through oxidative pathways), and regular heavy drinking leads to accumulation in liver cells (hepatocytes), progressive inflammation, fibrosis and eventually cirrhosis. The effects of drinking too much and too fast, usually to intoxication (binge drinking), on the liver are not clearly understood yet. Regular daily excessive drinking is however an established risk factor for cirrhosis, and the total amount (e.g. units or grams) of alcohol consumed is important rather than type (e.g. spirits vs. wine vs. beer). The risk of cirrhosis rises slowly and steadily in a linear pattern until a threshold of around 30 units per week is reached when there is a marked increase in risk thereafter. However, only a small proportion (10–20%) of all heavy drinkers will develop cirrhosis and do so for reasons that are not fully understood. Genetic, dietary, sex, ethnicity and socio-economic factors are likely to be important though. Women are more susceptible to the harmful effects of alcohol than men for similar levels of consumption, in part because they have a lower volume of distribution for equivalent volumes of alcohol and thus higher blood alcohol concentrations. Drinking alcohol without food appears to be more harmful than drinking with food, and the risk of cirrhosis is higher in smokers and obese individuals but lower in regular coffee drinkers.

The adolescent liver is particularly vulnerable to damage. Disturbingly, UK hepatologists report an increasing cohort of UK teenagers and young adults with established alcohol-related cirrhosis – a presentation unheard of 30 years ago.

Alcohol-related liver disease

The spectrum of ALD includes three widely recognised forms: alcohol-related fatty liver disease (steatosis), alcohol-related hepatitis (steatohepatitis) and alcohol-related cirrhosis (Figure 11.3).

ABC of Alcohol, Fifth Edition. Edited by Anne McCune.
© 2015 John Wiley & Sons, Ltd. Published 2015 by John Wiley & Sons, Ltd.

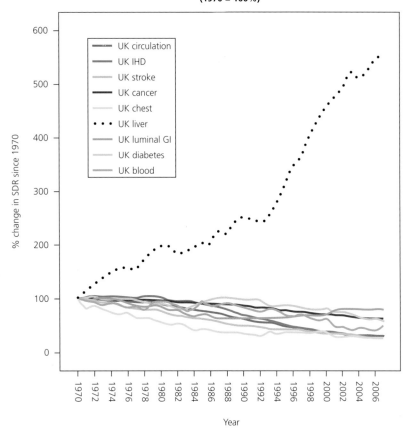

Figure 11.1 A rapid rise in liver-related deaths (mainly due to alcohol) in comparison with most other common diseases which have declined over time is detailed. Source: British Society of Gastroenterology (2010). Reproduced by permission of the British Society of Gastroenterology.

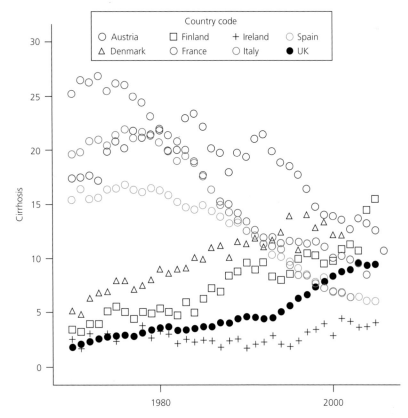

Figure 11.2 Standardised mortality (deaths/100,000 under age 64 years) from cirrhosis according to European country. There has been a rise in deaths in the United Kingdom, Ireland, Finland and Denmark compared to a steady fall in rates in France, Spain and Italy. In the former countries, there has been a relaxation in alcohol regulation; and in the latter countries, a fall in the consumption of cheap wine with meals over time. Source: Sheron et al. (2008). Reproduced by permission of BMJ Publishing Group Ltd.

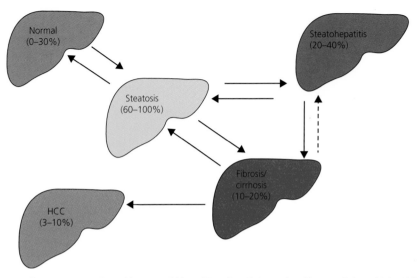

Figure 11.3 Histological spectrum of ALD. Source: Adapted from Kendrick and Day (2013). Reproduced by permission of John Wiley & Sons.

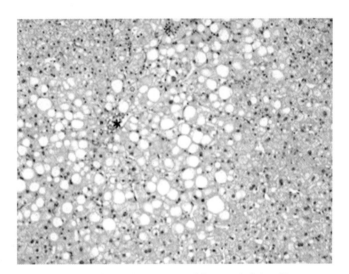

Figure 11.4 Alcohol-related steatosis. Small (microvesicular) and large (macrovesicular) droplets of fat are seen within the hepatocytes and most prominent near the central vein (asterisk). Source: Theise (2013). Reproduced by permission of John Wiley & Sons.

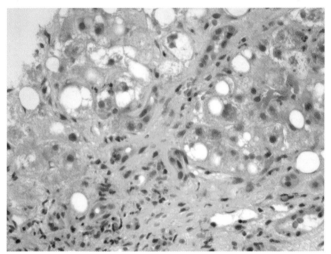

Figure 11.5 Histological findings typical of alcohol-related steatohepatitis. Macrovesicular steatosis, Mallory bodies, balloon degeneration of hepatocytes and inflammation (mainly neutrophils and lymphocytes) are seen. Source: Image courtesy of Dr Behrang Mozayani, Consultant Histopathologist, North Bristol NHS Trust.

The liver is the main site of metabolism, and alcohol is metabolised by two main pathways: by alcohol dehydrogenase to acetaldehyde and to a lesser extent by CYP2EI, an isoform of cytochrome P-450 (Chapter 3). Chronic alcohol misuse results in fat deposition in hepatocytes, lipid peroxidation, oxiditative stress with production of damaging free radicals and pro-inflammatory cytokines. Hepatocyte injury, loss and repair by fibrosis result.

Fatty liver disease (steatosis)

Fatty change is present almost universally in heavy drinkers (Figure 11.4) but can occur in many modest drinkers as well. The hepatocytes become swollen with triglycerides, but the steatosis can improve with cessation of alcohol and in some cases completely reverse. Patients with alcohol-related fatty liver disease do not usually have symptoms and tend to present when mild liver function abnormalities (raised aspartate ami-notransferase (AST) and alanine aminotransferase (ALT)) are detected on routine testing or when ultrasound imaging incidentally delineates a bright echogenic liver. The liver may become swollen and enlarged, detectable as hepatomegaly on examination. Stigmata of chronic liver disease (see below) are not generally seen.

Alcohol related hepatitis

Alcohol-related hepatitis (AH) is an acute florid manifestation of ALD and jaundice, coagulopathy and liver failure are clinical hallmarks of severe AH. The latter is associated with a high mortality of around 30–50%. AH is characterised histologically by parenchymal inflammation and hepatocellular damage (Figure 11.5). Some 80% of patients presenting with AH will also have underlying cirrhosis (Figure 11.6) but the differentiation

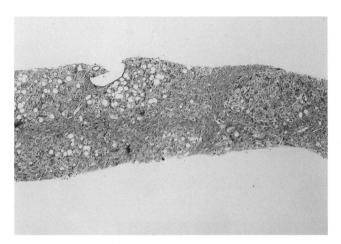

Figure 11.6 Alcohol-related cirrhosis (trichrome stain). Fibrous bands (blue) divide the liver into small regenerating regular nodules (micronodular cirrhosis). Fatty change is also seen. Source: Ed Uthman, Houston, TX, USA.

between AH and decompensated cirrhosis can be a difficult one even for experts. AH is likely if there is a history of significant alcohol misuse, no other explanation for jaundice and biliary obstruction excluded. Non-severe AH is common in alcohol misusers and may be asymptomatic but increases the risk of progression to cirrhosis.

Symptoms of AH include non-specific malaise, lethargy, fever, anorexia, abdominal discomfort and distension (due to ascites), confusion and bruising. Clinical signs include jaundice, temperature (usually <38.0°C), clinical ascites, encephalopathy (e.g. liver flap/asterixis, constructional apraxia, confusion) and tender hepatomegaly. Co-existent complications such as variceal bleeding and renal failure are common. As the majority of patients also have underlying cirrhosis, signs or stigmata of chronic liver disease are often found (see further). Liver transaminases are raised, but it is not typical for the ALT to exceed 300 IU/l.

Although AH is largely diagnosed clinically, mathematical scoring systems are often used to determine the severity of the condition, usually by utilising elevations of bilirubin and creatinine. The Maddrey discriminant function (MdF) has high positive predictive value for 30-day mortality. A score of 32 or more is indicative of severe disease and is often used as a threshold for the commencement of pharmacotherapy in these patients. Patients with severe AH require hospital treatment. Consensus guidelines currently recommend the use of corticosteroids (CS) in patients with severe AH although this is still the subject of on-going clinical study. Pentoxifylline (anti TNF-α agent) is sometimes prescribed when CS are contraindicated although there is limited randomised control trial data to support its use. A number of patients with severe alcohol-related hepatitis fail to respond adequately to steroid treatment and mortality is high in this group. Enteral nutrition is also important and as many patients with severe AH are unable to take sufficient calories by mouth, early nasogastric feeding is required. Protein restriction is no longer practised. Liver biopsy is not essential for diagnosis; but where there is clinical diagnostic doubt or co-existing aetiology, a biopsy should be undertaken.

Other tested treatments include monoclonal antibodies (infliximab and etanercept), antioxidants and artificial liver support devices, but no proven benefit has been shown in the studies to date.

Alcohol-related cirrhosis

With progressive liver injury, bands of fibrosis form with nodule formation and architectural distortion. Portal hypertension and liver failure result leading to decompensation, i.e. development of ascites, jaundice, encephalopathy and varices. Clinical findings (Table 11.1) include stigmata of chronic liver disease (as in cirrhosis of other aetiologies) and include spider naevi, palmar erythema, gynaecomastia, testicular atrophy (Figure 11.7). The presence of bilateral parotid enlargement, a pseudo-cushingoid appearance, Dupytren's contracture or peripheral neuropathy, favours alcohol aetiology.

Coagulopathy, hypoalbuminaemia (indicative of impaired liver synthetic function) and thrombocytopenia are common in patients with ALD cirrhosis. All patients with cirrhosis should be offered a gastroscopy to screen for varices. Cirrhotic patients with ascites should also have a diagnostic ascitic tap on admission to hospital, so spontaneous bacterial peritonitis (a common finding associated with high mortality) can be confidently excluded.

Overall, the prognosis of patients with cirrhosis depends on abstinence of alcohol. In a recent study, more than 80% of abstinent patients had extended survival after cessation of alcohol. Although the diagnosis of alcohol-related liver cirrhosis is generally a clinical and/or radiological one, a liver biopsy may be justified if there is diagnostic uncertainty, although non-invasive methods such as elastography (fibroscan®) are increasingly used to stage fibrosis. Elastography is best reserved for abstinent patients, as inflammation due to ongoing drinking can falsely elevate the readings.

Patients with severe malnutrition have a much poorer overall prognosis so, as for those with severe AH, nutritional support is

Table 11.1 Typical physical findings in alcohol-related liver cirrhosis

General	Parotid enlargement (usually bilateral)
	Cushingoid appearance (moon-shaped face)
	Cachexia
Skin	Jaundice
	Palmar erythema
	Spider naevi
	Telangiectasia
	Dupytren's contracture
	Finger clubbing
Abdomen	Tender swollen liver (especially if co-existent AH)
	Small shrunken liver (advanced cirrhosis)
	Ascites
	Splenomegaly
Musculoskeletal	Muscle wasting
	Proximal myopathy
Sex organs	Testicular atrophy
	Loss of body and pubic hair
	Gynaecomastia
Neurological	Seizures (alcohol withdrawal)
	Encephalopathy (confusion, drowsiness, asterixis, constructional apraxia)

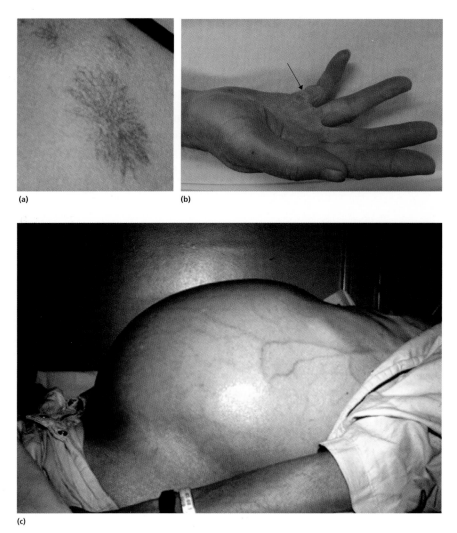

(a)   (b)

(c)

Figure 11.7 Some typical physical findings in alcohol-related liver cirrhosis. **(a)** Large cutaneous spider naevi with central arteriole and radiating vessels in a spoke-like fashion from the centre (gentle compression of the central area will lead to blanching). A few spider naevi (usually <6) can be seen in normal health in the distribution of the superior vena cava, and more can appear during pregnancy. Spider naevi in other sites (as on the abdominal wall in this case) should alert the clinician to the presence of chronic liver disease. Source: Fred HL, van Dijk HA. *Images of Memorable Cases: Case 114*. Available from http://cnx.org/content/m14900/1.3/. **(b)** Dupuytren's contracture resulting in the in-drawing of the fourth and fifth fingers due to changes within the palmar fascia. This finding has an association with chronic liver disease (mainly alcohol related) but can be idiopathic or related to manual labour/trauma. Image courtesy of James Heilman, MD. **(c)** Large-volume ascites – tense ascites likely to require drainage (paracentesis).

crucial. A low-salt diet is recommended in patients with ascites, but protein restriction is no longer prescribed as it exacerbates pre-existing malnutrition.

Alcohol cirrhosis and hepatocellular carcinoma

Patients with alcohol-related cirrhosis have a high life time risk of developing a hepatocellular carcinoma (HCC) because progressive cellular damage and fibrosis increase the risk of oncological change within the liver. A stable abstinent patient with cirrhosis has a 10% risk of developing an HCC over a 5-year period. HCC survival rates overall remain poor, although a small number of carefully selected patients with otherwise good performance status and well-compensated liver disease can have curative treatment (liver transplantation or resection). Patients presenting with HCC should

be managed in a multi-disciplinary team consisting of hepatologists, surgeons, oncologists and interventional radiologists amongst others. Loco-regional therapies are of a palliative nature but offer longer survival for patients as the modalities improve. Such therapies include radiofrequency ablation, percutaneous ethanol injection and transarterial chemo-embolisation (TACE). Abstinent cirrhotic patients should be considered for HCC screening and offered 6 monthly liver USS and alpha-fetoprotein measurement.

Treatment of ALD

Patients with ALD need to abstain from drinking alcohol completely, especially those with proven cirrhosis. Adequate psychological support is required; and for hospitalised patients, an alcohol nurse specialist plays a crucial pivotal role in their immediate care, facilitating follow-up support from local alcohol services. Any complications of cirrhosis are managed in the same manner as those patients with cirrhosis of other aetiology.

Alcohol withdrawal therapy in liver disease

Hospitalised patients with ALD should receive specialist input from an alcohol nurse specialist with experience in nursing hepatology patients. Alcohol withdrawal management (Chapter 17) can be complicated by the liver disease itself, encephalopathy and/or chronic alcohol-related brain injury. Withdrawal should be managed with short-acting benzodiazepines and as oxazepam has the shortest half-life, it may be the preferable agent. More frequent assessment will be required when short-acting preparations are used, and a symptom-triggered withdrawal regimen is particularly helpful in this situation (Chapter 17). Relapse prevention medications are often also required (NICE CCG 115) although baclofen is the only agent studied in cirrhotic patients.

Liver transplantation

Liver transplantation for patients with acute severe alcohol-related hepatitis and liver failure remains contentious, although a recent French study of highly selected patients showed promising results.

The demand for liver transplantation is rising as the prevalence of liver disease, especially ALD, continues to rise. Patients with ALD cirrhosis should be considered for transplantation if their liver disease has failed to recompensate sufficiently after 3 months' abstinence. An assessment for liver transplantation includes risk assessment of a return to drinking and adequate support for dependent patients should be in place. Patients are generally asked to sign an agreement to comply with follow-up and avoid alcohol. Outcomes after transplantation are similar to those after liver transplant for other liver diseases.

Further reading

British Society of Gastroenterology (lead author: Moriarty KJ). *Alcohol related disease. Meeting the challenge of improved quality of care and better use of resources* (A Joint Position Paper). 2010. http://www.bsg.org.uk/images/stories/docs/clinical/publications/bsg_alc_disease_10.pdf (accessed 18 September 2014).

European Association for the Study of the Liver. EASL clinical practice guidelines: management of alcoholic liver disease. *Journal of Hepatology* 2012; 57:399–420.

European Association for the Study of the Liver, European Organisation for Research and Treatment of Cancer. EASL-EORTC clinical practice guidelines: management of hepatocellular carcinoma. *Journal of Hepatology* 2012;56:908–43.

Glover L, Collins P, Gordon F, Holliwell K, Hunt V, Portal J, et al. Symptom triggered pharmacotherapy for acute unplanned alcohol withdrawal can be both clinically and cost-effective in a hospital setting: experience from a specialist hepatology unit. *Gut* 2011;60(Suppl 1):A48.

Kendrick S, Day C. Natural history and factors influencing the course of alcohol-related liver disease. *Clinical Liver Disease* 2013;2:61–63. doi: 10.1002/cld.145.

National Confidential Enquiry into Patient Outcome and Death (NCEPOD). *Measuring the units. A review of patients who died with alcohol-related liver disease.* 2013. www.ncepod.org.uk (accessed 18 September 2014).

National Institute of Health and Care Excellence. *Alcohol-use disorders: diagnosis and clinical management of alcohol-related physical complications* (NICE Guidelines CG100). 2010. http://guidance.nice.org.uk/CG100 (accessed 18 September 2014).

National Institute of Health and Care Excellence. *Alcohol-use disorders: diagnosis, assessment and management of harmful drinking and alcohol dependence* (NICE Guidelines CG115). 2011. http://guidance.nice.org.uk/CG115 (accessed 18 September 2014).

Sheron N, Olsen N, Gilmore I. An evidence-based alcohol policy. *Gut* 2008;57:1341–4.

Theise ND. Histopathology of alcoholic liver disease. *Clinical Liver Disease* 2013;2:64–7. doi: 10.1002/cld.172.

CHAPTER 12

Surgical problems

James S. Huntley

OVERVIEW

- Alcohol misuse is a cause of many 'surgical' conditions.
- Alcohol misuse complicates the management of patients with surgical conditions.
- Perioperative effects related to alcohol misuse include cardiac and autonomic dysfunction, deranged hepatic metabolism and altered coagulation.
- Postoperative effects related to alcohol misuse include magnified stress response, decreased haemostasis and wound healing, perturbed immune response and acute confusional state/ withdrawal syndrome.
- All patients presenting to hospital surgical services should be screened for alcohol misuse.

Alcohol misuse places a major burden on many health services, including surgery, where its consequences are complex and multi-factorial. Alcohol has acute and chronic effects on both body and mind (see Figure 12.1), which predispose to a number of surgical conditions. Additionally, alcohol has important social effects – for example, as a result of disinhibition, decreased judgement and increased risk-taking. Misuse may cause direct pathophysiological problems, or act indirectly being implicated in trauma and social harm.

Acutely intoxicated and chronic misusers run different risks, but the effects of alcohol are pervasive and interrelated. Alcohol misuse is implicated in a variety of surgical conditions: traumatic and non-traumatic. This chapter broadly considers these two groups of surgical problem though there is considerable overlap – for example, compartment syndrome can occur in the presence or absence of trauma.

Trauma

Trauma remains the largest cause of death in those under the age 40 years. Alcohol is a major factor for trauma of all types, both accidental (including road traffic accidents – either as driver or pedestrian) and non-accidental (e.g. suicide attempts, parasuicidal behaviour and self-harm), and also in increasing injury severity (e.g. cycling accidents). Alcohol is a major aetiological factor in violence – both as instigator and victim.

Alcohol-related trauma is common to all specialities, especially general, orthopaedic, plastic, maxillofacial, neurosurgical and ENT surgery. In the United Kingdom, the pattern has changed in recent decades with fewer accidents (perhaps because of legislation changes, enforcements and public education), but an increase in injuries due to violence (see Figure 12.2). Ninety per cent of assault victims sustain single or multiple lacerations and only 10% a fracture. Acutely intoxicated people are vulnerable targets – 'easy meat in the urban jungle'.

Head injuries are also common – of the approximately 1 million patients who attend emergency departments with a head injury each year (8% requiring admission), approximately 25% have drunk alcohol. Patients in this group often present a management/assessment dilemma in that the signs of intoxication and head injury may easily be confused.

Non-trauma

The pervasive effects of alcohol misuse on surgery can be thought of as occurring in three phases:

1 **Preoperative – alcohol-related harm managed by surgical specialities**
2 **Perioperative** – intraoperative problems include those of alcohol-related physiological perturbations – e.g. cardiac dysfunction, altered hepatic metabolism (e.g. of anaesthetic agents), altered coagulation and tissue quality derangements
3 **Postoperative** – increased risk of complications due to decreased immune response, poor wound healing, non-compliance

Intraoperative and postoperative effects may occur in patients undergoing surgery for conditions not overtly related to alcohol misuse – dependent drinkers are at high risk of developing withdrawal syndrome in the post-operative phase, classically manifesting as an acute confusional state. A recent report's principal recommendation included a statement that all patients

ABC of Alcohol, Fifth Edition. Edited by Anne McCune.
© 2015 John Wiley & Sons, Ltd. Published 2015 by John Wiley & Sons, Ltd.

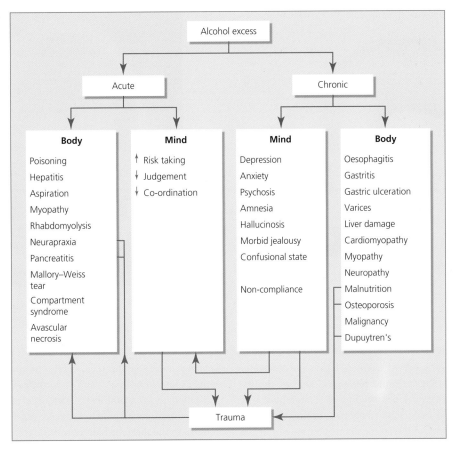

Figure 12.1 A web of causality.

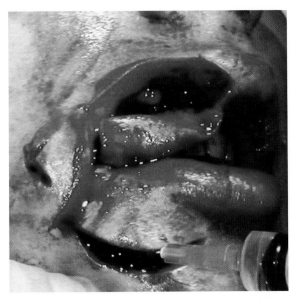

Figure 12.2 Eighty-five per cent of victims of alcohol-related assaults have a facial injury and 57% of individual injuries are to the face: lacerations right side of mouth.

presenting to hospital services should be screened for alcohol misuse routinely (NCEPOD Measuring the Units – see section Bibliography). See Chapters 6 and 17 for details of model alcohol histories.

Preoperative problems

Gastroenterology

Non-variceal upper gastrointestinal bleeding (NVUGIB) – Advancements in endoscopic and radiological techniques have revolutionised the management of NVUGIB such that salvage surgery is required in fewer than 4% of cases, mainly for uncontrolled peptic ulcer bleeding.

Variceal bleeding – see Chapter 11

Liver cirrhosis – Patients with liver disease, especially cirrhosis, who require surgery are at greater risk for surgical and anaesthetic complications and thus require careful pre-assessment by both surgeon and hepatologist. The precise risk of surgery is not possible to accurately quantify because there is little robust outcome data. Nevertheless, patients with severe alcohol-related hepatitis, Child–Pugh C cirrhosis or significant coagulopathy should not undergo elective surgery.

Pancreatitis – this is an inflammatory condition in which the endogenous enzymes are activated and digest the pancreatic parenchyma. The commonest causes are gallstones and alcohol. The pathogenesis is not completely understood, and the severity of the condition ranges from the mild and self-limiting to extremely toxic, with a profound systemic inflammatory response that can lead to multi-organ failure and death. When **acute**, onset is usually 12–48 h after an episode of binge drinking and is associated with nausea, vomiting and raised levels of plasma amylase.

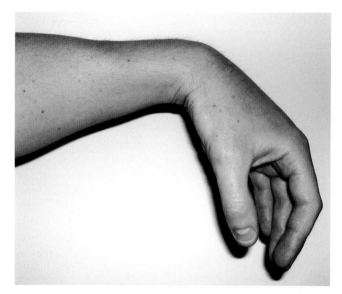

Figure 12.3 Radial nerve 'Saturday night' palsy – drunken sleep with arm over back of chair.

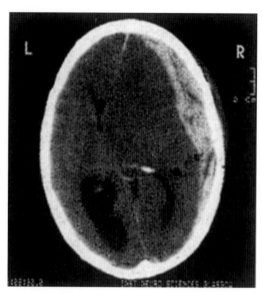

Figure 12.4 Right sided subdural haematoma with midline shift and left ventricular dilatation. Source: Driscoll et al. (2000). Reproduced by permission of John Wiley & Sons.

Severe disease should be managed by a multidisciplinary team involving gastroenterologists, intensivists, radiologists and surgeons. In **chronic** pancreatitis long-term morphological damage occurs to the pancreas, leading to exocrine (weight loss, steatorrhoea and hypoalbuminaemia) and endocrine (diabetes) dysfunction. The pain is chronic and severe – but some patients continue to drink alcohol despite this.

Orthopaedic surgery

Osteoporosis – alcohol is held responsible as a major aetiological factor for osteoporosis, especially in men, but the evidence is equivocal. Alcohol is certainly toxic to osteoblasts *in vitro*, but the situation *in vivo* may be different. Several epidemiological studies suggest that patients who chronically misuse alcohol have a lower bone density and a higher fracture risk. Osteoporosis is common in patients with alcohol-related cirrhosis. Alcohol in moderation may be beneficial, and the confounding roles of nutrition and smoking have not been elucidated.

Neuropathy, neurapraxia and myopathy – these conditions rarely require surgical treatment, but patients with them frequently present to the surgical team. Chronic alcohol misusers may develop bilateral symmetrical sensorimotor neuropathy – especially of the lower limbs; commonly, this is related to thiamine deficiency. Nerve conduction block (**neurapraxia**) – for example, of the radial nerve either at axillary or mid-humeral level (Figure 12.3) – can cause segmental demyelination. The loss of sensation and muscle power generally recovers over days to weeks, with the only treatment required being appropriate soft splintage, for example a wrist splint to keep the hand/fingers in a position of function.

Alcohol is implicated in both acute and chronic forms of **myopathy**. Proximal muscle pain (especially around hips/thighs and the shoulder girdle) with swelling and weakness may follow a period of acute intoxication. The severity varies, but typically the condition is mild and self-limiting, resolving fully with a period of abstinence. A more serious form is rhabdomyolysis

leading to myoglobinuria, acute tubular necrosis and renal failure (see later).

Compartment syndrome – this is a condition in which the intracompartmental pressure, usually in a limb, rises to such a level, relative to the diastolic blood pressure, that perfusion of intracompartmental structures is compromised, leading to hypoxia and tissue necrosis. Young athletic men are especially at risk. It is characterised by severe pain (especially on passive stretch of muscles passing through the compartment) and pain 'out of proportion' to that expected i.e. greater in severity than that expected for the injury sustained. Paraesthesiae, paralysis and pallor also occur. The presence of a distal pulse is not reassuring; indeed, this is normal in a compartment syndrome. People who misuse alcohol are at high risk of this important condition. If the diagnosis is a possibility, compartment pressure monitoring should be instigated as it expedites emergency and limb-saving fasciotomies.

Rhabdomyolysis – this condition, fortunately uncommon, involves damage to the sarcolemmal membrane of skeletal muscle, resulting in leakage of myoglobin and other intracellular contents (including creatine kinase and potassium ions) into the circulation. A variety of triggers exist: the two most common being mechanical injury (due to local compression and crushing) and alcohol misuse. Alcohol-related rhabdomyolysis may be because of a mechanical effect (trauma or seizures) or a direct toxic effect on the membrane. Myoglobin is nephrotoxic and can precipitate acute tubular necrosis and renal failure. Hyperkalaemia, which may lead to cardiac arrest, occurs due to leakage of potassium ions from the muscle, nephrotoxic effects and renal failure.

Avascular necrosis of the femoral head – non-traumatic osteonecrosis of the femoral head in the mature skeleton, most often bilateral, occurs mainly in men aged 35–45 years. A high index of suspicion should be maintained for patients with hip pain (especially at night), the severity of which is out of proportion to the clinical and radiological findings. The aetiology is multifactorial, with 40% being idiopathic. Known precipitants include alcohol, corticosteroids, irradiation, sickle cell disease, decompression sickness (the 'bends') and the genetic lysosomal storage disease Gaucher's disease.

Dupuytren's contracture – in this condition, there is excessive fibrosis and contracture of the palmar fascia, more often in men, and is usually bilateral. Case-control studies suggest that alcohol is an independent risk factor, but that smoking is more important.

Neurosurgery

People who misuse alcohol are at high risk of intracranial (especially subdural) haematomas (Figure 12.4). Chronic misusers may have coagulopathy and a degree of cortical atrophy. The latter renders the bridging veins more susceptible to damage.

Obstetrics

Misuse of alcohol in pregnancy is associated with **foetal alcohol syndrome** (FAS), unfortunately occurring 1 in every 750 live-births, and reflecting the ability of alcohol to freely cross the placenta. Other maternal factors influence the FAS phenotype severity, including age, nutrition and metabolic efficiency of alcohol metabolising pathways. Although smaller amounts of alcohol may be associated with less severe manifestations (foetal alcohol spectrum disorders), interventricular haemorrhage and white matter damage are more likely in foetuses of women who drink more than three units on a single occasion. Recent NICE guidelines advise alcohol abstinence in women who are pregnant or who are planning to conceive.

Urology

Alcohol is implicated in erectile dysfunction, impotence and loss of libido.

Intraoperative problems

Alcohol misusers may present a poorer surgical substrate in terms of frailty of tissues. In emergency situations, anaesthesia may be required in an intoxicated patient, but with little knowledge of relevant history or recent metabolic status.

A level of 'basal narcosis' may mean that less general anaesthetic agent is required in the acutely intoxicated patient to induce and maintain anaesthesia. In the context of chronic misuse, however, the central nervous system and metabolism may undergo considerable alterations: clearance of some drugs – for example propanolol, pentobarbital, amitryptiline, warfarin and diazepam – may be enhanced dramatically by enzyme induction. Induction involves up to a 10-fold increase in the microsomal ethanol oxidising system (MEOS), with an associated increase in toxic aldehyde and oxygen free radical products, as well as conversion of certain xenobiotics (including paracetamol, enflurane and methoxyflurane) to toxic metabolites.

With advanced liver disease such as severe fibrosis or cirrhosis, drugs that are metabolised considerably by 'first-pass' mechanisms undergo diminished metabolism because of altered hepatic blood flow due to portosystemic shunting and reduced hepatocellular function. If synthetic function is compromised to the point of hypoalbuminaemia, the handling of protein-bound drugs, such as corticosteroids, is also altered.

Postoperative complications

Patients who misuse alcohol are at high risk of complications after surgery (Figure 12.5). For instance case-match studies show that misusers with ankle fractures have substantially more in-hospital complications (33 v. 9%), longer hospital stays, more long-term complications and greater requirements for further surgery. The increased risk is probably multifactorial. Similar outcomes have been documented for colorectal, upper gastrointestinal, prostate, subdural and gynaecological surgery.

Stress response

Surgery and alcohol both activate the hypothalamo–pituitary–adrenal axis, and surgery increases activity of this axis to a greater degree in long-term misusers than those who drink within recommended levels. Indicators of surgical stress such as interleukin 6 levels are increased much less in heavy drinkers if they have abstained for 1 month before surgery. Such a period of abstinence also reduces post-operative morbidity considerably.

Wound healing

Alcohol misusers have a high risk of wound complications because of decreased immune function, altered haemostasis, nutritional and healing deficiencies.

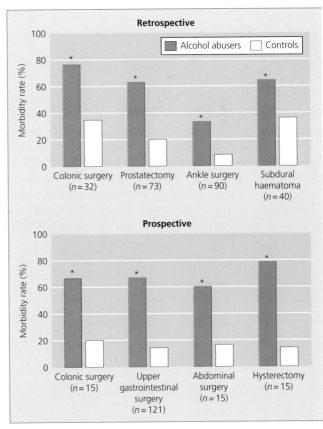

Figure 12.5 Retrospective and prospective studies of postoperative morbidity in people who misuse alcohol and controls. Source: Tønnesen and Kehlet (1999). Reproduced by permission of John Wiley & Sons.

Bone healing

Myopathy, neuropathy, decreased osteoblast function, nutritional deficiency and poor co-ordination/compliance (e.g. concerning mobilisation and weightbearing) may contribute to delayed bone healing.

Haemostasis

Alcohol has multiple effects on both coagulation and fibrinolytic systems, which increase the bleeding time; this can manifest before, during and after surgery. Chronic misuse of alcohol reduces platelet numbers and platelet aggregation. Moderate drinking decreases fibrinogen levels and increases fibrinolytic activity.

Cardiovascular physiology

Alcohol misuse can cause myocardial damage and arrhythmia. One-third of chronic drinkers are alleged to have a low ejection fraction because of cardiomyopathic changes. Previously subclinical defects may be unmasked by the increased physiological costs of surgery.

Immune system

Chronic alcohol misuse is associated with an increased risk of infection and malignancy. Activation of T-cells and T-cell-dependent processes are impaired. Mobilisation of macrophages, mononuclear cells and neutrophils is reduced.

Alcohol withdrawal syndrome

Alcohol withdrawal is a common cause of the acute confusional state postoperatively and should be considered in all patients who present with features suggestive of this condition (see Chapter 17).

Conclusion

Clinical inertia is the failure of healthcare workers or systems to offer, initiate or intensify therapy when indicated. A large amount of identifiable alcohol misuse in undetected or undocumented. Referrals to alcohol liaison services are offered only infrequently. Problem drinkers are often seen as awkward nuisances rather than patients with an identifiable and potentially treatable problem.

Patients who misuse alcohol are rarely optimised with a supported abstention period before elective surgery, surely an opportunity missed to decrease perioperative risk. Other possibilities for intervention at a 'moment of crisis' (when patients are amenable to change) are also missed.

Early (and preoperative) recognition of alcohol-misusing patients allows anticipation of possible complications. This is a critical point of communication from primary to hospital care: the importance of alcohol-related morbidity. Peri-operative support can be optimised, for example with a period of abstinence. Operative plans can be altered (e.g. surgical approach and femoral head size can be changed at total hip arthroplasty to decrease the chance of post-operative dislocation). Post-operative sequelae can be anticipated and hopefully avoided.

Further reading

Bullock R. Head Injuries. In: Driscoll P, Skinner D, Earlam R, eds. *ABC of major trauma*, 3rd edn. London: BMJ, 2000:34–41.

Driscoll P, Skinner D, Earlam R, eds. *ABC of major trauma*, 3rd edn. London: BMJ, 2000.

Frossard JL, Steer ML, Pastor CM. Acute pancreatitis. *Lancet* 2008;371: 143–52.

National Confidential Enquiry into Patient Outcome and Death (NCEPOD). *Measuring the units. A review of patients who died with alcohol-related liver disease.* 2013. www.ncepod.org.uk (accessed 18 September 2014).

National Institute of Health and Care Excellence. *Alcohol-use disorders: diagnosis and clinical management of alcohol-related physical complications* (NICE Guideline CG100). 2010. http://guidance.nice.org.uk/CG100 (accessed 18 September 2014).

Oppedal K, Moller AM, Pedersen B, Tonnesen H. Preoperative alcohol cessation prior to elective surgery. *Cochrane Database of Systematic Reviews* 2012;7:CD008343.

Rushbrook J, Pennington N. The effects of alcohol in orthopaedic patients. *Orthopaedics & Trauma* 2013;27:164–70.

Tønnesen H, Kehlet H. Preoperative alcoholism and postoperative morbidity. *British Journal of Surgery* 1999;86:869–74.

Tønnesen H, Nielsen PR, Lauritzen JB, Moller AM. Smoking and alcohol intervention before surgery: evidence for best practice. *British Journal of Anaesthesia* 2009;102:297–306.

Tønnesen H, Rosenberg J, Nielsen HJ, Rasmussen V, Hauge C, Pedersen IK, et al. Effect of preoperative abstinence on poor postoperative outcomes in alcohol misusers: randomised controlled trial. *BMJ* 1999;318:1311–6.

Touquet R, Csipke E, Hollaway P, Brown A, Patel T, Seddon AJ, et al. Resuscitation room blood alcohol concentrations: one-year cohort study. *Emergency Medicine Journal: EMJ* 2008;25:752–6.

CHAPTER 13

Alcohol, maxillofacial trauma and prevention of personal violence

Jonathan Shepherd and Paul Jordan

OVERVIEW

- Sharing basic information from trauma patients with relevant authorities leads to a reduction in levels of violence.
- Alcohol misuse is a key factor in violent injury.
- Having a simple, structured conversation with patients can motivate them to reduce their chances of injury and other alcohol-related harms.
- Brief interventions lead to a reduction in repeat attendances in hospital clinics.
- Implementing information sharing and alcohol brief interventions can be done without the need for additional resources.

Introduction

Alcohol consumption and violence are closely linked, and there is a causal link between alcohol misuse and a range of health conditions. Evidence from Cardiff University's Violence Research Group suggests that it is possible for staff in the NHS to have a direct impact on levels of violence as well as alcohol misuse. Findings of randomised controlled trials (RCTs) of brief interventions resulted in fewer repeat injuries as well as reduced alcohol consumption. Intoxication decreases physical capacity to avoid confrontation, causes poor decision-making, causes isolation in risky urban environments and decreases capacity of the injured to identify assailants, thereby protecting them from prosecution.

Alcohol plays a key role in the social, cultural and economic life in the United Kingdom. Fifty years ago the United Kingdom had one of the lowest drinking levels in Europe and many people continue to drink sensibly. However in recent decades, a culture of overuse has developed and the United Kingdom is now one of the few countries in Europe where consumption has increased during that period. There were over 1.2 million alcohol-related hospital admissions in 2010/2011 alone. According to the Government's Alcohol Strategy, published in 2012, in a community of 100,000 people, 2000 will be admitted to hospital with an alcohol-related condition and 1000 will be a victim of an alcohol-related crime. And a total of 21,500 will regularly drink over the lower-risk recommended levels. In the long-term, excessive drinking contributes to a range of health conditions which include cancers of the mouth, heart disease, diabetes, gastro intestinal diseases and liver disease, of which there was a 25% increase in between 2001 and 2009. Accident and emergency departments, in the main, see the more immediate impact of excess alcohol consumption, both unintentional (accidents) and intentional injuries (violence). Some of the more common alcohol-related injuries which are treated in maxillofacial clinics include glassings, broken noses, fractured zygoma and jaw and even injuries sustained through biting. All of which stem from violence, which is entirely preventable (Figure 13.1).

The collection and use of straightforward data concerning assaults and the delivery of brief inventions to patients who misuse alcohol can prevent violence and injury as well as reduce consumption. Therefore, in addition to their therapeutic role, maxillofacial and other trauma surgeons can play an effective part in violence prevention. This chapter highlights the need to rethink the responsibilities of both surgeons and nurses in oral and maxillofacial departments to achieve this. Alcohol misuse and violence affects all sectors of society, it really is everybody's business.

Data sharing for violence prevention: The Cardiff Model

The Cardiff Violence Prevention Model is based on information sharing between emergency departments (EDs), local government and the NHS. For all ED patients reporting injury in violence, information about the precise location of the incident (name of bar, nightclub, street, park, etc.), time and day and type of weapon is captured electronically in the ED by reception staff when patients first present. These data are then anonymised and shared by hospital IT personnel with crime analysts who work in the police service or in local authorities. The crime analyst then combines these data with police intelligence to provide a comprehensive list of precise

ABC of Alcohol, Fifth Edition. Edited by Anne McCune.
© 2015 John Wiley & Sons, Ltd. Published 2015 by John Wiley & Sons, Ltd.

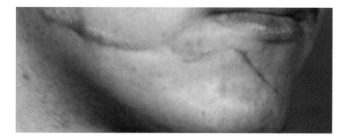

Figure 13.1 The aftermath of an alcohol-related assault.

locations and times where violence is concentrated. This allows police and local authorities to target resources more effectively than is achievable using police intelligence alone. There are many practical examples of successful prevention strategies flowing from this approach: deployment of closed-circuit television cameras, traffic flow and public transportation alterations, a switch to toughened and polycarbonate glassware in high-risk pubs and clubs, pedestrianisation of city entertainment streets and alcohol licence revocation.

In a 7-year experiment, this approach in Cardiff was compared with traditional violence prevention methods in 14 'most similar' cities identified by the UK Home Office in terms of a range of social and economic indicators. Compared to these control cities, Cardiff experienced significantly fewer hospital admissions and serious violence recorded by the police. Between 2003 and 2007, the average admission rate following violence per 100,000 of the population was 89 in Cardiff compared with 135 in the comparison cities where the model was not implemented. Compared to the control cities 42% fewer woundings were recorded by the police. The Cardiff Model led to a substantial reduction in costs associated with violence, for health services, criminal justice and society at large, providing a substantial return on investment and demonstrates the benefits of multi-agency information sharing partnerships to guide violence prevention planning, policies and activities. Moreover, the fact that the reduction in woundings and the cost-benefit savings were documented at the community-level underscores the public health significance of the Cardiff Model. Current economic realities mean that limited resources are available for prevention, making collaboration across sectors, including health and law enforcement as well as transportation, education, social services and others, a necessity.

Maxillofacial surgeons can contribute to this process by ensuring that their EDs record violence prevention information electronically and that ED software is modified to facilitate this. This involves incorporating specific training for ED receptionists, identifying a hospital IT lead who can anonymise and share the data, making connections between the IT lead and the local community crime analyst, and ensuring that these unique ED data are actually used continuously by the police and local authorities. Maxillofacial surgeons and emergency physicians can also contribute by organising and sustaining regular meetings with senior police officers and local government officials where month to month decisions about targeting resources are made. These contributions are very rewarding professionally, particularly when it is realised that the communities and cities involved are being made safer.

Alcohol brief interventions

Brief interventions are short, structured conversations lasting around 5 minutes between patient and health professional designed to motivate patients to reduce their alcohol consumption. They have been found to be effective in a wide range of healthcare settings including maxillofacial clinics, as research from Cardiff University has found. The World Health Organisation and the Royal College of Surgeons recommend that screening and brief interventions for alcohol misuse should be adopted as a routine part of clinical practice. The intention is to prompt the patient to recognise the harm which their drinking has caused, especially the wound being treated; to review their drinking; to set themselves drinking limits; and to make and act on decisions to reduce their hazardous drinking. For some patients, the intervention will prompt those who have relapsed in their drinking behaviour to drink sensibly once more.

Timing is crucial. Brief interventions work best when there is a '*teachable moment*', when a person is faced with the consequences of their actions and therefore more receptive to the suggestion of behaviour change. Nowhere is this opportunity more obvious than during suture removal in a maxillofacial clinic in the week following injury whilst intoxicated (Figure 13.2). In another context, the return from holiday to find that work clothes are tighter is a key moment when suggestions about diet adjustments are taken more seriously than usual.

Brief interventions should be personalised and offered in a supportive, non-judgemental manner; using the FRAMES approach (Box 13.1; for more information on this read William Miller's book on motivational interviewing).

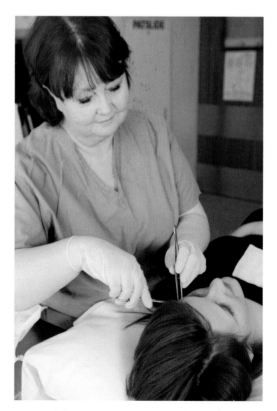

Figure 13.2 Maxillofacial clinic nurse removing sutures from a patient whilst delivering a brief intervention.

Box 13.1 **The FRAMES agenda**

Feedback: helping the patient make the link between their current injury and their alcohol misuse.

Responsibility: encouraging the patient to take responsibility for their own drinking.

Advice: providing the patient with individually tailored advice on issues such as keeping consumption within safe limits.

Menu: providing the patient with options to enable them to reduce their drinking, for example choosing a small glass of wine instead of a large one, avoiding drinking in 'rounds' and not relying on alcohol drinks alone to quench thirst.

Empathy: using an empathetic approach rather than lecturing the drinker, for example, saying 'we all like a drink but being in A&E on Saturday night can't have been much fun'.

Self-efficacy: emphasising for patients that they *can* change their drinking habits, in the same way, for example, that patients can and often do give up smoking.

Kathryn Bridgeman, Nurse Manager, Cardiff University Health Board, who was involved in the initial trials, said:

The intervention starts as a normal conversation and it is only when it develops and the patient engages with you, they realise that there is a structure to the conversation and an agenda. At the point of realisation it is important for the nurse to re-evaluate the engagement of the patient. It may be necessary to re-group and assure the patient that you're not being judgemental about their drinking habits. It is often at this point that full realisation dawns on the patient and the process of intervention can truly begin.

Brief interventions work

Controlled trials indicate that on average, for every eight people drinking at hazardous levels who receive an alcohol brief intervention, one will reduce their drinking to within safe drinking limits as a result of a brief intervention. Effectiveness is even greater if the intervention is delivered in the maxillofacial clinic as described earlier; one in four reverted to safe drinking levels as a result of brief intervention in this setting. Since brief interventions are opportunistic and incorporated into routine clinical work without the need for additional clinical resources, they represent a very worthwhile use of nurses' time and are therefore cost effective. However, maxillofacial nurses and other health professionals incorporating brief advice into their standard work need high-quality training and support if they are to be effective in this prevention role.

The challenges of embedding these models

There are some misconceptions about data sharing and brief interventions. Involvement in community prevention has in the past been wrongly labelled as 'medical paternalism'. The General Medical Council guidance makes specific provision for data sharing in order to detect and prevent community violence. Prevention of violence and future injury is just as important as treatment. Logistical barriers to the collection of data include a lack of appropriate software in ED reception, lack of links with crime analysts working in crime reduction partnerships as well as lack of knowledge amongst receptionists. These barriers can be overcome by receptionist training, simple adjustments to software and the establishment of formal links between ED consultants and local crime reduction partnerships. Data sharing can be achieved at no extra cost to ED and maxillofacial clinics since simple software solutions for data recording can be provided by hospital IT personnel. Brief interventions can be delivered without the need for additional resources since the conversation can take place at the same time as suture removal and does not require specialist knowledge of substance misuse. Some professionals might feel hypocritical delivering interventions if they themselves drink above the guidelines but, clearly, a professional approach to real health risks for patients should include helping them to reduce these risks. Nevertheless, the screening and brief intervention process may perhaps be helpful to the health professionals themselves as a challenge to their own health behaviours. So why not, in the spirit of the Welsh alcohol brief intervention campaign, 'Have a Word'?

Further reading

Dines C. Using A&E data to prevent violence in communities. *Nursing Times* 2011;107(13):16–8.

Florence C, Shepherd J, Brennan I, Simon T. Effectiveness of anonymised information sharing and use in health service, police, and local government partnership for preventing violence related injury: experimental study and time series analysis. *BMJ (Clinical Research Ed.)* 2011;342:d3313.

Gentilello LM, Rivara FP, Donovan DM, Jurkovich GJ, Daranciang E, Dunn CW, et al. Alcohol interventions in a trauma center as a means of reducing the risk of injury recurrence. *Annals of Surgery* 1999;230:473–80.

Miller WR, Rollnick S. *Motivational interviewing: preparing people to change addictive behavior.* New York: Guilford Press, 1991.

Raistrick D. *Review of the effectiveness of treatment for alcohol problems.* London: National Treatment Agency for Substance Misuse, 2006.

Smith AJ, Hodgson RJ, Bridgeman K, Shepherd JP. A randomized controlled trial of a brief intervention after alcohol-related facial injury. *Addiction* 2003;98:43–52.

CHAPTER 14

Neurological and neurosurgical complications of alcohol

Jane Alty and Jeremy Cosgrove

OVERVIEW

- Wernicke's encephalopathy is a medical emergency and requires urgent treatment with high-dose intravenous thiamine.

- Give high-dose intravenous thiamine to any patient with a history of possible chronic alcohol misuse before giving glucose in order to avoid precipitating Wernicke's encephalopathy. If in doubt, give thiamine!

- Alcohol withdrawal seizures are one feature of acute alcohol withdrawal syndrome and should be treated with benzodiazepines.

- Chronic alcohol excess is a risk factor for central pontine myelinolysis – hyponatraemia of greater than 24 h duration should be corrected cautiously.

- Consider head injury in any problematic drinker with a neurological presentation.

Introduction

Taking an alcohol history is crucial in all neurological presentations because alcohol misuse is so common and can cause a wide range of nervous system damage. This chapter outlines common neurological and neurosurgical complications of alcohol and emphasizes conditions that may have serious consequences without prompt management. The information is presented within defined sections, but patients will often present with overlapping clinical phenotypes such as peripheral neuropathy and cerebellar degeneration or Wernicke–Korsakoff syndrome and alcohol withdrawal seizures; so if you detect one complication of alcohol, look carefully for others that may require additional treatment.

Seizures

How to differentiate alcohol withdrawal seizures from epilepsy?

When someone with a history of chronic alcohol misuse suddenly stops drinking or markedly reduces alcohol intake, withdrawal seizures can occur. Seizures are one feature of acute alcohol withdrawal. Other features include anxiety, agitation, autonomic instability and tremor; this is covered in more detail in Chapter 18 on 'Management of acute unplanned alcohol withdrawal'.

By contrast, epileptic seizures may be precipitated in susceptible individuals after heavy alcohol ingestion. Table 14.1 outlines the features that help differentiate between the two types of seizure.

In dependent drinkers with concurrent epilepsy, antiepileptic drugs such as levetiracetam, lamotrigine and topiramate tend to be prescribed because they have fewer liver and drug–drug interactions. However, it must be emphasized that continued heavy drinking will make these drugs less effective because of associated poor compliance with drug regimens and lowering of the seizure threshold.

Treatment of alcohol withdrawal seizures

Alcohol withdrawal seizures tend to be brief and self-limiting. A reducing regimen of oral benzodiazepines should prevent further seizures, but sometimes seizures cluster together and very occasionally progress into status epilepticus. Always consider other causes of seizures such as head injury and electrolyte imbalance. Anti-epileptic medications other than benzodiazepines are not usually required.

Driving regulations and alcohol withdrawal seizures

The Driver and Vehicle Licensing Agency (DVLA) regulations state that a group one licence (car or motorcycle) will be revoked for a minimum of 6 months following a single alcohol withdrawal seizure. Multiple alcohol withdrawal seizures are covered under the DVLA's epilepsy regulations. It is advisable to keep up to date with the DVLA driving rules and consult them if in doubt.

All patients who have a seizure of any type should be advised not to drive and to declare their licence to the DVLA. This conversation should be documented in the medical records.

Table 14.1 Differentiating features of alcohol withdrawal seizures and epileptic seizures

	Alcohol withdrawal seizures	Epileptic seizures
Time of seizure	Most likely to occur 12–24 h after abstinence (range 8–48 h)	More likely to occur the morning after acute intoxication
Type of seizure	Generalized tonic–clonic seizures A focal seizure suggests a structural brain problem and is extremely unlikely to be an alcohol withdrawal seizure	Generalised or focal – reflects the underlying cause of epilepsy
Pattern of seizures	More likely to cluster together i.e. several seizures over a few hours. Status epilepticus is uncommon but possible	Any pattern possible – reflects the underlying cause and severity of epilepsy
Electroencephalogram (EEG) changes	Ictal[a] EEG: global changes compatible with generalized seizure Interictal[b] EEG may be subtly abnormal during the alcohol withdrawal period	Ictal EEG: reflects the seizure type, i.e. global changes during generalized seizure, focal abnormalities during focal seizure Interictal EEG: may show evidence of genetic/idiopathic epilepsy or focal brain abnormality depending on cause of epilepsy

[a] Ictal means *during* a seizure.
[b] Interictal means *between* seizures, i.e. not during a seizure.

Neuropathy

Alcoholic neuropathy

Peripheral nerves can be damaged directly by alcohol and also through associated nutritional deficiency (especially thiamine). Classically this causes a length-dependent, sensorimotor axonal polyneuropathy resulting in a symmetrical 'glove and stocking' distribution (see Figure 14.1) of burning, lancinating pain with mild weakness.

In early alcoholic neuropathy, abstinence combined with vitamin supplementation can reverse symptoms; but in more advanced cases, this will only prevent further damage. Neuropathic medications such as amitriptyline, gabapentin and pregabalin may reduce sensory symptoms and physiotherapy can improve gait.

Compression neuropathy

A reduced level of consciousness caused by acute alcohol intoxication prevents awareness of discomfort, and this predisposes to nerve compression. The classic example is 'Saturday night palsy' – radial nerve compression against the humerus when the arm is hung over a hard surface such as a bar edge or bench. Nerve dysfunction is usually temporary, caused by focal damage to the myelin sheath but not the underlying axon (neuropraxia).

Cerebellar disease

Almost everybody has seen transient acute cerebellar dysfunction caused by acute alcohol intoxication. This manifests as slurred speech (dysarthria), jerky eye movements (nystagmus), tremor (intention tremor), wide-based gait and in-coordination (ataxia), which resolves once the blood alcohol level drops. However, chronic alcohol misuse can cause irreversible cerebellar atrophy. As with alcoholic neuropathy, there is evidence to suggest that associated thiamine deficiency is integral to this process.

Wernicke–Korsakoff syndrome

This term is used to describe the combination of Wernicke's encephalopathy and Korsakoff's syndrome. Both conditions are caused by thiamine deficiency and can be considered different manifestations of the same disease process.

Wernicke's encephalopathy: The classic triad of symptoms only occurs in one-third of cases:

 (i) Ocular dysfunction: ranges from multidirectional nystagmus to complete ophthalmoparesis.
 (ii) Gait ataxia: ranges from subtle difficulties with tandem walking to an inability to stand unaided.
(iii) Acute confusion: usually global confusion characterized by apathy, inattention, disorientation and agitation. Stupor may also occur.

Timely thiamine replacement usually leads to reversal of confusion and ocular dysfunction within hours. Delayed treatment may lead to irreversible signs and can result in the development of Korsakoff's syndrome.

All patients with suspected Wernicke's encephalopathy should be treated with high-dose intravenous thiamine immediately. Those at risk of developing Wernicke's encephalopathy should also be offered treatment with thiamine – refer to NICE guidance CG100 for doses.

Korsakoff's syndrome: Feature of Wernicke's encephalopathy can be disguised by alcohol withdrawal syndrome, delirium tremens, head injury or infection. Afterwards, the clinical features of Korsakoff's syndrome may be discovered:

 (i) Profound anterograde amnesia: Patients are unable to retain new information. Working memory (the holding of information for very brief periods of time) is usually intact, but transferring this to a semi-permanent or permanent memory is impaired. A patient may be able to register and repeat a sequence of numbers when asked, but moments later cannot recall the sequence or being asked to perform the task in the first place. Alternatively, patients might repeat themselves or read the same page of a book for hours.
 (ii) Varying degrees of retrograde amnesia: Episodic memory – places, times and emotions within a person's life (autobiographical) – is severely impaired, for example a patient may be unable to recall 20 or 30 years of their life. Earlier memories are retained more than recent ones. Semantic memory loss – the memory for meaning and facts – differs in severity between patients and is usually not as dramatic as episodic memory loss.
(iii) Confabulation: This refers to the replacement of memory with information a patient is able to recall at that time. The patient believes what they are saying, and the problem is driven by profound deficits in episodic memory.

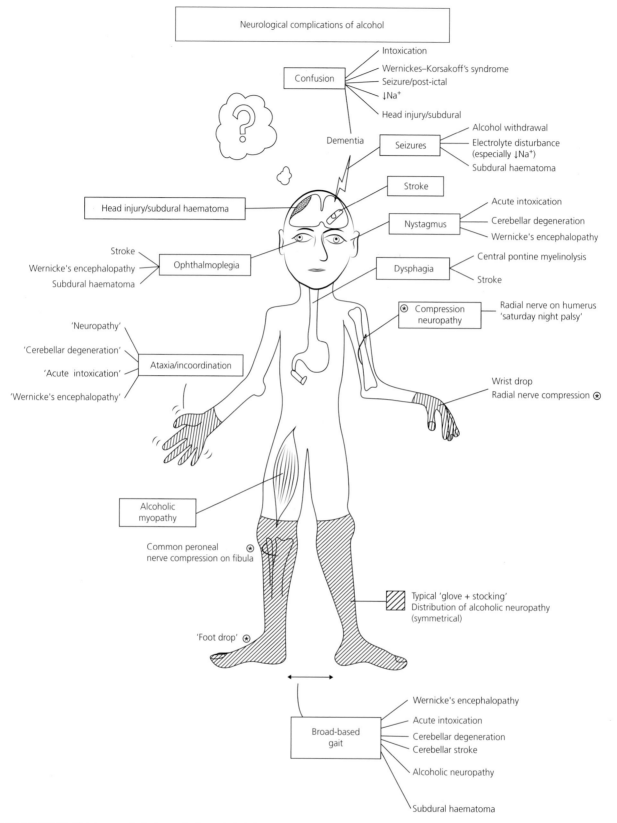

Figure 14.1 Summary of main neurological complications of alcohol.

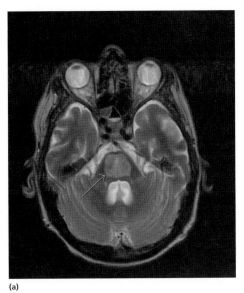
(a)

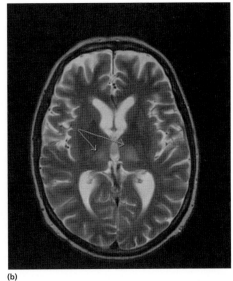
(b)

Figure 14.2 Osmotic demyelination syndrome. Axial T$_2$-weighted MRI of the brain of a middle-aged problematic drinker who presented to hospital with variceal bleeding and then developed flaccid quadraparesis, reduced consciousness, dysphagia and dysarthria. Note the diffuse abnormal high-signal pontine change typical of CPM **(a)** with associated high-signal abnormality in both thalami consistent with EPM **(b)**.

Characteristically, patients with Korsakoff's syndrome lack insight into their memory deficits and may be apathetic. Their level of consciousness is normal. Magnetic resonance imaging (MRI) scans often show changes consistent with focal areas of microhaemorrhage and gliosis in the brainstem, mammillary bodies and thalamus.

Abstinence and nutritional replacement are the cornerstones of treatment in Korsakoff's syndrome. If established, chances of any recovery are low, but a proportion of patients do show improvement and new learning is sometimes possible.

Alcoholic dementia

It is recognized that 50–70% of problematic drinkers have global cognitive impairment on neuropsychological testing. It remains unclear how much is due to the direct neurotoxic effects of alcohol and how much other factors such as nutritional deficiency, repeated head injuries and liver disease contribute. No distinct brain pathology has been reported and generalized cerebral atrophy is the typical finding.

Stroke

Alcohol misuse increases stroke risk by raising lipid levels, increasing the risk of diabetes, raising blood pressure and inducing atrial fibrillation. By contrast, a small amount of alcohol may reduce cerebrovascular disease risk.

Central pontine myelinolysis

Central pontine myelinolysis (CPM) refers to non-inflammatory demyelination within the anterior pons. Sometimes, similar pathology affects other areas of the brain such as the cerebellum, thalamus and basal ganglia and this is referred to as 'extrapontine myelinolysis'

(EPM). CPM and EPM are collectively called 'osmotic demyelination syndrome' (ODS); see Figure 14.2. The susceptibility of specific brain regions to demyelination probably relates to the interdigitation between grey and white matter at these sites.

ODS is caused by a rapid shift in serum osmolality. It is most often seen when hyponatraemia (usually sodium <120 mmol/l) that has been present for at least 24 h is corrected too rapidly. A sudden increase in serum osmolality results in rapid water loss from cells, causing them to shrink and die. Problematic drinkers have increased risk of ODS because they drink large volumes of fluid, have poor dietary intake and may have impaired liver and renal function.

The presentation of ODS depends on the location and severity of the myelinolysis. The 'classic' description of severe CPM involves the development of flaccid, areflexic quadraparesis with associated dysphagia and dysarthria approximately 24–48 h after rapid correction of hyponatraemia. Diffuse damage to the anterior pons in CPM can occasionally result in 'locked-in syndrome'. With the advent of MRI, many more patients with mild or asymptomatic cases are identified and prognosis is variable, ranging from complete recovery to death.

In all patients with hyponatraemia for 24 h or more, correction of sodium should not exceed 10 mmol/l in any 24 h period.

Alcoholic myopathy

Acute alcoholic myopathy occurs after binge drinking. It is characterized by myalgia, proximal weakness and occasionally dysphagia that develop over 24–48 h. Muscles become swollen and tender. Creatine kinase (CK) levels are markedly elevated and rhabdomyolysis may occur. Recovery takes weeks to months.

Chronic alcoholic myopathy evolves over weeks to months with progressive, often painless, proximal muscle weakness and atrophy. CK is usually normal, but hypokalaemia and hypophosphataemia often occur. Incomplete recovery occurs over months.

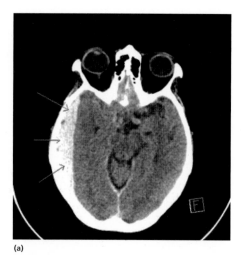 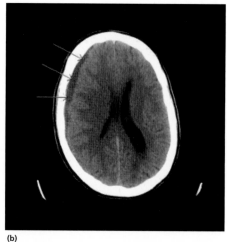

(a)   (b)

Figure 14.3 Acute and chronic subdural haematomas: Axial computerised tomography (CT) scans demonstrating acute **(a)** and chronic **(b)** right-sided subdural haematomas. Remember that acute blood appears hyperdense (bright) on CT imaging and chronic blood appears hypodense (dark).

Treatment is supportive – hydration, abstinence, correction of associated electrolyte abnormalities and nutritional supplementation.

Head injury and subdural haematoma

Head injury as a result of alcohol intoxication or alcohol-related damage to the nervous system is common. The symptoms of head injury – such as unsteadiness, headache, fluctuating confusion, lethargy and apathy – can mimic alcohol withdrawal or Wernicke's encephalopathy and should be considered in any problematic drinker with a neurological presentation.

Subdural haematoma (SDH) is a specific type of head injury caused when bridging veins (connecting superficial cortical veins to dural venous sinuses) rupture; see Figure 14.3. Blood fills the subdural space and increases intracranial pressure. There are a number of predisposing physiological and anatomical changes in people who misuse alcohol that increase the risk of SDH. These include blood clotting abnormalities secondary to liver disease, the direct toxic effect of alcohol on the bone marrow causing thrombocytopenia and the increased vulnerability of bridging veins secondary to cerebral atrophy.

Acute SDH sometimes requires surgery to remove clotted blood and/or repair damaged veins. Chronic SDH presents more insidiously and may not be associated with head injury. Often chronic SDH is managed conservatively but may require surgery.

All subdural haematomas should be discussed with a neurosurgeon.

Further reading

Driver and Vehicle Licensing Agency. *DVLA at a glance guide to the current medical guidelines for professionals, 2013*. https://www.gov.uk/government/collections/current-medical-guidelines-dvla-guidance-for-professionals (accessed 18 September 2014).

Harper C. The neuropathology of alcohol-related brain damage. *Alcohol & Alcoholism* 2009;44:136–40.

Kopelman MD, Thomson AD, Guerrini I, Marshall EJ. The Korsakoff syndrome: clinical aspects, psychology and treatment. *Alcohol & Alcoholism* 2009;44:148–54.

National Institute of Health and Care Excellence. *Alcohol-use disorders: diagnosis and clinical management of alcohol-related physical complications* (NICE Guidelines CG100). 2010. http://www.nice.org.uk/guidance/CG100 (accessed 18 September 2014).

Welch KA. Neurological complications of alcohol and misuse of drugs. *Practical Neurology* 2011;11:206–19.

CHAPTER 15

Alcohol and cancer

Sarah L. Williams

OVERVIEW

- Alcohol causes at least seven types of cancer.
- A total of 12,500 cases of cancer a year in the United Kingdom are caused by alcohol.
- There is no 'safe' limit of alcohol drinking, below which cancer risk isn't increased.
- The risk of cancer increases with the average amount a person drinks.
- Alcohol worsens the effects of other carcinogens such as tobacco, raises oestrogen levels, and has a carcinogenic metabolite (acetaldehyde).

Types of cancer

Alcohol has been established as a cause of cancer for over 25 years. The International Agency for Research into Cancer (IARC, part of the World Health Organisation) is the world's leading body in determining whether an agent causes cancer, and have classified alcohol as something that causes cancer (a carcinogen) in humans, since 1988. Alcohol is now known to increase the risk of seven types of cancer (Figure 15.1): oral, pharyngeal, laryngeal, oesophageal, colorectal (bowel), liver (hepatoma/hepatocellular carcinoma) and female breast cancers. And there is gathering evidence that alcohol (at least in heavy drinkers) could be a cause of pancreatic cancers too.

A comprehensive report on lifestyle and cancer (Parkin, 2011) calculated that alcohol is responsible for 4% of UK cancers – 12,500 cases a year (Figure 15.2). Alcohol causes proportionally more upper aerodigestive tract (UADT) cancers – that is, oral, pharyngeal, laryngeal and oesophageal cancers – compared to other types of cancer. But alcohol causes a higher number of cases of colorectal and breast cancer, because these cancer types are much more common overall.

The higher the intake, the higher the risk

Although risk of cancer increases with the amount a person regularly drinks, it's not only heavy drinkers who are affected (Figure 15.3). Drinking up to one small drink (about 1.5 units of alcohol) a day increases the risk of female breast cancer by 5%, oral and pharyngeal cancer by 17% and one type of oesophageal cancer (squamous cell carcinoma) by 30%.

At higher levels of drinking, around six units a day, the risks for oesophageal and laryngeal cancer double, and the risk of oropharyngeal cancer triples (Corrao et al., 2004). In terms of normal UK drink strengths and measures, six units (Figure 15.4) is 2 pints of premium lager, or 2 large (250 ml) glasses of wine.

Alcohol and breast cancer

Breast cancer is the most common cancer in the United Kingdom, and many UK women drink alcohol. Because of this, the alcohol–breast cancer link is particularly important in terms of public health, even though the relative risk of breast cancer per unit of alcohol is small.

Among 1000 non-drinking women, around 111 will be diagnosed with breast cancer at some point in their lifetime. If those 1000 women each drank up to 12.5g of alcohol a day (around 1.5 units and within UK guidelines), there'd be around an extra six cases of breast cancer. And if they drank 40g of alcohol each day (5 units), you would expect to see 32 extra cases (Table 15.1).

Drinking patterns

Most epidemiological research on alcohol and cancer has looked at the association with average daily drinking. There hasn't been enough research into the effect of drinking patterns to know whether the pattern of drinking – binge drinking or drinking mainly with meals – affects the risk of cancer. For now, the clear message from epidemiology is that the more someone drinks on average, the higher the risk of cancer.

How alcohol can cause cancer

It's likely that alcohol causes different types of cancer through different mechanisms. No mechanism has yet been thoroughly established, but there are several theories that are supported by good evidence (Table 15.2).

Acetaldehyde

Alcohol (ethanol) is metabolised to acetaldehyde, which is in turn converted into acetate. Acetate is non-toxic, but acetaldehyde is a known mutagen and IARC has classed it as carcinogenic to humans, when it's formed after drinking alcohol. Acetaldehyde is thought to be a particularly important mechanism for causing UADT cancers (Figure 15.5).

Alcohol is mostly metabolised to acetaldehyde through the action of the alcohol dehydrogenase (ADH) family of enzymes. Aldehyde dehydrogenase (ALDH) then detoxifies acetaldehyde to acetate, which mostly happens in the liver.

There are seven known classes of human ADH, which are expressed in nearly all human tissues. Different classes are more common at some sites than others. Most ethanol metabolism takes place in the liver, which expresses high levels of the class 1 ADHs. But ADHs are also expressed by the stomach and upper gastrointestinal mucosa – including the oesophagus, gingiva, mouth and tongue.

Small amounts of alcohol may be metabolized immediately after it is drunk, by the upper gastrointestinal mucosa or in the stomach, but the majority will be absorbed into the body through the small intestine and carried to the liver in the bloodstream.

However, particularly with heavier drinking, not all ethanol will be metabolised the first time it passes through the liver. This circulating systemic ethanol is then available for metabolism by ADH present at other sites – for example the oral mucosa – and

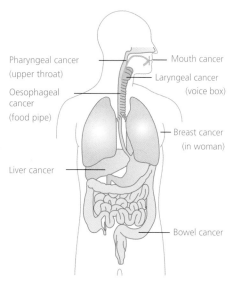

Figure 15.1 Alcohol causes seven different types of cancer.

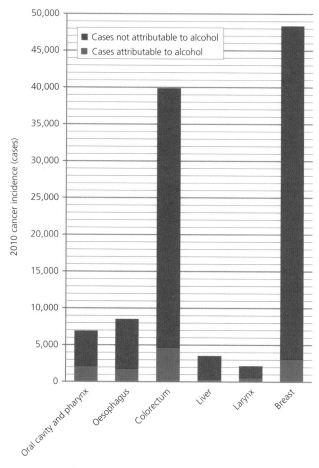

Figure 15.2 The total incidence of alcohol-related cancers in the United Kingdom in 2010, highlighting the number of cases attributable to alcohol consumption. Data from Parkin (2011).

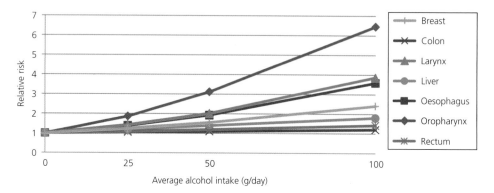

Figure 15.3 The risk of cancer increases with alcohol intake. Data from Corrao et al. (2004).

2 units
A pint of ordinary strength (3–4%)
lager, cider or bitter

3 units
A pint of premium strength (5–5.5%)
lager, cider or extra strength bitter

9.5 units
1 bottle of wine (12.5%)

3 units
A large 250 ml glass of wine (12.5%)

2 units
A 175 ml glass of wine (12.5%)

Just under 3 units
A large 2 x 35 ml double measure
of spirits (40%)

1 unit
A small 25 ml single measure of spirits
(40%) with or without a mixer

Just under 1.5 units
A 275 ml bottle of alcopop (5%)

Figure 15.4 A UK unit is equivalent to 10 ml (8 g) of pure alcohol. There is relatively poor public understanding of how many units of alcohol are in a given drink.

Table 15.1 Impact of alcohol on breast cancer incidence rate in women

Grams of alcohol a day	Expected lifetime cases of breast cancer per 1000 women	
	Linked to alcohol	In total
0	0	111
up to 12.5	6	117
20	16	127
30	24	135
40	32	143

At a population level, the impact of alcohol on the number of women developing breast cancer is appreciable, because many women drink alcohol and breast cancer is a common disease. Calculation by Cancer Research UK, based on current literature.

Table 15.2 Mechanisms by which alcohol could cause cancer

Site	Mechanisms supported by good evidence
Oral cavity	Acetaldehyde
	Co-carcinogenic action (especially with tobacco)
Pharynx	Acetaldehyde
	Co-carcinogenic action (especially with tobacco)
Larynx	Acetaldehyde
	Co-carcinogenic action (especially with tobacco)
Oesophagus	Acetaldehyde
	Co-carcinogenic action (especially with tobacco)
Liver	Immune-mediated injury including damage from reactive oxygen species
	Repair leads to fibrosis and eventually cirrhosis.
	Increased mutagenesis in damaged liver cells
	Co-carcinogenic action (viral hepatitis (B & C), tobacco)
Colorectum	Reduced folate
Breast (female)	Raised oestrogen

There are several theories for how alcohol can cause cancer that are supported by good evidence. It is likely that alcohol causes cancer through different mechanisms at different sites.

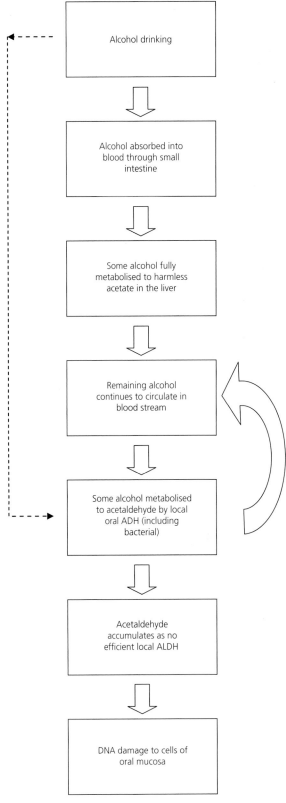

Figure 15.5 Alcohol could cause oral cancer through its primary metabolite, acetaldehyde. ADH, alcohol dehydrogenase; ALDH, acetaldehyde dehydrogenase.

by oral bacteria in saliva. The acetaldehyde this produces in the mouth and throat is not readily converted to harmless acetate, as the oral and pharyngeal mucosa lacks ALDH activity. This means that the concentration of carcinogenic acetaldehyde can be increased in the mouth and throat for some time after alcohol consumption.

In one study, acetaldehyde concentration in the saliva increased markedly after drinking alcohol, but the use of an antibiotic mouthwash by participants reduced this response – highlighting an important role oral bacteria play in the production of endogenous acetaldehyde. And a pilot study found high levels of DNA-acetaldehyde adducts in oral cells of volunteers after drinking alcohol, providing the first direct evidence for a link between consuming alcohol and DNA damage in the mouth (Balbo et al., 2012).

Oestrogen

Compared to non-drinkers, women who drink alcohol tend to have higher levels of sex hormones, including oestrogens, and lower levels of sex hormone binding globulin (Endogenous Hormones and Breast Cancer Collaborative Group, 2011). Oestrogen is a key driver of breast cancer and this is one likely explanation for how alcohol increases the risk of developing the disease.

The effects of alcohol on oestrogen levels may be particularly important in post-menopausal women, because they have naturally lower oestrogen levels than pre-menopausal women. Therefore, oestrogen produced as a result of alcohol drinking could have a bigger impact on post-menopausal women.

Co-carcinogenic effects of alcohol

Alcohol can also work together with other carcinogens, increasing the risk of cancer even further than either on its own. There is a great deal of evidence that alcohol worsens the effects of tobacco (Figure 15.6). People who both drink alcohol and use tobacco have far higher risks of UADT cancers than those who do neither. Tobacco carcinogens are more readily absorbed in the presence of

alcohol both through a solvent effect and by an increase in the permeability of the oral mucosa.

Patients with alcohol-related liver cirrhosis have an increased risk of developing primary liver cancer (hepatoma/HCC) – see Chapter 11. Patients infected with viral hepatitis (hepatitis B and C) also have a high lifetime risk of cirrhosis and in patients who drink the risk of both cirrhosis and HCC is higher than in non-drinkers. People with chronic hepatitis B and C are advised to avoid drinking alcohol.

Reducing the risk of cancer

People can reduce the risk of developing cancer by reducing the amount they drink on average. Despite being a scientifically well-established cause of cancer, many people are unaware of the link with alcohol. Many also mistakenly believe that only heavy drinkers are at risk. There is a need to raise public awareness of the risks of moderate and even light drinking, and to advise and support people to cut down on alcohol – and there are many simple changes people can make to cut down on the amount they drink on average (Box 15.1).

Understanding units

In the United Kingdom, the alcohol content of a drink is often measured in units. One unit is the equivalent of 10 ml, or 8 g, of pure ethanol. The UK government advises that people do not regularly drink more than three to four units in a day for men, or two to three units in a day for women. However, there does not seem to be good public understanding of what is meant by a unit, or how many units different drinks contain (Figure 15.4).

Broadly, the government advice can be interpreted as no more than two standard drinks a day for men, or one for women. The risk of cancer is smaller, the less alcohol someone drinks. Although drinking alcohol within the guideline amounts can still increase the risk of cancer, the impact on the absolute risk of

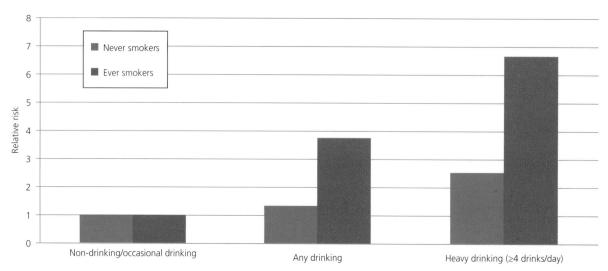

Figure 15.6 Compared to non- or occasional drinkers, alcohol increases the risk of oropharyngeal cancer more amongst smokers than non-smokers. The effect is stronger among heavy drinkers with intake four or more drinks per day (Turati et al., 2013).

Box 15.1 **Tips on reducing drinking**

- Don't keep white wine or beer in the fridge – chill it as you want to drink it.
- Try to avoid keeping a big stock of alcohol at home.
- If you tend to drink with a particular person, such as your partner, agree some non-drinking days that you'll both stick to.
- Try not to "top up" your drink – it makes it harder to keep track of your drinking.
- In pubs and bars, stay out of big rounds so you can control if and when you have another drink.
- Alternate alcoholic drinks with soft drinks, or try spritzers and shandys.
- Keep track of your drinking, you may find you're having more than you thought. There are online and mobile app trackers, including one from the NHS.

developing the disease is small. For people who drink over the guidelines, the risk of cancer is a key reason to recommend they reduce their alcohol intake.

Further reading

Bagnardi V, Rota M, Botteri E, Tramacere I, Islami F, Fedirko V, et al. Light alcohol drinking and cancer: a meta-analysis. *Annals of Oncology* 2013;24:301–8.

Balbo S, Meng L, Bliss RL, Jensen JA, Hatsukami DK, Hecht SS. Kinetics of DNA adduct formation in the oral cavity after drinking alcohol. *Cancer Epidemiology, Biomarkers and Prevention* 2012;21:601–8.

Boyle P, Autier P, Bartelink H, Baselga J, Boffetta P, Burn J, et al. European code against cancer and scientific justification: third version (2003). *Annals of Oncology* 2003;14:973–1005.

Corrao G, Bagnardi V, Zambon A, La Vecchia C. A meta-analysis of alcohol consumption and the risk of 15 diseases. *Preventive Medicine* 2004;38: 613–9.

Endogenous Hormones and Breast Cancer Collaborative Group; Key TJ, Appleby PN, Reeves GK, Roddam AW, Helzlsouer KJ, Alberg AJ, et al. Circulating sex hormones and breast cancer risk factors in postmenopausal women: reanalysis of 13 studies. *British Journal of Cancer* 2011;105:709–22.

Homann N, Jousimies-Somer H, Jokelainen K, Heine R, Salaspuro M. High acetaldehyde levels in saliva after ethanol consumption: methodological aspects and pathogenetic implications. *Carcinogenesis* 1997;18:1739–43.

Parkin DM. Cancers attributable to consumption of alcohol in the UK in 2010. *British Journal of Cancer* 2011;105(Suppl 2):S14–8.

Personal habits and indoor combustions. Volume 100E. A review of human carcinogens. IARC monographs on the evaluation of carcinogenic risks to humans. Lyon: IARC, 2012.

Seitz HK, Pelucchi C, Bagnardi V, La Vecchia C. Epidemiology and pathophysiology of alcohol and breast cancer: update 2012. *Alcohol and Alcoholism* 2012;47:204–12.

Turati F, Garavello W, Tramacere I, Pelucchi C, Galeone C, Bagnardi V, et al. A meta-analysis of alcohol drinking and oral and pharyngeal cancers: results from subgroup analyses. *Alcohol and Alcoholism* 2013;48:107–18.

CHAPTER 16

Alcohol and the heart

Nitin Kumar, Yasmin Ismail and Julian Strange

OVERVIEW

- The relationship between alcohol intake and the cardiovascular system is complex, with light to moderate alcohol consumption known to reduce the incidence of coronary heart disease, ischaemic stroke, peripheral arterial disease, coronary heart disease mortality as well as all-cause mortality, whilst heavy alcohol consumption has been shown to be detrimental causing cardiomyopathy, cardiac arrhythmias and increasing cardiovascular mortality.

- Chronic alcohol intake is associated with malnutrition; deficiencies in specific electrolytes and trace elements may predispose to arrhythmias.

- Alcohol septal ablation in hypertrophic cardiomyopathy (HCM) highlights a therapeutic application of alcohol in cardiology.

- In the absence of robust data from randomised controlled trials specifically assessing the impact on alcohol consumption on cardiovascular health, patients should not be encouraged to initiate drinking. There is however little reason to routinely recommend abstinence

Introduction

According to the World Health Organization, the population of Europe are the heaviest consumers of alcohol in the world with over one-fifth of the European population aged greater than or equal to 15 years, reporting heavy episodic drinking at least once a week. Such 'binge' drinking is widespread across all ages and all European nations. In addition, it has been estimated that 38% of men and 16% of women in the United Kingdom consume more alcohol than the recommended sensible limit and 3.6% of the adult population are thought to be dependent on alcohol. As illustrated in previous chapters, alcohol has detrimental effects throughout the body; and in this chapter, we will explore the complex effects of alcohol on the cardiovascular system.

Relationship of alcohol and all-cause mortality

A large number of observational studies have consistently demonstrated a J-shaped relationship between alcohol consumption and all-cause mortality, that is those with no alcohol consumption have higher total mortality than those drinking one to two drinks per day.

A large meta-analysis of 34 studies, incorporating data from more than 1,000,000 patients conducted by Di Castelnuovo et al., confirmed the J-shaped relationship between alcohol and total mortality, which had been described in multiple previous studies. Specifically, the study showed that low levels of alcohol intake (one to two drinks/day for women and two to four drinks/day for men) are inversely associated with total mortality, whilst heavy alcohol consumption correlates with increased total mortality due to its association with several kinds of cancer, liver cirrhosis and pancreatitis, as well as accidents, suicide and homicide.

Alcohol and cardiovascular mortality

Alcohol consumption and cardiovascular outcomes also exhibit a J-shaped distribution (Figure 16.1). Interestingly however, the significant reductions in coronary artery disease as defined by reduction in cardiac events seen with light–moderate alcohol consumption are also present with heavy alcohol consumption. However, stroke incidence and mortality (especially haemorrhagic strokes) increase substantially with heavier drinking, explaining the steep rise in cardiovascular mortality with increased alcohol consumption. The adverse association between heavy alcohol consumption and hypertension may account, in part, for the higher risk of haemorrhagic stroke associated with heavier drinking.

The exact mechanisms by which low–moderate alcohol consumption mediates its beneficial effects on cardiovascular mortality are complex and are yet to be clearly defined but are thought to include its effects on increasing HDL cholesterol, tissue plasminogen activator and improving endothelin function and decreasing platelet aggregability,

ABC of Alcohol, Fifth Edition. Edited by Anne McCune.
© 2015 John Wiley & Sons, Ltd. Published 2015 by John Wiley & Sons, Ltd.

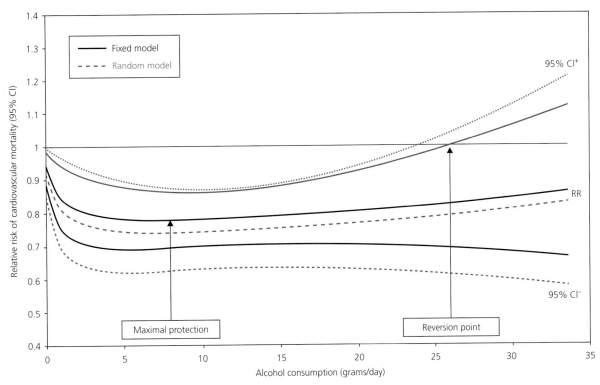

Figure 16.1 Alcohol consumption in relation to cardiovascular mortality in cardiovascular disease patients. Source: Costanzo et al. (2010). Reproduced by permission of Elsevier.

fibrinogen and lipoprotein(a). It is noteworthy that the effects of alcohol on cardiovascular mortality are not consistently replicated across all populations with studies in African-American, Asian Indian and Chinese populations showing a positive correlation between alcohol consumption and mortality/coronary heart disease.

Coronary artery disease

There is no direct relationship between coronary artery disease and alcohol consumption. The effects of alcohol on other established modifiable risk factors such as hypertension and lipid metabolism, as well as the indirect link with smoking may account for the association of atherosclerosis and alcohol consumption.

Various studies have found that moderate alcohol intake is associated with reduced risk of coronary artery disease. The INTERHEART study demonstrated regular moderate alcohol consumption (defined as consumption of alcohol three or more times per week) was associated with decreased risk of myocardial infarction. The Spanish EPIC study was a large prospective cohort study of over 40,000 subjects with a median follow-up period of 10 years and suggested in men aged 29–69 years alcohol intake (moderate (5–30 g/day), high (30–60 g/day) and very high (>90 g/day)) was associated with 30% lower incidence of coronary heart disease (CHD).

Alcohol and hypertension

Chronic alcohol intake can lead to hypertension. This association was first reported by Lian in 1915 when he studied a group of French servicemen and found three times higher frequency of

hypertension in heavy as compared with moderate drinkers. Various epidemiological studies have further confirmed this association. The exact mechanism of this has not been definitively established, but effects on the renin–angiotensin–aldosterone axis, adrenergic nervous system discharge, heart rate variability, ionic fluxes, cortisol secretion or insulin sensitivity have been proposed as underlying mechanisms of action.

Alcohol and lipid metabolism

Moderate alcohol intake is associated with increase in high-density lipoprotein (HDL) 1 and 2 levels both of which have a cardioprotective effect. A Norwegian study (CONOR) disputed this beneficial effect on HDL after taking into account all the confounding factors and suggested serum HDL level was not an important variable in association of alcohol and CHD.

Studies have also shown a possible antioxidant effect of alcohol on the low-density lipoprotein (LDL). The flavonoids and phenolic compounds in red wine inhibit the production of the oxidised form of LDL, which is more atherogenic.

Alcohol and the coagulation system

An improvement of endothelial function, reduction in plasma viscosity, inflammation and platelet aggregation may explain the benefits of alcohol consumption on coronary heart disease. In addition, moderate alcohol intake (up to two drinks per day) has been shown to decrease fibrinogen levels, which decreases the risk of CHD.

Alcohol and heart failure

Alcohol is an important cause of cardiomyopathy and comes under toxic causes in the classification. The toxic effects of ethanol and its metabolites can affect ventricular function through its effect on cardiac calcium homeostasis, mitochondrial respiration, myocardial protein and lipid synthesis, as well as signal transduction. Prolonged ethanol exposure of myofibrils leads to their degeneration resulting in eventual replacement with fibrosis. Myocardial inflammation is detectable on cardiac MRI following binge drinking. Such binge drinking has also been shown to cause chronic myocardial inflammation.

Any person presenting with signs and symptoms of heart failure with a history of excess alcohol consumption should strongly be suspected of having alcoholic cardiomyopathy (AC). Usually it manifests in patients who have been ingesting more than 80–90 g (eight to nine units) alcohol/day for 5 years or more. The blood alcohol concentration in women is higher than the men for similar level of alcohol intake owing to the high proportion of body fat and consequently women may develop AC earlier than men. As discussed earlier, excess alcohol consumption is associated with hypertension which is an important cause of heart failure. In addition to standard heart failure treatment, cessation of alcohol is recommended with studies suggesting improvement in cardiac function with alcohol abstinence.

Cardiac arrhythmias

Alcohol affects cardiac conduction, both acutely and chronically precipitating both supraventricular tachycardias such as atrial fibrillation (AF), as well as more serious ventricular arrhythmias. The Copenhagen City Heart Study showed that consumption of more than five standard alcoholic drinks/day increased the risk of AF. AF is commonly encountered in the setting of the emergency department after episodes of binge drinking causing what is commonly known as the 'holiday heart'.

In addition, alcohol abuse can lead to electrolyte abnormalities, which can in turn affect cardiac conduction. Hypocalcaemia and hypomagnesaemia can both cause QTc prolongation (Figure 16.2) and increase the risk of serious arrhythmias. QTc interval prolongation, secondary to electrolyte abnormalities, is also seen in chronic alcoholics, which predisposes them to *torsades de pointes* (Figure 16.3), which is a form of polymorphic ventricular tachycardia and can lead to sudden death.

Alcohol excess is associated with falls, poorer compliance with medication and liver disease including portal hypertensive bleeding, making anticoagulation for AF potentially hazardous. The decision to anticoagulate such patients should be made on a case-by-case basis. The use of risk calculators such as CHADS-Vasc score and the HAS-BLED score should be used to assess the risks involved as recommended by the European Society of Cardiology guidelines for anticoagulation in AF. If there is a strong indication to use anticoagulation, then warfarin is preferred as there are as yet no clinically applicable reversing agents for life-threatening bleeding induced by the novel oral anticoagulant agents.

Therapeutic effects of alcohol in cardiovascular medicine

Alcohol septal ablation or the *Sigwart procedure* was first performed in 1994 by Ulrich Sigwart at the Royal Brompton Hospital in the United Kingdom and since has become very popular in the management of medically refractory cases of hypertrophic cardiomyopathy (HCM) (Figure 16.4). It lowers the outflow tract obstruction by therapeutically infarcting a carefully selected part of the intraventricular septum. The procedure uses techniques familiar to coronary angioplasty. An early septal branch of the left anterior descending (LAD) that supplies part of the intraventricular septum is initially identified, and then 2 ml of neat alcohol is injected resulting in a therapeutic myocardial infarct. This results in atrophy of part of the septum.

A recent Danish observational study found patients treated with alcohol septal ablation had improved survival and reduced

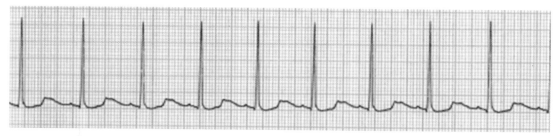

Figure 16.2 QT prolongation.

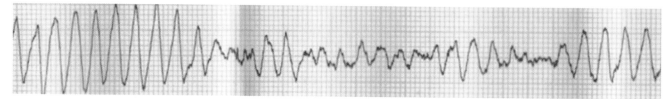

Figure 16.3 QT prolongation predisposes to *torsades de pointes*.

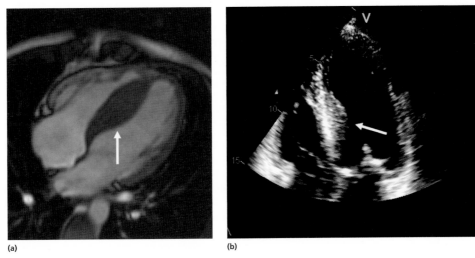

Figure 16.4 Septal hypertrophy (arrow) demonstrated on four chamber MRI **(a)** and on four chamber two-dimensional (2D) echocardiography **(b)** Source: ten Berg et al. (2010). Reproduced by permission of BMJ Publishing Group Ltd.

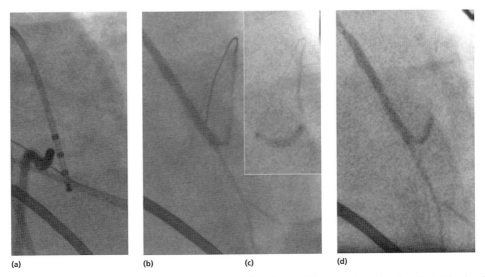

Figure 16.5 (a) Fluoroscopic image (LAO 30 projection) of mapping catheter in the right ventricle at entrainment pacing site (white arrow). **(b)** Fluoroscopic image (PA projection) showing BMW guidewire positioned in target mid-septal branch of the native LAD. Access is retrograde via the LAD saphenous vein graft. **(c)** Fluoroscopic image (PA projection) of contrast injection into the target vessel following balloon inflation. **(d)** Fluoroscopic image (PA projection) of the occluded target vessel following ethanol administration. Image Courtesy: Dr Tom Johnson.

symptoms. The prevalence of non-sustained ventricular tachycardia and incidence of sudden cardiac death was also reduced.

There are also descriptions of trans-coronary ethanol ablation of ventricular arrhythmias in the literature, and the technique has been used succesfully to treat medical and catheter ablation refractory arrhythmias (Figure 16.5).

Effect of type of alcoholic beverage

Rimm et al. systematically reviewed ecological, case-control and prospective studies to see individual effect of beverages. The ecological studies suggested reduced risk of mortality in comparison with beer, wine or spirits, whereas prospective cohort studies found evidence for the beneficial effects of beer and spirits. The case-control studies did not reveal advantage of one drink over the other. Overall, data suggest that it is the alcohol component of beverages that confers any beneficial health effects.

Alcohol consumption and diet

Through its effect on the kidney, alcohol increases the urinary excretion of both magnesium and calcium. It is also recognised that harmful and hazardous drinkers do not have a balanced diet and, therefore, suffer from various degrees of malnutrition. Nutritional deficiencies in such electrolytes as well as B-complex vitamins and trace elements such as selenium can impact on cardiac function and conduction as discussed earlier in this chapter. Interestingly the addition of cobalt chloride to improve the foaming quality of beers led to a local epidemic of heart failure in chronic heavy drinkers in Quebec in the 1960s.

Conclusion

There is a complex relationship between alcohol consumption and cardiovascular health, with both positive and negative effects dependent on the levels consumed. In the absence of robust, large randomised controlled trials routine ingestion of alcohol cannot be recommended for its cardiovascular benefits; similarly, the benefits of abstinence must not be over-promoted unless related to alcohol-related cardiovascular disease.

Further reading

Arriola L, Martinez-Camblor P, Larrañaga N, Basterretxea M, Amiano P, Moreno-Iribas C, et al. Epic study – epidemiology: alcohol intake and the risk of coronary heart disease in the Spanish EPIC cohort study. *Heart* 2010;96(2):124–30.

ten Berg J, Steggerda RC, Siebelink H-MJ. The patient with hypertrophic cardiomyopathy. *BMJ Heart* 2010;96:1764–72. doi:10.1136/hrt.2009.190124.

Bonow RO, Mann DL, Zipes DP, Libby P. Braunwald's heart disease: a textbook of cardiovascular medicine, 9th edn. London: Saunders, 2012.

Camm AJ, Lüscher TF, Serruys PW. ESC textbook of cardiovascular medicine. Malden, MA: European Society of Cardiology, 2006.

Costanzo S, Di Castelnuovo A, Donati M, Iacoviello L, de Gaetano G. Alcohol consumption and mortality in patients with cardiovascular disease: a meta-analysis. *Journal of the American College of Cardiology* 2010;55(13): 1339–47. doi:10.1016/j.jacc.2010.01.006.

Di Castelnuovo A, Costanzo S, Bagnardi V, Donati MB, Iacoviello L, de Gaetano G. Alcohol dosing and total mortality in men and women: an updated meta-analysis of 34 prospective studies. *Archives of Internal Medicine* 2006;166(22):2437.

Movva R, Figueredo VM. Alcohol and the heart: to abstain or not to abstain? *Cardiology Faculty Papers* 2013;164:267–76. http://jdc.jefferson.edu/cardiologyfp/28 (accessed 18 September 2014).

Rimm EB, Klatsky A, Grobbee D, Stampfer MJ. Review of moderate alcohol consumption and reduced risk of coronary heart disease: is the effect due to beer, wine, or spirits. British Medical Journal 1996;312(7033): 731–736.

CHAPTER 17

Drug–alcohol interactions

Dan Harris

OVERVIEW

- Potentially the majority of adults will consume alcohol with prescribed or illicit drugs at some point in time.
- Taking careful note of the past and current alcohol history in all patients, not just alcohol dependent ones, will help guide safe prescribing.
- The efficacy of all drugs that undergo hepatic metabolism will be affected by alcohol to a positive or negative degree.
- Significant pharmacodynamic interactions can occur even after a single episode of moderate alcohol consumption.
- The purposeful mixing of alcohol and illicit drugs by many people leaves them at great risk of physical harm.

Alcohol is consumed on a weekly basis by over half of all adults in the United Kingdom. It is therefore inevitable that many people will drink alcohol immediately before, during or after they have taken prescribed, over-the-counter or illicit drugs. This chapter provides a guide as to where and when interactions may occur and the potential adverse consequences.

Prescribed and over-the-counter drugs

Clinicians routinely take a drug history when prescribing new or adjusting existing medications, in part to prevent predictable interactions occurring. Alcohol should also be considered a drug, yet prescribers often fail to consider the patient's alcohol history unless they are known to be chronically alcohol-dependent. We may then fail to predict the interactions between prescribed drugs and the moderate amounts of alcohol consumed by many patients during their treatment.

Broadly divided into pharmacokinetic or pharmacodynamic interactions, outcomes can be additive, synergistic or antagonistic and result in the alcohol altering the drug effect or vice versa. Pharmacokinetics relate to a drug's absorption, distribution, metabolism and excretion (what the body does to the drug) and pharmacodynamics to a drug's physiological effects and mechanism of action (what the drug does to the body) (Figure 17.1).

Pharmacokinetic elements

Most interactions relate to the changes in liver enzyme function that alcohol cause, primarily to the cytochrome P450 (CP450) group which is inextricably linked to drug metabolism. Predicting interaction outcomes is made more complex as the diminution or enhancement of a drug's effect can be influenced by

- whether a person is a moderate drinker or long-term heavy alcohol user;
- whether they do or do not have impaired liver function;
- whether they are intoxicated or sober at the time of drug ingestion (Table 17.1).

One must then also consider whether the metabolites produced from the initial drug are active, inactive, toxic or safe.

In a moderate alcohol user who drinks whilst on a course of medication that undergoes CP450 liver-based metabolism, there is competition for normal quantities of enzyme between the drug and alcohol. The resultant reduction in drug metabolism leads to a higher-than-expected concentration of remaining active substrate. This may increase the blood pressure-lowering effect of antihypertensive medication, the cardiovascular side effects of tricyclic antidepressants or the anticoagulant effect of warfarin.

Long-term heavy alcohol users without impaired liver function will have enhanced CP450 activity and so drug interactions will follow an 'enzyme induction'-enhanced metabolism pathway (Figure 17.2). This can be further influenced by whether the patient is intoxicated or not at the time of drug ingestion.

A sober patient with enhanced CP450 will have a marked increase in enzyme-mediated metabolism, thereby reducing substrate concentration and decreasing the clinical effect of the drug. However if the patient is using alcohol simultaneously the drug must compete with the ingested alcohol for CP450 with a resulting reduction in substrate metabolism causing the opposite outcome of increased clinical effect.

Alcohol-induced cirrhosis patients with impaired liver function have opposite dosing issues. These patients have reduced enzyme production and, therefore, a reduced ability to metabolise substrates, resulting in an increased drug concentration and effect.

ABC of Alcohol, Fifth Edition. Edited by Anne McCune.
© 2015 John Wiley & Sons, Ltd. Published 2015 by John Wiley & Sons, Ltd.

Further attention must be given to drugs such as paracetamol whose CP450-related metabolite (N-acetyl-p-benzoquinone imine) is hepato-toxic. The enzyme-inducing alcohol-dependent patient is more vulnerable to toxicological side effects at prescribed doses through the increased CP450 plus reduced conjugating glutathione levels (Figure 17.3).

In cases of paracetamol overdose in 'chaotic' or heavy drinkers the accurate estimation of the timing and quantity of overdose is often impossible. This reduces the usefulness of tools such as the paracetamol nomogram and factors such as physiological state; acid–base balance; and renal, liver and clotting results should be carefully reviewed alongside the plasma paracetamol concentration which if viewed alone may not be a useful guide for initiating treatment.

This potential for day-to-day variability added to the pre-existing problems of basic medication compliance in alcohol-dependent patients makes drug dosing more complex than most consider it to be.

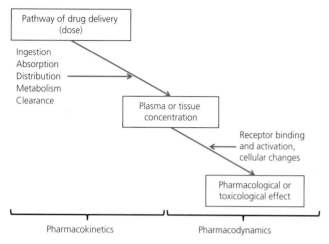

Figure 17.1 Pharmacokinetics and pharmacodynamics.

Table 17.1 Likely drug–alcohol interaction outcomes

Type of drinker	Liver impairment	Drinking with medication	Substrate concentration
Moderate	No	No	Normal
Moderate	No	Yes	Increased
Heavy	No	No	Decreased
Heavy	No	Yes	Increased
Heavy	Yes	No	Increased
Heavy	Yes	Yes	Increased

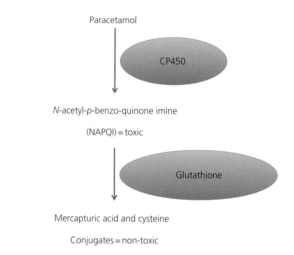

Figure 17.3 Paracetamol metabolism.

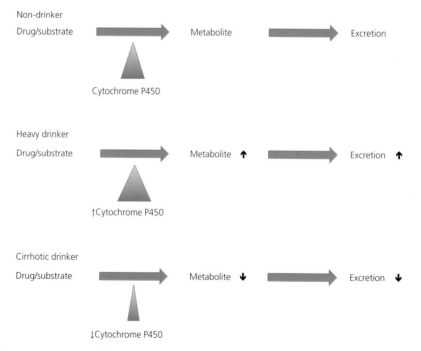

Figure 17.2 Cytochrome P450-mediated drug metabolism.

Pharmacodynamic elements

Some basic additive pharmacodynamic interactions cause clinical problems early on in the ingestion phase. Alcohol is a gastric irritant and so will worsen the erosive effects of drugs such as prednisolone or non-steroidal anti-inflammatory drugs (NSAIDs) if taken concurrently. The poor outcome will be most pronounced in the cirrhotic patient whose deranged blood clotting will make any resulting gastrointestinal haemorrhage more severe.

The majority of pharmacodynamic interactions occur in the central nervous system. Alcohol can synergistically enhance the sedative effect of many drugs including benzodiazepines, opioids and some tricyclic antidepressants through common receptor agonism. This mechanism makes such pharmacodynamic interactions more likely to occur than pharmacokinetic ones during periods of intermittent alcohol use or even single episodes (Figure 17.4).

Some interactions will increase the blood alcohol level expected for the amount consumed by increasing the amount absorbed from the small intestine. Drugs that increase the rate of gastric emptying such as metoclopramide, erythromycin and histamine-2 receptor antagonists reduce the percentage of alcohol eliminated by gastric alcohol dehydrogenase metabolism. Patients may then become more intoxicated than expected, with the accompanying risks and cognitive changes (Table 17.2).

Illicit drugs

Illicit drug use remains common in the United Kingdom with the NHS Information Centre publication on drug use in 2011 showing 8.8% of UK adults used illicit drugs in the preceding year, with over half of those people using multiple illicit drugs simultaneously. Home Office studies also found that people who drink alcohol are between 3 and 6 times more likely to use illicit drugs than non-drinkers; increasing to 14 times for people who visit nightclubs four or more times a month.

The range of drugs available is continuously increasing, with a surge in the popularity of MDMA, synthetic cathinones and benzylpiperazines; plus the resurgence of drugs such as cocaine, ketamine and amphetamines (Figure 17.5). For the majority of illicit drugs the combined use of the drug with alcohol will have a simple additive effect and increase the natural risks that accompany the associated cognitive impairment. However the concomitant use of alcohol and certain specific illicit compounds can result in the production of unique metabolites or alter the expected metabolism of the drug. Whilst many drug users may see this as a beneficial augmentation, the combination can make dosing unpredictable and severe acute toxicity more likely.

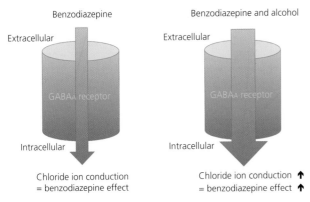

Figure 17.4 Benzodiazepine and alcohol interaction.

Table 17.2 Likely interactions between alcohol and commonly used medications

Interactions between alcohol and prescribed or over-the-counter drugs		
Drug group	**Drugs involved**	**Possible effect**
Antacids	H$_2$ blockers	Increased blood alcohol level
Analgesics	Opioids	Enhanced sedative effect
	NSAIDs	Enhanced gastrointestinal irritation
Antibiotics	Erythromycin	Increased blood alcohol level
	Metronidazole	Flushing, vomiting through acetaldehyde accumulation
Anticoagulants	Warfarin	Decreased effect with short-term alcohol use
		Increased effect with long-term alcohol use
Anticonvulsants	Phenytoin	Reduced effect
	Carbamazepine	Enhanced central nervous system effects
Antidepressants	Tricyclics	Increased sedation and plasma levels
	Monoamine oxidase inhibitors	Tyramine reaction (severe hypertension)
Antidiabetics	Metformin	Increased risk of lactic acidosis
Antihistamines	Chlorpheniramine	Increased sedation
Antihypertensives	ACE inhibitors	Enhanced hypotensive effect
	Beta blockers	Enhanced hypotensive effect
	Calcium channel blockers	Enhanced hypotensive effect, increased blood alcohol level (verapamil only)
	Angiotensin II antagonists	Enhanced hypotensive effect
Benzodiazepines	All	Increased sedation acutely
		Tolerance with chronic alcohol use
Muscle relaxants	Baclofen	Dizziness, agitation, confusion

ACE, angiotensin-converting enzyme; H$_2$ blockers, histamine H2 receptor antagonists; NSAIDs, non-steroidal anti-inflammatory drugs.

Figure 17.5 Photo of illicit drugs that can interact in an additive or synergistic way with alcohol.

Cocaine prevalence has climbed steadily in the United Kingdom from 0.6% of 16–59-year-olds in 1996 to 2.5% in 2010, with the figure rising to 11.6% in 16–24-year-olds; making it the second most commonly used illicit drug after cannabis (7% of 16–59-year-olds). The 2010 MI×Mag survey on club drug use found that over 60% of people using cocaine always consume alcohol with it.

Cocaethylene is a unique compound formed when alcohol and cocaine are combined producing a heightened euphoria amongst users, with a more prolonged effect than taking cocaine on its own. The resulting 30% increase in blood cocaine levels is associated with a significant rise in the incidence of neurological and cardiac emergencies including myocardial ischaemia and infarction, cardiac arrhythmias and intracranial haemorrhage.

As well as the direct physical and psychological risks associated with combined cocaine and alcohol use, the stimulant effect of using cocaine reduces the user's sense of alcohol intoxication and allows greater quantities of alcohol to be consumed. The ensuing alcohol-related disinhibition combined with the cocaine-induced self-confidence results in a far greater risk of impulsive and violent behaviour than in people who have taken either drug alone.

Gamma hydroxybutyrate (GHB) is a recreational psychoactive that at low dose has an affect similar to alcohol, causing social disinhibition, elevated mood and relaxation. Higher doses cause increased music appreciation and euphoria making it a popular 'dance-drug'. However, the dosing difference between the euphoric stage and overdose with associated vomiting, CNS and respiratory depression, apnoea and seizures can be as little as 1 g.

Although the exact mechanism is unclear, alcohol is known to have a synergistic effect making unintentional overdose more likely as well as accurate dosing of GHB less precise due to the intoxicating effects of alcohol consumption.

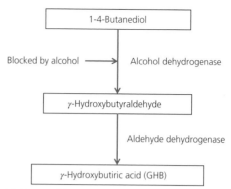

Result of 1-4-Butanediol accumulation: delayed metabolism resulting in high serum levels of GHB with associated severe toxicity

Figure 17.6 1-4-Butanediol metabolism.

1-4-Butanediol (1-4-B) is an increasingly available and popular pro-drug of GHB. Its metabolism into the active GHB form is dependent upon alcohol dehydrogenase. Concomitant alcohol consumption results in the competitive inhibition of alcohol dehydrogenase by ethanol, causing a potentially life-threatening build up of unmetabolised 1-4-B. This becomes active when the user stops drinking, resulting in the delayed onset of severe, and in some recorded cases, lethal GHB toxicity (Figure 17.6).

Cannabis remains the most widely used illicit drug in the United Kingdom. The combined use of alcohol and cannabis is common although less so in people who consume the greatest quantities of cannabis. This is because alcohol causes a significant increase in the rate of absorption of tetrahydrocannabinol, the psychoactive component of cannabis. This results in the cannabis having a far stronger and more rapid effect with large increases in associated rates of nausea, vomiting, postural hypotension, anxiety, paranoia and acute psychosis.

Conclusion

Statistically adults in the United Kingdom are almost more likely to consume alcohol whilst taking a course of prescribed medication than not. It is therefore essential that even moderate drinkers be warned about the potentially significant interactions that can occur so that drinking behaviour can be modified for the duration of treatment. For those patients known to be most likely to drink whilst on medication greater vigilance will be required to ensure the therapeutic outcomes are achieved with minimal adverse side effects.

Acknowledgements

I thank Professor Robin Touquet for his support and advice during the writing of this chapter.

Further reading

Baxter K, Preston C. *Stockley's drug interactions*, 10th edn. London: Pharmaceutical Press, 2013.

Blumenthal DK, Garrison JC. Pharmacodynamics: molecular mechanisms of drug action. In: Brunton L, Chabner B, Knollman B, eds. *Goodman &*

Gilman's the pharmacological basis of therapeutics, 12th edn. New York: McGraw-Hill, 2011:41–72.

Buxton ILO, Benet LZ. Pharmacokinetics: the dynamics of drug absorption, distribution, metabolism, and elimination. In: Brunton L, Chabner B, Knollman B, eds. *Goodman & Gilman's the pharmacological basis of therapeutics*, 12th edn. New York: McGraw-Hill, 2011:17–40.

Hansten P, Horn J. *Drug interactions, analysis and management 2011*. St. Louis: Wolters Klewer Health, 2011.

Nutt D, King L, Phillips L. Drug harms in the UK: a multicriteria decision analysis. *The Lancet* 2010;376(9752):1558–65.

Weathermon R, Crabb D. Alcohol and medication interactions. *Alcohol Research & Health* 1999;23(1):40–54.

CHAPTER 18

Management of acute unplanned alcohol withdrawal

Adrian Brown and Anne McCune

OVERVIEW

- An increasing number of dependent drinkers present to acute hospital services, but doctors, nurses and allied healthcare professionals are often inexperienced in the recognition and management of dependency.

- An alcohol history appropriate for the patient's presentation is mandatory for all patients presenting to acute hospital services.

- Around 40% of all alcohol misusers will develop unpleasant symptoms on stopping drinking. Delirium tremens (DTs) is a severe manifestation of acute alcohol withdrawal and is associated with considerable mortality if untreated.

- Withdrawal symptoms should be treated with a benzodiazepine, such as chlordiazepoxide, using a symptom-triggered regimen in hospital wherever possible. A tool (i.e. CIWA-AR or CIWA-AD) should be utilised as an adjunct to clinical judgement.

- Alcohol nurse specialists play a central role in the assessment, management and support of patients presenting to acute services with alcohol withdrawal.

Introduction

The number of dependent drinkers in the United Kingdom has increased dramatically (6% men and 2% women) and as a group commonly present to hospital services either with the direct consequences of dependency, with a condition attributable to alcohol such as falls, personal injury, liver disease or with an entirely unrelated condition.

In the community, a person who realises they are exhibiting signs of alcohol withdrawal may become anxious or agitated and unsure what to do. Some will approach their General Practitioner, whilst others will attend their local emergency department (ED) seeking help. Before a severe state of withdrawal is reached, there is opportunity to intervene either with medication or, as many dependent drinkers do, by drinking again to control symptoms. The latter of course perpetuates the cycle of addiction but may be a very important interim step in preventing medical emergencies such as seizures

or delirium tremens (DTs) and allow time for a planned assessment by specialist alcohol services. Doctors may feel uneasy advising a patient to return to drinking to prevent symptoms, but this may be the least risky option for the patient in the short term until an elective withdrawal can be arranged.

Finally, a clinician may decide to admit a patient to hospital before his or her drinking is recognised as problematic. Signs and symptoms of withdrawal can emerge within hours or even a few days after cessation of alcohol but without vigilance may only be recognised once the individual is in an advanced state of withdrawal. Sadly, many doctors, nurses and allied healthcare professionals are not adequately experienced in the recognition and management of dependency in the healthcare settings they work.

Signs of withdrawal

It is crucial all healthcare professionals have some detailed knowledge of the symptoms and signs of withdrawal (Table 18.1). The onset of withdrawal symptoms after stopping drinking is variable, but some individuals develop uncomfortable symptoms as early as 6–8 h after their last alcoholic drink. DTs are thankfully rare but associated with considerable mortality (Table 18.1). Most episodes of DTs are avoidable especially if the patient is managed promptly by experts in withdrawal management. In acute trusts multidisciplinary teams or 'alcohol care teams' led by an experienced consultant and supported by one or more alcohol nurse specialists are crucial.

Screening and assessment of the dependent drinker

All patients presenting to acute hospital services should be screened for alcohol misuse (NCEPOD, NICE) and an alcohol history appropriate for the patient's presentation is mandatory. Medical and nursing staff in all acute hospital settings require training and skills to recognise the dependent drinker. At a minimum the history should indicate the number of units drunk weekly, the pattern of drinking and recent drinking behaviour, the time of last drink (crucial for risk assessment of withdrawal) and indicators of dependence (Table 18.2).

ABC of Alcohol, Fifth Edition. Edited by Anne McCune.
© 2015 John Wiley & Sons, Ltd. Published 2015 by John Wiley & Sons, Ltd.

Table 18.1 Typical withdrawal symptoms and onset

Mild dependency	Seizures uncommon but can occur before stopping drinking if there is a rapid reduction in alcohol.
	Mild withdrawal symptoms can occur within 8 h but usually within 12–24 h of last drink.
	Symptoms and signs include fine tremors, sweating, anxiety, hyperactivity, hypertension, tachycardia, mild pyrexia, anorexia, nausea and retching, disturbed sleep.
	Withdrawal symptoms generally peak at 24 h and subside by 36 h.
Moderate dependency	As above. Seizures possible especially within first 24–48 h.
	Symptoms and signs as above and coarse tremor, shaking, agitation, confusion, hyperventilation, dehydration, disorientation, paranoia. Resolution usual by day 5.
	Auditory and visual hallucinations are uncommon but may start any time, usually peaking within this period but occasionally prolonged.
Severe dependency	As above, but more severe and prolonged symptoms. Resolution usually within 7 days but may be longer
	Patients with severe dependency are at particular risk of developing DTs. Onset is usually around 48 h and common are severe agitation and anxiety, confusion, disorientation, delusions, fever and florid visual hallucinations specifically tactile – 'crawling insects'. Severe circulatory collapse and death can occur

Table 18.2 Components of a brief alcohol history

- Units of alcohol consumed per day/week
- Drinking pattern – daily/continuous vs. episodic/binge pattern
- Drinking pattern in previous week and 6 months
- Time of last drink
- History of previous withdrawal symptoms such as tremor, sweating, anxiety, hallucinations, nausea or vomiting, insomnia or previous DTs (Table 18.1)
- Symptoms/behaviour suggestive of dependence: cravings or compulsion to drink; priority over other pursuits or social activities; morning drinking to alleviate or avoid withdrawal symptoms

There are a number of tools available to help with screening for alcohol misuse and dependency and these include AUDIT, AUDIT-C, FAST, PAT and SADQ (Chapter 6). If the patient's history reveals excessive alcohol use then a risk assessment of withdrawal is mandatory – allowing safe withdrawal from alcohol in a calm environment with relief of the patient's uncomfortable symptoms whilst also avoiding potentially violent scenarios and minimising the risks to other patients and staff. The use of a tool is recommended such as the Clinical Institute Withdrawal Assessment Scale for Alcohol, Revised (CIWA-AR) or shortened version CIWA-AD (see Figure 18.1 and the following text). Alcohol nurse specialists (ANS) play a vital role in the further assessment of dependent drinkers. The use of withdrawal tools is usually embedded in their practice and the ANS offers invaluable support to both patients and clinical teams on the ward alike. The ANS is able to offer regular review and undertake more comprehensive assessments, planning further follow up and referral as appropriate. Acute trusts should offer a 7-day ANS service as part of a multidisciplinary 'alcohol care team'.

The early recognition of alcohol dependence is a vital part of both emergency and planned admissions. Not all patients who attend the emergency department will require admission to hospital.

The following criteria (NICE CG100) are useful when deciding whether a patient with symptoms of alcohol withdrawal requires admission to hospital:

- Offer admission if a patient is at high risk of developing alcohol withdrawal seizures or delirium tremens.
- Consider a lower threshold for admission for certain vulnerable people – for example those who are frail, have cognitive impairment

or multiple comorbidities, lack social support, have learning difficulties or are 16 or 17 years.

- For young people under 16 years who are in acute alcohol withdrawal, offer admission to hospital for physical and psychosocial assessment, in addition to medically assisted alcohol withdrawal.

Assessment and management of withdrawal symptoms

Not all patients at risk of developing acute alcohol withdrawal symptoms will require pharmacotherapy. However, it is important to monitor physical signs and symptoms where severe withdrawal symptoms are predicted. The best choice of drug to manage withdrawal symptoms and prevent seizures is a benzodiazepine, usually chlordiazepoxide or less commonly diazepam. A symptom-triggered regimen should be utilised in an acute setting (see the following text) and individualised according to the patient's age, associated co-morbidities (e.g. cirrhosis) and severity of dependence or withdrawal symptoms.

Symptom-triggered regimen

In a symptom-triggered withdrawal (STW) regimen the signs and symptoms of withdrawal are monitored regularly utilising a tool (e.g. CIWA-AR, Figure 18.1), and the pharmacotherapy dose is varied according to the calculated score.

Although this regimen does require nurse training (in completion of scores which are usually 1–4 hourly depending on symptom severity), patients benefit from regular pre-defined assessment of withdrawal symptoms and vital signs according to the CIWR score – this is usually lacking in fixed-dose regimens where nursing staff administer medication generally without any formal assessment of withdrawal symptoms (see the following text). STW regimens require less pharmacotherapy over a shorter time period. A third of patients managed on such a regimen do not require any pharmacotherapy at all, allowing earlier discharge from hospital and early engagement with community alcohol services. Each hospital should have written alcohol withdrawal protocols which include prescribing guidance for the young, elderly and cirrhotic patient. The use of trained staff, supported by the ANS, and a withdrawal tool ensures patients are managed as safely as possible without risk of over-sedation.

The main advantage of STW is that rising withdrawal severity scores alert clinical staff and prompt them to change the dosing regimen (in a manner akin to an insulin 'sliding scale'), thus avoiding

Nausea and vomiting

0 - No nausea and vomiting
1
2
3
4 - Intermittent nausea with dry heaves
5
6
7- Constant nausea, frequent dry heaves vomiting

Paroxysmal sweats

0 - No sweat visible
1 - Barely perceptible sweating, palms moist
2
3
4 - Beads of sweat obvious on forehead
5
6
7- Drenching sweats

Agitation

0 - Normal activity
1 - Somewhat more than normal activity
2
3
4 - Moderate fidgety and restless
5
6
7 - Paces back and forth during most of the interview or constantly thrashes about

Visual disturbances

0 - Not present
1 - Very mild photosensitivity
2 - Mild photosensitivity
3 - Moderate photosensitivity
4 - Moderately severe visual hallucinations
5 - Severe visual hallucinations
6 - Extreme severe visual hallucinations
7 - Continuous severe visual hallucinations

Tremor

0 - No tremor
1 - Not visible, but can be felt at finger tips
2
3
4 - Moderate when patient's hands extended
5
6
7 - Severe, even with arms not extended

Tactile disturbances

0 - None
1 - Very mild paraesthesias
2 - Mild photosensitivity
3 - Moderate paraesthesias
4 - Moderately severe hallucinations
5 - Severe hallucinations
6 - Extremely severe hallucinations
7 - Continuous hallucinations

Headache

0 - Not present
1 - Very mild
2 - Mild
3 - Moderate
4 - Moderately severe
5 - Severe
6 - Very severe
7 - Extremely severe

Auditory disturbances

0 - Not present
1 - Very mild harshness or ability to frighten
2 - Mild harshness or ability to frighten
3 - Moderate harshness or ability to frighten
4 - Moderately severe hallucinations
5 - Severe hallucinations
6 - Extremely severe hallucinations
7 - Continuous hallucinations

Orientation and clouding of the sensorium

0 - Oriented and can do serial additions
1 - Cannot do serial additions
2 - Disoriented for date by no more than 2 calendar days
3 - Disoriented for date by more than 2 calendar days
4 - Disoriented for place/person

Cumulative scoring

Cumulative score	Approach
0–8	No medication needed
9–14	Medication is optional
15–20	Definitely needs medication
>20	Increased risk of complications

Figure 18.1 Clinical Institute Withdrawal Assessment Scale for Alcohol, Revised (CIWR-AR). Source: NCEPOD (2013).

escalating agitation, confusion and emergence of fits/DTs. On occasion patients will require higher than British National Formulary doses of chlordiazepoxide (>200 mg daily). These individuals should be managed by a senior clinician, require at least hourly measurement of vital signs and on occasion need critical care. Additional agents such as haloperidol, olanzapine or risperidone may also be required in the delirious patient. Hospital alcohol withdrawal protocols should also include advice on the management of alcohol withdrawal with delirium (DTs).

The emergence of DTs and seizures should be preventable, especially if screening and assessment is thorough. The majority of patients in this situation have been prescribed inappropriately low medication doses. In the event of a seizure the pharmacotherapy dose (e.g. chlordiazepoxide) should be increased. A short-acting benzodiazepine, such as lorazepam, can be a useful adjunct in this situation reducing the likelihood of further fits. Anticonvulsants are not indicated, being of no proven benefit in management of alcohol withdrawal seizures.

Other withdrawal regimens

Front-loaded regimen – a single high dose of chlordiazepoxide or diazepam medication is given to provide sedation at the start of treatment and further doses are given as required.

The initial dose needs to be individually tailored, and many junior doctors find it challenging to chose an appropriate initial starting dose. This regimen is not widely used in the United Kingdom.

Fixed dose regimen – an initial starting dose of medication is chosen and then reduced steadily over a defined time period.

Fixed regimen protocols usually offer two or three dosing regimens for suspected mild, moderate or severe dependence and allow additional 'as-required' doses of sedation – usually chlordiazepoxide. These regimens require little nurse training as a withdrawal tool is not generally utilised. This regimen can be somewhat inflexible and tends to encourage a 'one-size-fits-all' approach. Patients generally receive sedation every 6 h, but symptoms can arise rapidly between drug rounds and escalate. Fixed regimens can also result in a premature reduction of medication without considering the onset of withdrawal. Some also encourage prescribing based on a calculation of daily units of alcohol consumed. However there is much variation in the extent and severity of withdrawal symptoms, so this at best should only be considered an approximate measure of dose.

The prevention and management of Wernicke's encephalopathy

Hazardous and harmful drinkers are at risk of developing Wernicke's encephalopathy (WE), a neuropsychiatric condition which can lead to irreversible brain damage (Korsakoff's syndrome) – see Chapter 13. WE is in large part due to thiamine deficiency although other, as-yet undetermined, factors are likely also to be important in its development.

WE is characterised by the following:
1 Confusion and disorientation
2 Poor balance, ataxia
3 Eye disturbances, nystagmus
The classic triad however is uncommon.

Making a diagnosis can be a challenge especially if patients have a co-existent condition leading to confusion such as intoxication, sepsis, hepatic encephalopathy and so on. A high degree of suspicion of the possibility of WE is essential and when there is doubt intravenous thiamine should be administered (see the following text).

Patients suspected of having WE should receive treatment with intravenous high-dose thiamine supplements on admission to hospital. The licensed preparation in the United Kingdom is Pabrinex®, which also contains ascorbic acid, nicotinamide and other B vitamins, and is administered over a 30-min period to minimise any risk of anaphylaxis (an IM form is available for those patients who are too agitated or confused to keep an IV line in, but should be avoided in those with cirrhosis and coagulopathy).

Patients should receive two of each ampoule of Pabrinex® intravenously three times per day, for 5 days or until complete resolution of symptoms has occurred (NICE CG100). This should be clearly prescribed on the drug chart as '2 pairs of Pabrinex®, three times daily' or '2 × (vial I + vial II) of Pabrinex®, three times daily'. Oral thiamine follows intravenous dosing (at least thiamine 100-mg, three times per day) – the optimum length of treatment is unknown, but a minimum course of 1 month is advisable, noting that absorption is reduced if a patient returns to drinking.

Problem drinkers may also be at risk of developing WE during their admission even though they may not display any overt symptoms or signs of WE on admission to hospital. Those at high risk should be given prophylactic thiamine (Table 18.3).

Table 18.3 Prevention of Wernicke's encephalopathy (based on NICE CG100 guidance)

- Offer prophylactic oral thiamine (e.g. at least thiamine 100 mg t.d.s.) to harmful or dependent drinkers
  - if they are malnourished or at risk of malnourishment **or**
  - if they have decompensated liver disease **or**
  - if they are in acute withdrawal **or**
  - before and during a planned medically assisted alcohol withdrawal
- Offer prophylactic parenteral thiamine (1 pair (vial I and II) i.v. daily) followed by oral thiamine (e.g. at least thiamine 100 mg t.d.s.) to harmful or dependent drinkers
  - if they are malnourished or at risk of malnourishment **or**
  - if they have decompensated liver disease
- **and in addition**
  - attend an emergency department **or**
  - are admitted to hospital with an acute illness or injury

Figure 18.2 Alcohol nurse specialists are experienced, nursing-focused clinicians. Source: photograph by Adrian Brown.

The role of the alcohol specialist nurse in managing patients with acute alcohol withdrawal

Alcohol nurse specialists (Figure 18.2) are experienced, nursing-focused clinicians, familiar with clinical aspects of medical care. This is important when delivering interventions of the highest quality as they can enhance consistency of care – advising medical and nursing colleagues about complex needs (including mental health assessments). They generally have more time to monitor the patient's withdrawal symptoms and the motivation to follow up with abstinence support. Other than direct assessment and care planning of patients, the ANS is also able to offer teaching and training (e.g. anticipation and recognition of withdrawal symptoms, advice and monitoring of detoxification regimes, education on physical effects of excessive drinking) to all multidisciplinary groups within an acute setting. The ANS provides crucial advocacy for the alcohol-dependent patient and can give useful feedback to staff on the progress of patients, thus ensuring a high-quality service is maintained. Their knowledge is a resource to encourage colleagues to overcome reluctance in what is often seen as a specialist field and deliver better care for patients with alcohol problems.

Further reading

BSG/BASL/AHA (lead author: Moriarty KJ). *Alcohol related disease: meeting the challenge of improved quality of care and better use of resources* (A Joint Position Paper). 2010. www.bsg.org.uk (accessed 18 September 2014).

Glover L, Collins P, Gordon F, Holliwell K, Hunt V, Portal J, et al. Symptom triggered pharmacotherapy for acute unplanned alcohol withdrawal can be both clinically and cost-effective in a hospital setting: experience from a specialist hepatology unit. *Gut* 2011;60(Suppl 1):A48.

National Confidential Enquiry into Patient Outcome and Death (NCEPOD). *Measuring the units. A review of patients who died with alcohol-related liver disease.* 2013. www.ncepod.org.uk (accessed 18 September 2014).

National Institute of Health and Care Excellence. *Alcohol-use disorders: diagnosis and clinical management of alcohol-related physical complications* (NICE Guidelines CG100). 2010. http://guidance.nice.org.uk/CG100 (accessed 18 September 2014).

National Institute of Health and Care Excellence. *Alcohol-use disorders: diagnosis, assessment and management of harmful drinking and alcohol dependence* (NICE Guidelines CG115). 2011. http://guidance.nice.org.uk/CG115 (accessed 18 September 2014).

CHAPTER 19

The role of alcohol care teams in district general hospitals

Kieran J. Moriarty

OVERVIEW

Every District General Hospital should establish the following:

- A consultant-led alcohol care team to collaborate with key stakeholders and patient groups
- Coordinated policies across A&E and Acute Medical Units
- A 7-day alcohol specialist nurse service
- Liaison and addiction psychiatry input
- An alcohol assertive outreach team
- Collaborative, multidisciplinary, timely, responsive and patient-centred care
- Integrated treatment pathways between primary and secondary care
- Training, education, audit and research

Introduction

Alcohol misuse, binge drinking and alcohol-related liver disease (ALD) are major public health concerns. Between 1970 and 2006, there was a 500% increase in liver-related deaths, mainly due to alcohol. By contrast, mortality from most common diseases decreased (Figure 19.1). Gastroenterologists and hepatologists are now caring for teenagers with end-stage ALD.

The annual cost of alcohol-related harm to the NHS in England is around £3.5 billion, with 78% of the costs incurred by hospitals, inpatient costs alone accounting for 45%. Alcohol services could be more cost-effective and person-centred if evidence-based, integrated primary and secondary care was delivered in the most appropriate setting.

Future hospital-based alcohol services

In 2010, the British Society of Gastroenterology (BSG), the Alcohol Health Alliance UK and the British Association for Study of the Liver published a paper, detailing 11 Key Recommendations for typical British District General Hospitals (DGHs), serving a population of 250,000 (Box 19.1). If implemented, they should improve quality and efficiency of care, lower mortality and reduce alcohol-related admissions and readmissions. The paper provides the evidence base for effective policies and the workforce expansion required to implement them.

Alcohol care teams

The principal recommendation is for a multidisciplinary, consultant-led alcohol care team (ACT). The evidence base for ACTs has been enhanced by the quality, innovation, productivity and prevention (QIPP) case study, which was scored highly on implementability, evidence of change, quality and savings by NHS Evidence and NICE (Figure 19.2).

The Royal Bolton Hospital ACT comprises four consultant gastroenterologists, a liaison psychiatrist, alcohol specialist nurses (ASNs) and relevant healthcare professionals, including a dedicated social worker. The consultants devote 2-week blocks entirely to inpatient care, conducting daily ward rounds and multidisciplinary team meetings, and seeing all acute gastroenterology admissions and ward consultations. Consequently, length of stay has reduced from 11.5 to 8.9 days, inpatient mortality from 11.2 to 6.0% and ward discharges increased by 37%.

Accident and emergency

St Mary's Hospital, London has trained staff to give Brief Advice to patients presenting to A&E (see also Chapter 8). They have designed the 1-minute Paddington alcohol test to identify and educate patients with an alcohol-related problem, "the teachable moment". This resulted in a 10-fold increase in referrals to their alcohol health worker, who gave brief interventions, resulting in a 43% reduction in alcohol consumption. Every two interventions resulted in one fewer reattendance during the following year. If appointments were offered on the same day, two-thirds attended; but if delayed for 48 h, only 28% attended.

ABC of Alcohol, Fifth Edition. Edited by Anne McCune.
© 2015 John Wiley & Sons, Ltd. Published 2015 by John Wiley & Sons, Ltd.

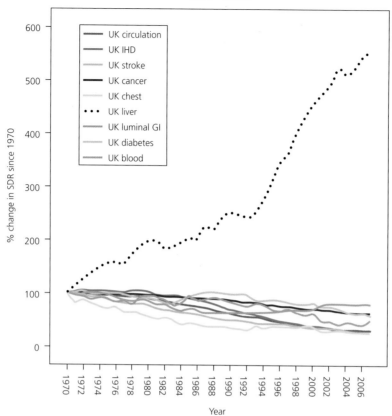

**UK under 65 standard death rate for various diseases
(1970 = 100%)**

Figure 19.1 Trends in standard death rates for major diseases since 1970. Data are from the World Health Organisation Health for All Database. Death rates normalised to 100% in 1970. Courtesy of Dr. Nick Sheron. Source: Moriarty et al. (2010). Reproduced by permission of the British Society of Gastroenterology.

Box 19.1 **Key recommendations for hospital-based alcohol care**

In a typical British District General Hospital, serving a Population of 250,000, there should be:

1. A multidisciplinary 'alcohol care team', led by a consultant, with dedicated sessions, who will also collaborate with Public Health, Primary Care Trusts, patient groups and key stakeholders to develop and implement a district alcohol strategy.
2. Coordinated policies on detection and management of alcohol-use disorders in Accident and Emergency departments and Acute Medical Units, with access to brief interventions and appropriate services within 24 h of diagnosis.
3. A 7-day alcohol specialist nurse service and alcohol link workers' network, consisting of a lead healthcare professional in every clinical area.
4. Liaison and addiction psychiatrists, specialising in alcohol, with specific responsibility for screening for depression and other psychiatric disorders, to provide an integrated acute hospital service, via membership of the 'alcohol care team'.
5. Establishment of a hospital-led, multi-agency assertive alcohol outreach team, including an emergency physician, acute physician, psychiatric crisis team member, alcohol specialist nurse, drug and alcohol action team member, hospital/community manager and Primary Care Trust Alcohol Commissioner, with links to local authority, social services and third sector agencies and charities.
6. Multidisciplinary, person-centred care, which is holistic, timely, non-judgmental and responsive to the needs and views of patients and their families.
7. Integrated alcohol treatment pathways between primary and secondary care, with progressive movement towards management in primary care.
8. Adequate provision of consultants in gastroenterology and hepatology to deliver specialist care to patients with alcohol-related liver disease.
9. National indicators and quality metrics, including alcohol-related admissions, readmissions and deaths, against which hospitals should be audited.
10. Integrated modular training in alcohol and addiction, available for alcohol specialist nurses and trainees in gastroenterology and hepatology, acute medicine, accident and emergency medicine and psychiatry.
11. Targeted funding for research into detection, prevention and treatment strategies and outcomes for people with alcohol-use disorders.

Source: Moriarty et al. (2010).

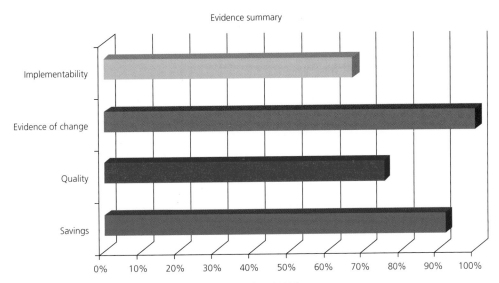

Figure 19.2 NHS evidence summary for alcohol care teams QIPP. Source: Moriarty (2014).

Alcohol specialist nurses

The alcohol specialist nurses (ASN) service implemented in Nottingham reduced admissions for detoxification by 66%, clinical incidents by 75%, gamma GT levels by 50% and Bed Day occupancy in cirrhotic patients by 50%.

Bolton Hospital's two ASNs provided comprehensive assessment, inpatient care plans or rapid outpatient appointments with the Community Alcohol Team, saving the Trust 1000 bed days annually, equivalent to £250,000, in reduced inpatient detoxifications alone. This provided the evidence base to establish a 7-day ASN service to rapidly assess patients at peak week-end periods.

The ASNs have trained a Network of 50 Trust Alcohol Link Workers and 600 staff to use the Short AUDIT C Alcohol Questionnaire and deliver Brief Advice. All inpatients are routinely asked about alcohol consumption, facilitating identification of problem drinkers, patients with previously undiagnosed ALD and a 63% increase in referrals to the ASNs for more comprehensive assessment.

Psychiatry services

There should be a consultant-led liaison psychiatry service in all DGHs (see also Chapters 20–23). A consultant psychiatrist should liaise closely with A&E and Acute Medical Units to ensure that patients are assessed for possible psychiatric illness, especially depression and suicidal ideation. This involves training and collaboration between A&E staff, the Mental Health Crisis Team, ASNs and the Community Alcohol Team. There should be clear pathways for rapid referral to a psychiatrist specialising in alcohol dependency.

Alcohol assertive outreach teams

The Salford alcohol assertive outreach team (AAOT) is a multidisciplinary team, comprising medical, psychiatric, substance misuse, psychology, nursing and social work specialists. The AAOT worked with 54 complex, poorly compliant 'frequent attenders' and case-managed them in a community setting for 6 months. Following the intervention, hospital admissions fell by 67% and A&E attendances by 59%. The team also works proactively with patients, who have had two alcohol-related admissions within a short period of time, the so-called 'fast risers'.

Collaborative, multidisciplinary, person-centred care

Collaborative, integrated care especially between specialists working in gastroenterology, hepatology, psychiatry, A&E, acute medicine and primary care is essential (Box 19.2).

Integrated alcohol treatment pathways

Integrated alcohol treatment pathways or ATPs (see also Chapter 19) help drive the shift from secondary care to community care, reducing costs. Enhanced services should be developed in primary care to screen and detect alcohol misuse and alcohol-related harm, especially liver disease, at an early stage. ATPs should be developed for drug and alcohol misusers, since patients often have multiple problems, requiring co-ordination of treatment by several specialists and generic service providers. All ATPs need a coordinated strategy to address both the medical and psychiatric aspects of actual or potential alcohol-related harm.

Consultant gastroenterology and hepatology expansion

As recommended in the National Plan for Liver Services 2009, there must be a major expansion of the consultant hepatology workforce. Each DGH should have at least six consultants in gastroenterology and hepatology, of whom at least two should have specialist hepatology training.

Box 19.2 **Collaborative alcohol care**

Collaborative care is a multidisciplinary team approach to assessing, planning, implementing and evaluating care, in collaboration with the patient and family, and is developed around an anticipated length of stay, or episode of care. Patients are empowered to make lifestyle changes.

Key elements of the Royal Bolton Hospital Model
- Consultant Gastroenterologists and a Liaison Psychiatrist, with a special interest in substance and alcohol misuse, provide joint inpatient and outpatient care.
- A psychiatric alcohol liaison nurse (PLN) and a liver nurse practitioner (LNP) work in close partnership, together with the Emergency and Acute Medical Units, the specialised gastroenterology ward nurses and consultants.
- A multidisciplinary team, which meets daily to discuss all inpatients and any outpatient or service issues. The meeting is consultant-led, together with the ward doctors, nurses, ASNs, social worker, dietician, physiotherapist and occupational therapist. All healthcare professionals write in the same notes. The team working ethos makes everyone feel valued and optimises and unifies patient-centred, collaborative care.
- A dedicated social worker greatly influences length of stay and facilitates discharge to a suitable environment. Discharge and ongoing care of inpatients, who are out of-area, may be problematic. Daily involvement of the appropriate social worker is vital. There is particular difficulty in providing care for the homeless and rough sleepers. There are increasing numbers, particularly of young men with alcohol-related dementia, including Wernicke–Korsakoff Syndrome, for whom there is a major shortage of suitable long-term care.
- Daily consultant gastroenterology input into the Acute Medical Receiving Units facilitates the rapid triage and clinical and endoscopic management of gastroenterology emergencies and their transfer to the gastroenterology ward or critical care area.
- Coordinated care pathways across the hospital, including A&E.
- Access to brief interventions within 24 h of detection of alcohol-related problems. This structured advice lasts for 20–40 min and involves individualised personalised feedback to the patient about their level of health risk due to alcohol, with practical advice about reducing their alcohol intake. Patients are managed daily from the day of admission to discharge, with continued review in outpatients.
- Collaborative working with local Liver Units.
- Joint outpatient clinics, by a multidisciplinary medical, nursing and psychiatric team, facilitate 'one-stop clinics', reducing DNA rates.
- Telephone hotline, rapid access is provided to GPs, patients, their families and carers, either directly to the LNP or PLN, or via the secretaries or ward, where a close relationship has developed.
- Unified primary, secondary and community alcohol care, including nurse-supervised home detoxifications, often commenced in hospital.
- Transparent, No-blame Clinical Governance Meetings.
- A seamless flow for a patient from Tier 1 (General Practice) to Tier 4 (Hospital) care, and back again, using Tier 3 (Community Alcohol Team).
- A close working relationship with Regional Addiction and Liaison Psychiatrists, who provide inpatient psychiatric care in residential settings.
- Health promotion, education, training, audit and research, under a governance framework, which has had a significant impact on both alcohol-dependent patients and those with liver disease.
- Educational updates in diverse settings, from wards to tents, to improve awareness and engagement. Accessibility is paramount, overcoming any barrriers.
- Partnership with Link/Community workers to overcome the alcohol stigma in our Asian community.

Source: Moriarty (2011).

National indicators and quality metrics

National indicators and quality metrics should be established to facilitate audit and evaluate service delivery. Quality metrics should include a systematic patient evaluation of the service. The National Liver Plan advocates the development of Managed Clinical Networks.

Networks can establish databases, which capture activity and outcomes, to develop strategies for future care models for alcohol-related problems.

In 2012, the BSG produced 'Commissioning evidence-based care for patients with gastrointestinal and liver disease'. This provides commissioning guidelines for the highest standards of clinical care in gastroenterology and hepatology.

Modular training

Modular training, with assessment and accreditation of competencies, should be developed for all doctors, nurses and healthcare personnel treating people with alcohol and drug-related problems.

The Academy of Medical Royal Colleges has published a set of core competencies for all doctors in all medical and surgical specialties to attain (Box 19.3). Undergraduate curricula are introducing similar training.

Alcohol specialist nurses deliver interventions with competencies, in accordance with Drugs and Alcohol National Occupational Standards (DANOS). These include competencies in motivational approaches and brief interventions. These will be enhanced by the DH and Royal College of Nursing publication of core competences for liver specialist nurses (Box 19.4).

Research and education of the public

Research into the causes, prevention, consequences and treatment of alcohol-use disorders should be a priority. Research must engage patients and patient groups in service delivery and the most effective public education strategies. These might include Department of Health (DH) and Alcohol Charity campaigns, advertising to different age groups, health promotion leaflets in various languages and patient fora with patient advocates.

Box 19.3 **Alcohol and other drugs core competencies for all doctors**

Key recommendations

This working group has developed a consensus across 13 medical and surgical colleges and faculties on the following core competencies, which it recommends should be incorporated into postgraduate curricula for all doctors:

1. Knowledge
   - Effects, common presentations and potential for harm of alcohol and other drugs.
   - Addictive potential of alcohol and other drugs, including prescribed and over-the-counter medicines.
   - Range of interventions, treatments and prognoses for use of alcohol and other drugs.
   - Effects of alcohol and other drugs on the unborn child, children and families.
   - Recommended limits on alcohol intake.
2. Skills
   - Be competent to make an assessment of alcohol and other drug use, including taking a history and using validated tools.
   - Recognise the wide range of acute and long-term presentations involving use of alcohol and other drugs (e.g. trauma, depression and hypertension).
   - Provide brief advice on use of alcohol and other drugs.
   - Provide management and/or referral where appropriate.
3. Behaviour/attitudes
   - Work in a supportive, empathic and non-judgemental manner without collusion.
   - Be confident and comfortable discussing alcohol and drug use with patients.
   - Act appropriately on any concerns about own or colleagues' use of alcohol and/or other drugs.

Source: Royal College of Psychiatrists (2012).

Box 19.4 **Core competencies for liver specialist nurses**

The nine liver care core competencies:

1. Provides empathy and understanding and works with the patient (and their family/carers), particularly those with chronic liver disease as experts in their own condition.
2. Signposts and supports patients (and families/carers) in their understanding of their condition, through patient education and health promotion.
3. Undertakes a comprehensive clinical assessment, including risk profiling and follows up with appropriate action, including referral to specialists, for relevant acute and chronic health care conditions.
4. Assesses, in collaboration with the patient (young people, adults, family/carers), their health care needs, taking into account the impact of their age, vulnerability, their lifestyle, cultural and ethnic background.
5. Develops and evaluates a self-management plan with the patient, who has predisposing factors to liver disease.
6. Works alongside and with the patient (and families/carers) to address the psychological and social impact of their condition.
7. Provides specific diagnostic/treatment options safely:
   7.1 undertaking phlebotomy and cannulation in the patient with difficult access associated with their liver disease.
   7.2 nutrition and fluid management/hydration in patients with liver disease
   7.3 pharmacological treatment and side effects
   7.4 non-invasive diagnostics and treatment options.
   7.5 invasive diagnostics and treatment options.
8. Uses early warning tools/approaches to identify the patient's changing and deteriorating condition, and takes appropriate action.
9. Actively improves and promotes liver services across the appropriate care pathway.

Source: Royal College of Nursing (2013).

Low levels of public awareness of alcohol, units of alcohol, liver disease and alcohol-related problems need to be addressed with a national, comprehensive public education and health promotion strategy to reduce the population risk of alcohol-related harm. Education of the public about alcohol and alcohol-related problems should begin in childhood, both in the home and at school, with particular emphasis on people and their families affected by alcohol misuse. Link worker networks should be developed in the community. A non-judgmental attitude will help to overcome barriers, by removing the stigma traditionally associated with alcohol-use disorders. Hopefully, this will encourage people to present for care at an early stage.

Cost-effective alcohol strategies

Strategies involve the intelligent coordination of services. However, investment is needed to expand consultant and ASN numbers and ACTs. The DH has identified 7 High Impact Changes (Box 19.5). Psychosocial treatment for dependent drinkers may save the public sector £5 for every £1 spent on treatment.

Box 19.5 **Department of Health High Impact Changes**

The Department of Health has identified 7 High Impact Changes, which are calculated to be the most effective actions for those local areas that have prioritised the reduction in alcohol-related harm:

1. Work in partnership.
2. Develop activities to control the impact of alcohol misuse in the community.
3. Influence change through advocacy.
4. Improve the effectiveness and capacity of specialist treatment.
5. Appoint an alcohol health worker.
6. Identification and brief advice – provide more help to encourage people to drink less.
7. Amplify national social marketing priorities.

Source: Department of Health 2009b.

The HubCAPP on the Alcohol Learning Centre gives more detail. HubCAPP is the Hub of Commissioned Alcohol Projects and Policies, commissioned by the DH and run in partnership through Alcohol Concern. The DH estimates that delivery of these High Impact changes can produce average annual savings for a PCT of £650,000.

Source: Department of Health (2009a).

Box 19.6 **Alcohol and health inequalities**

Emerging data are beginning to identify the effects of alcohol misuse in specific groups, allowing for more targeted intervention:

- The most deprived 20% of the UK population suffer two to five times greater alcohol-related admissions to hospital or alcohol-related mortality, compared to the least deprived.
- The most deprived lifestyle group have 4–15 times greater alcohol-specific mortality and up to 10 times greater alcohol-specific admissions to hospital.
- Men aged over 35, unskilled or manual workers or unemployed, are at the highest risk of being admitted to hospital with an alcohol-related problem.
- Fifty per cent of homeless people are dependent upon alcohol.
- Psychiatric co-morbidity is common among problem drinkers – up to 10% for severe mental illnesses and 50–80% for personality or neurotic disorders.

Source: Association of Public Health Observatories (2007).

Alcohol and health inequalities

Liver transplantation is the final, definitive treatment for patients with end-stage liver disease. The greatest proportion of patients listed for liver transplants have ALD. All patients, regardless of geography, should be offered good and equal access to liver healthcare and liver transplantation. There is an urgent need for more liver donors (Box 19.6).

Future care

Currently, alcohol treatment services are not adequately equipped to cope with the nation's alcohol problem. However, there are hopeful signs. In 2009, only 42% of hospitals had ASN support. Encouragingly, in the 2013 NCEPOD report, the figure had increased to 79%.

Moreover, specialist alcohol care can pull people back from the brink of the most devastating consequences of alcohol misuse, especially alcohol-related liver disease, give them back their self-respect and restore them to their families and communities. The development of high-quality, integrated prevention and treatment services for people with alcohol-related disease will prove to be a wise investment for the future health of our nation, especially that of our young people.

Further reading

Association of Public Health Observatories. *Indications of public health in the English regions 8: alcohol.* Liverpool: NWPHO, 2007.

British Association for the Study of the Liver (BASL), British Society of Gastroenterology (BSG) (Liver Section). *A time to act: improving liver health and outcomes in liver disease. The national plan for liver services UK.* London: BASL, 2009. http://www.bsg.org.uk/attachments/1004_National%20Liver%20Plan%202009.pdf (accessed 18 September 2014).

British Society of Gastroenterology. *Commissioning evidence-base care for patients with gastrointestinal and liver disease.* 2012. http://www.bsg.org.uk/clinical/general/commissioning-report.html (accessed 18 September 2014).

Department of Health. *NHS 2010–2015: from good to great. Preventative, people-centred, productive.* London: Department of Health, 2009a.

Department of Health. *Signs for improvement: commissioning interventions to reduce alcohol-related harm.* London: Department of Health, 2009b.

Hughes NR, Houghton N, Nadeem H, Bell J, McDonald S, Glynn N, et al. Salford alcohol assertive outreach team: a new model for reducing alcohol-related admissions. *Frontline Gastroenterology* 2013;4:130–4.

Moriarty KJ. Collaborative liver and psychiatry care in the Royal Bolton Hospital for people with alcohol-related disease. *Frontline Gastroenterology* 2011;2:77–81.

Moriarty KJ. *Alcohol Care Teams: reducing acute hospital admissions and improving quality of care.* Published on behalf of the British Society of Gastroenterology and Bolton NHS Foundation Trust. 2014. Quality, Innovation, Productivity and Prevention (QIPP) Publication on NHS Evidence website. http://www.evidence.nhs.uk/quality and productivity (accessed 18 September 2014).

Moriarty KJ, Cassidy P, Dalton D, et al. *Alcohol-related disease. Meeting the challenge of improved quality of care and better use of resources.* A Joint Position Paper on behalf of the British Society of Gastroenterology, Alcohol Health Alliance UK & British Association for Study of the Liver. 2010. http://www.bsg.org.uk/images/stories/docs/clinical/publications/bsg_alc_disease_10.pdf (accessed 18 September 2014).

Royal College of Nursing. *RCN competences: caring for people with liver disease: a competence framework for nursing.* 2013. RCN Online www.rcn.org.uk (accessed 18 September 2014).

Royal College of Psychiatrists. *OP85. Alcohol and other drugs: core medical competencies.* Final report of the Working Group of the Royal Colleges. 2012. www.rcpsych.ac.uk/publications/collegereports/op/op85.aspx (accessed 18 September 2014).

CHAPTER 20

Management in primary care

Carsten Grimm

OVERVIEW

- Alcohol misuse and the majority of alcohol-dependent patients can be safely and cost effectively managed in primary care.
- Screening tools and training is widely available.
- GPs as generalists are ideally placed to deal with the consequences of drinking.
- Reducing harm is an important element of dealing with problem drinkers.
- Do not forget safeguarding of children.

Introduction

General practice is an ideal place to screen and initially deal with alcohol-related health problems. Assuming that a GP will see between 40 and 50 patients on an average day, two or three will be alcohol dependent and between 6 and 16 will be drinking to a hazardous level. The exact number will depend on a variety of factors, including deprivation, ethnic and gender mix. In a white male population between 25 and 34 years up to 46% are hazardous drinkers.

In addition, most British GPs are already set up for the screening and treatment of chronic or relapsing conditions. Hypertension, which was once the domain of secondary care, is now nearly exclusively screened, diagnosed and treated in primary care. Smoking cessation programmes are widely available and often conducted by practice nurses or health care assistants. Teaching programmes, local and national initiatives trying to address screening and treatment of alcohol misuse are well established; however, there are considerable local and regional variations.

Despite this, alcohol is sadly still not on the top of the agenda for GPs. This chapter will concentrate on how primary care can deal with this issue in a pragmatic way. The National Institute for Health and Care Excellence (NICE) has published a set of comprehensive guidelines that address clinical issues, as well as making the case for screening and brief interventions again. There is now overwhelming evidence that screening and brief intervention is beneficial.

How do you diagnose drinking problems in primary care?

The best way is to use one of the well-established screening questionnaires. The gold standard measurement remains the AUDIT tool/questionnaire, with several other variations in use like FAST, AUDIT-C, AUDIT-PC and so on (see Chapter 6). It is a matter of personal preference which one to use. Bearing in mind that the AUDIT takes about 10 min to complete, it is worth considering using a shortened version as an initial screening tool, and only continue if this is positive. I recommend AUDIT-C as initial screening tool, followed by AUDIT.

Using these will reliable identify hazardous and harmful drinking and both can be done by anyone who is trained to use these. There are numerous local training programmes available, alternatively the alcohol learning centre or the RCGP have free online training.

Pitfalls

There are some pitfalls: Firstly, although harmful drinker are bound to present frequently with various illnesses or symptoms that are alcohol related, patients often don't admit that they have a drinking problem or refuse to do anything about it. There is little point in forcing someone who smells of alcohol at 10 a.m. to go through a structured screening questionnaire if they deny any drinking from the start.

Secondly, most screening questionnaires use the term of a unit of alcohol – and most patients have no idea what a unit of alcohol is. Even worse, most healthcare professionals struggle to calculate units themselves. It is worth considering using the built-in calculators of electronic health record systems that are in use in UK primary care or to use the Internet. Therefore, it is often down to the professional to learn and then ask what kind of alcohol a patient consumes and in what quantities, then translate this into units. To make matters even more confusing, UK units are slightly different to the ones used in the United States and other countries.

So what do you need to know about units? It is a measure of alcohol in a drink, like the numbers 130/70 are a measure of blood pressure. It is not as daunting to calculate units as you might think and certainly does not require any complex calculations. It is

ABC of Alcohol, Fifth Edition. Edited by Anne McCune.
© 2015 John Wiley & Sons, Ltd. Published 2015 by John Wiley & Sons, Ltd.

important to get a feel for the numbers and what they mean. I remember two benchmarks:

1 1 can or pint of lager = approximately 2 units
2 1 bottle of wine = approximately 10 units

Please bear in mind that the exact alcohol content will vary and some lagers, beers and wines have a slightly different percentage volume (see Chapter 4 for more details on absolute alcohol content in common beverages). Everything else can be looked up. As a general rule, anyone consuming considerable amounts of spirits or high volumes is likely to be drinking harmfully and needs a further assessment anyway.

When and whom to screen

Anyone who presents with a symptom that could be alcohol related should be screened – see Table 20.1 of the commonest presentations in primary care that should trigger screening. Alternatively, screening can be conducted more strategically, for example as part of a chronic disease management review. Screening of newly registered patients was encouraged by a direct enhanced service (a commissioning method to incentivise GPs), but the overall results were inconsistent, partly because it was structured insufficiently and poorly implemented.

Screening – and then?

There are four possible outcomes of using the AUDIT:

1 Abstinent or low-risk drinking (0–7 points) – positive feedback
2 Hazardous drinking (8+ points) – brief intervention
3 Harmful drinking (and possible mild/moderate dependency) – (16–19 points) – further assessment
4 Likely dependency (20+ points) – further assessment

I think of dependency as a subgroup of harmful drinking.

Giving feedback and brief interventions

For the low-risk drinker, positive feedback should encapsulate that drinking is never without risk; but at the current level, it is unlikely to cause any harm in the future – hence the term 'low-risk drinking'. Reiterate recommended drinking limits (four units for men, three units for women, two alcohol-free days a week) and no further action is needed.

Brief interventions are straight forward. The most important thing to remember about brief interventions is that it should be relevant to the patient. A 25-year-old will be little impressed by the increased risk of cardiovascular disease, whilst this might be very important to a 60-year-old. The acronym FRAMES (Table 20.2) is often used to give brief interventions a structure.

Table 20.1 Common presentations or conditions that should trigger alcohol screening in primary care

Hypertension
Abnormal LFTs
Indigestion
Sleep disorders (insomnia)
TATT (tired all the time)
Low mood/depression
Cardiovascular disease

Brief interventions are typically between 5 and 10 min, so are usually delivered as part of the assessment. They can also be the first step to address alcohol consumption in harmful drinkers, but be careful not to advise rapid reduction and abstinence before ensuring that patients are not either moderately or severely dependent on alcohol – withdrawal can kill!

Further assessment

Harmful drinking generally requires an extended brief intervention, which won't be part of the routine GP appointment. I would also recommend looking at physical health aspects, which should include brief examination looking for stigmata of chronic liver disease, blood pressure and routine blood tests (FBC and LFTs). This could be combined with seeing a nurse or healthcare assistant who are trained to deliver an extended brief intervention and a further assessment, including screening for symptoms of alcohol dependence (see the following text).

Extended brief intervention is in principle no different from a brief intervention – just less brief. It lasts typically 20–30 min and can be delivered in one or two sessions as required. The FRAMES approach can be useful for this as well. See also Box 20.1.

Table 20.2 FRAMES

Feedback	About personal risk or impairment
Responsibility	Emphasis on personal responsibility for change
Advice	To cut down or abstain if indicated because of severe dependence or harm
Menu	Of alternative options for changing drinking pattern and, jointly with the patient, setting a target; intermediate goals of reduction can be a start
Empathy	Listening reflectively without cajoling or confronting; exploring with patients the reasons for change as they see their situation
Self efficacy	An interviewing style which enhances peoples' belief in their ability to change

---

Box 20.1 **A case for motivational interviewing**

'I lack willpower' she says, and you can't prescribe it.
Is willpower something you are born with in your genes and you are helpless? Or is this an excuse for a choice she has made, but doesn't like the consequences, so she dumps the blame elsewhere?
Can you do anything constructive?
Yes

- Accept you cannot do it for her. If she wants it different, she must find some way (her way, not yours) of making it so.
- Don't threaten her, she will only defend herself.
- She does what she does because she likes it. Find out what she gets out of it and appreciate it – she will feel understood.
- So where is the problem? Not your problem, hers. There must be some disadvantages to her choice; she knows this, but hasn't admitted it.
- Once she has looked at the good things and the bad consequences, does she want to change?
- If she does, you are in business. If she doesn't, at least she has made a choice. It is her own – you will both feel better for accepting it.
- She doesn't lack willpower, but she is not yet ready to move. It may take a crisis to shift her.

If an extended brief intervention is insufficient, or the patient has moderate-to-severe dependence, it is advisable to refer on to a specialist service as long as the surgery has not signed up to a shared care scheme.

Dependent drinking

What AUDIT is to the diagnosis of hazardous or harmful drinking, the Severity of Alcohol Dependence Questionnaire (SADQ) is to the diagnosis of the severity of alcohol dependence in an individual patient. There are three levels, with the prevalence in the general adult population:

1 Mild dependence (5.4%) – SADQ less than 15
2 Moderate dependence (0.4%) – SADQ 15–30
3 Severe dependence (0.1%) – SADQ 30+

Only a relatively small proportion of patients with alcohol problems are physically dependent on alcohol and require a medical-assisted withdrawal during their treatment. NICE has published ample guidance how to do this safely. A typical patient who would require medical-assisted withdrawal would:

- Consume at least 15 units daily and drink throughout the day.
- Have physical signs of alcohol withdrawal when trying to stop abruptly.
- Score at least 15 on SADQ.
- Aim for abstinence for at least 3 months

Most patients are able to reduce their drinking in a controlled manner to some degree and reduce the risk to their health. It is advisable not to reduce too fast, that is not more than 10% every couple of days, to avoid withdrawal or anxiety.

Medical-assisted withdrawal in primary care

Medical-assisted withdrawal as a stand-alone treatment is nearly always bound to fail, if no appropriate aftercare plan is in place. It should always be undertaken as part of a larger treatment package and never *ad hoc*.

It only makes sense when both the patient and the environment are ready and supportive. Individuals who are so unfortunate to be surrounded by other dependent drinkers, that is in bedsits and deprived areas, are bound to fail and relapse quickly. This can be discouraging for all parties involved and possibly dangerous, as even a short period of abstinence can reduce tolerance and lead to relatively high levels of intoxication on relapse with often fatal consequences. For those who see abstinence as an achievable and realistic goal, it is an important treatment modality. The Fresh Start clinics in Wandsworth have shown good results with patients having rapid and appropriate access to a well organised and supported medical assisted withdrawal.

Medical-assisted withdrawal is nearly always conducted in a shared care scheme nowadays, and it should only be undertaken by appropriately trained staff or as part of an agreed treatment protocol with specialist services.

In a community setting, fixed-dose regimes are best. Front-loaded or symptom triggered dosing schemes require a level of supervision that is unrealistic and often unnecessary, as complex cases and severely dependent individuals would require inpatient treatment.

Supervision does not necessarily require home visits, but should be at appropriate intervals. For straightforward cases, a review every other day might be sufficient with daily telephone contact. For more complex cases, daily or even twice daily home visits might be required. As a general rule, the higher the SADQ score is and the older and more comorbidities a patient has, the more likely a patient requires intensive monitoring. I would also recommend that a close friend or relative is able to stay with the patient for the first 48 h. This is the dangerous period when things can go wrong, and it is important to have a responsible adult who can call for help if needed.

It comes down to the competence and confidence of the team, and the GP in deciding which cases can be treated in the community. There are some absolute contraindications to offering medical assisted withdrawal in the community:

- History of withdrawal seizures or epilepsy
- History of delirium tremens or severe withdrawal syndrome
- Lack of supervision at home

Medication used in primary care

The following medication is used routinely in the treatment of problematic drinking. Apart from disulfiram and benzodiazepines, all are relatively benign with a limited amount of side effects and risks (Table 20.3).

Training

The RCGP Certificate in the Management of Alcohol Problems in Primary Care consists of e-learning modules and a face-to-face training day. It is designed to enable clinicians working in primary care who are interested in the diagnosis and treatment of alcohol problems or want to work as part of a shared care scheme. It is also suitable for other clinical staff such as practice nurses.

Tips

- Train all practice staff, especially healthcare assistants and nurses in the use of AUDIT.
- Use AUDIT-C or FAST as initial screening tool, followed by AUDIT.

Table 20.3 Medication used in primary care

Thiamine	Prescribe 100 mg TDS per day for patients at risk of malnourishment or malnourished indefinitely
Vitamin B compound	Prescribe to anyone with signs of peripheral neuropathy indefinitely
Chlordiazepoxide	Used for medical-assisted withdrawal – 5 or 10 mg capsules (cheaper than tablets)
Diazepam	Used as alternative to chlordiazepoxide
Acamprosate	Both used as part of drinking down schemes
Naltrexone	or as relapse prevention following withdrawal
Nalmefene	Used as part of drinking down schemes
Disulfiram	Relapse prevention (usually started in specialist services)

- Consider the use of electronic screening tools like drinkcheck. co.uk or drugsmeter.com.
- Remember 1 can or pint of lager = approximately 2 units, 1 bottle of wine = approximately 10 units.
- Never offer medical-assisted withdrawal to patients without a full assessment and an aftercare plan in place.

Further reading

Bien TH, Miller WR, Tonigan JS. Brief interventions for alcohol problems: a review. *Addiction* 1993;88:315–36.

Coetzee J, Penfold M. GP-led services for alcohol misuse – the Fresh Start Clinic. *London Journal of Primary Care* 2011;4:11–5.

Grimm C. Alcohol in primary care – what GPs need to know. *The Digest: The Journal of the Primary Care Society for Gastroenterology.* Spring/Summer 2014;(3):11–2.

Kaner E, Bland M, Cassidy P, Coulton S, Dale V, Deluca P, et al. Effectiveness of screening and brief alcohol intervention in primary care (SIPS trial): pragmatic cluster randomised controlled trial. *BMJ* 2013;346:e8501.

National Institute of Health and Care Excellence. *Alcohol-use disorders: diagnosis, assessment and management of harmful drinking and alcohol dependence* (NICE Clinical Guideline CG115). February 2011. http:// guidance.nice.org.uk/CG115 (accessed 18 September 2014).

CHAPTER 21

Advice and counselling

Nicola Taylor

OVERVIEW

- Identification and engagement of the patient is fundamental.
- Awareness of the cycle of change can be key.
- Motivational interviewing works. And it works in partnership *with* the patient.
- Harmful alcohol use is rarely only the patient's problem.

Introduction

Harmful alcohol use has far-reaching biological, psychological and social consequences, and as such should routinely be asked about by any health worker. People can feel sensitive and defensive when asked about their drinking, and so it should be done in a routine, non-judgemental way. It is helpful to remember that when people are drinking alcohol at harmful levels, they are doing so for a reason. To change their drinking habits, they need a better reason.

Engagement and enquiry

Key to the success of any intervention is the initial engagement with the patient. This means that they have to trust the clinician enough to give honest answers to the questions without feeling they are going to be judged or treated in a detrimental way. If a patient does feel judged, then they may become defensive and the opportunity for any real engagement has been lost.

Routine tools for identifying who is at risk can be in the form of questionnaires, as well as clinical interview. See Chapter 6 for more information on validated questionnaires.

The patient and the doctor

It can be frustrating to believe that a patient is underestimating the problem, or underestimating their intake. They might use phrases such as 'social drinker', but one man's social drinker is another's alcohol dependent drinker. It is important to clarify, without judging, exactly how much they are consuming, of what type and how often.

It is tempting to try and scare people into 'coming clean' about how much they drink, and acknowledging that they have a problem: this is rarely helpful. More often it says something about the frustration of the doctor who feels helpless (because of work pressures, time pressures or intransigence on the part of the patient) than it does about the patient. Remember, the goal of any clinical interaction is not to make the doctors feel better, but to help the patient.

Awareness of the 'cycle of change' can help here.

The cycle of change

Modifying alcohol use is a big decision for many people; and like all big decisions, there is a process of thinking about the decision and putting the decision into action (Figure 21.1).

For the clinician, it's important to be able to identify where on the cycle the patient is so that the most useful motivational interviewing techniques can be applied (Box 21.1).

Pre-contemplative

At this stage, no overt problem has been acknowledged by the patient. It may be obvious to family or work colleagues, but the patient is in a state of 'ignorant bliss'.

In this stage, forcibly pointing out the dangers of their actions is unlikely to result in any movement. They are more likely to become defensive and argue against any change. In the very worst circumstances, they will become distressed by what they perceive as attack, and disengage completely. They are not thinking about changing anything in the foreseeable future.

If any phrase will help the clinician recognise this stage it is 'yes, but …' This is evident when the patient says 'yes, but …' in reply to any solution or point of view offered by the doctor.

Although the patient seems to be agreeing with whatever is being said, they are not. It is not an invitation for argument: the patient is making it clear they are not ready to change.

The most helpful thing the clinician can do is
- Validate: that is, to acknowledge the patient's difficulties in, in a non-judgemental way.
- Encourage self exploration.

ABC of Alcohol, Fifth Edition. Edited by Anne McCune.
© 2015 John Wiley & Sons, Ltd. Published 2015 by John Wiley & Sons, Ltd.

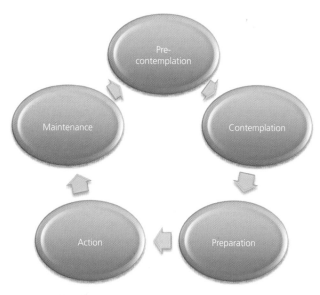

Figure 21.1 The cycle of change.

Box 21.1 **Principles of motivational interviewing**

It is most powerful if the patient says it.
Roll with resistance.
Be non-judgemental.
Encourage self-efficacy.
Encourage patient-generated solutions.

Examples:
- 'It must be difficult to hear your wife being so upset with your drinking.'
- 'It sounds very stressful at work just now.'
- 'Do you think there is anything you could do to help this?'
- 'What do you think might be going on here?'

Contemplation

In this stage, the patient might still be ambivalent about change: they are not sure if it is the right thing for them, but they're considering changing in the next 6 months. Phrases that may alert the clinician are 'I was wondering …', or 'I thought about maybe …'.

The most helpful thing the clinician can do is the following:
- Acknowledge the ambivalence, and the difficult decision the patient has to make. At this stage, drawing up a list of pros and cons can be useful.
- More powerful than the clinician telling the patient that they need to change is the patient coming to the conclusion of their own accord. It matters that *they* say 'I need to so something about this', rather than anyone else.

As part of the acknowledgement of the difficulties in change, open 'I wonder …?' type questions can be helpful.
Examples:
- 'I wonder what would be different if you did manage to cut down on your drinking.'
- 'I wonder what might be better.'
- 'I wonder if you'd like some more information about help that's around' (see Chapter 23).

Preparation

Patients here are 'testing the waters'. They might have done some exploratory work in thinking about the practicalities of change, what support they might need and what life would be like. The list of pros and cons can be reviewed and added to. A more detailed exploration of what life is going to be like for them without alcohol, and the benefits they can expect is useful here.

It is also worthwhile to think about the difficulties they might face: loss of social group, disruption to routine and so on and how they are going to cope with that. If they have family at home, then it will be difficult for everyone: even good change is stressful. They may also face pressure from 'drinking friends' not to change. This loss of social support should not be underestimated.

The most helpful thing the clinician can do is the following:
- At this stage, encouragement and validation of the hard work so far is key.
- More detailed discussion about specific psychotherapies may be useful.

Examples:
- 'Well, I really impressed with what you've done so far.'
- 'It's brave of you to make such difficult decisions.'
- 'Tell me how you have managed so far.'
- 'What did you think of the information I gave you?' (about the sources of help)

Action

At this stage, the patient will have made the changes to their behaviour, and will need encouragement to continue. They may be actively engaged in counselling or psychotherapy. Acknowledging any losses, while focusing on gains and benefits, is important.

Patient-generated solutions to their own problems are important. And credit should be given to them for doing so.

The most helpful thing the clinician can do is the following:
- The prospect of relapse is real, and clinicians should help the patient guard against feelings of complacence while encouraging them on.

Examples:
- 'So, tell me how did you manage to not go to the pub after work on that stressful day.'
- 'Is that going to work every time – do you have a plan B?'
- 'It must be odd not spending so much time with your friends, but how's things with your husband now?'

Maintenance

By now the changes should be more routine, and hopefully the patient will be feeling more confident in their choices. Work now is about ongoing encouragement, and more guarding against complacence. The difficult decisions shouldn't be taken for granted, and they should get lots of credit for the work they have done so far.

Examples:
- 'Well, I'm so pleased to see you looking so well: I hope you feel proud of yourself.'
- 'How are you keeping going with the new you?'

Relapse

Return to drinking can feel catastrophic, but it doesn't have to be. It's better framed as part of the recovery process: an opportunity for

Box 21.2 **Questions to explore the circumstances of relapse**

What was happening just before?
How were you feeling?
Where were you?
Who were you with?
Can you remember what made you decide to drink?
What do you think now?

Box 21.3 **Families and children**

When there are families and children in the support network, their need should be considered.
A carer's assessment should be offered if appropriate.
The needs and welfare of any children should be considered.
A referral to social services may be appropriate and can be framed as seeking further help and support for the family.

people to reflect again on how far they have come, and what caused them to slip into old habits. Looking again at the cycle of change, they can enter in at any stage, even straight back to the 'action' of abstinence using the same sort of techniques and motivational interviewing style outlined earlier.

Emotional, environmental and situational triggers for relapse can be identified, with the purpose of avoiding them in the future, not making the patient feeling guilty in the present (Box 21.2).

What to aim for?

For people who are dependent on alcohol, or who have significant physical disease associated with alcohol, abstinence is the ultimate aim. However, some people may prefer to try and reduce their alcohol intake first.

It's more important to engage them in the discussion about their alcohol use than argue them into aiming for abstinence. They should be supported with harm reduction strategies.

Involve the network

Harmful and dependent alcohol use affects everyone around the patient. The views of people in this network are important. People closest to the patient need to be 'on board' to increase the chance of success (Box 21.3).

It's tempting to assume that all family members or friends want the patient to stop drinking too, but this isn't the case. Perhaps they also have alcohol problems and are not thinking about stopping. Sometimes, a spouse will feel actively threatened in their position at home by the patient becoming abstinent and re-engaging in family life. The behaviours of people who are alcohol dependent can sometimes be more easily predicted and managed than those of a sober family member.

In short, relationships are complicated, and not everyone will be supportive of change.

Who to turn to?

Informing the patient of services available in their own area is best done in the contemplative and preparation parts of the cycle of change. Here the clinician can act as a 'signpost', and let the patient take the lead in what services might be best for them. Some of these different types of services are outlined in Chapter 23.

Withdrawal and detoxification

Emergency detoxification should be avoided if possible. If the patient's health requires admission to hospital (general or mental health), then pharmacological support for alcohol withdrawal is likely (see Chapter 17). Otherwise, patients do better when the alcohol withdrawal is planned. This may be through shared care arrangements (local substance misuse services and general practice), or through a more specialised detoxification program.

Referral to specialist secondary care alcohol services, where detoxification may be considered as an in-patient or outpatient, is discussed in Chapter 22.

Further reading

Miller WR, Rollnick S. *Motivational interviewing: helping people change*, 3rd edn. New York: The Guildford Press, 2013.

National Institute for Health and Care Excellence. *Alcohol-use disorders: diagnosis, assessment and management of harmful drinking and alcohol dependence* (NICE Guidelines CG115). London: National Institute for Health and Care Excellence, 2011.

Prochaska JO, Velicer WF. The Transtheoretical Model of health behavior change. *American Journal of Health Promotion* 1997;12(1):38–48.

CHAPTER 22

Psychological treatment and relapse prevention

Nicola Taylor

OVERVIEW

- Relapse prevention can be helped by psychotherapies, medication or both.
- Patients need to 'be on board' to get the most use from psychotherapy.
- Medication can't take the place of motivation, but can help.

Introduction

For all people with alcohol misuse problems, psychological or talking therapies can be useful in harm reduction and abstinence. In the 'cycle of change' mentioned in Chapter 21, this is in the 'action' and 'maintenance' part of the cycle. Therapies with the most evidence tend to be ones which are structured, time limited and deal with specific problems in the 'here and now'. Patients with alcohol misuse do not exist in a vacuum; and wherever possible, the inclusion of supportive family, partner and friends is beneficial. The social context of excessive alcohol use is also important – when all of someone's social contact revolves around drinking and the pub, we are not only asking them to give up alcohol but for some, a way of life.

People may also need pharmacological assistance in maintaining abstinence.

Psychotherapies

Cognitive behavioural therapy

Cognitive behavioural therapy is a time-limited talking therapy – working on problems in the 'here and now'. It looks at the relationship between thoughts, feelings (emotions), behaviours and physical sensations. Simple explanations of a cognitive model might be around the recognition that symptoms of withdrawal (physical sensations such as palpitations, sweating and tremor) can cause strong feelings of anxiety. This anxiety is linked to worry (thoughts), and these thoughts lead to behaviours such as drinking. Thoughts, feelings, behaviours and physical perceptions can be linked together in a number of different ways, and drawing out this web of connections can be helpful during therapy. Some of the automatic thoughts triggered by physical perceptions and feelings can be isolated and challenged, helping break down the entrenched connections.

One commonly used diagram is seen in Figure 22.1. Therapists can use this very basic diagram with the patient to map out the individual connections. As with all psychotherapies, people need to 'be on board' with the concepts, and be willing to engage in the sessions and the homework that is given. This homework may include alcohol diaries, mood diaries or exercises that use evidence to challenge unhelpful automatic thoughts.

It can be offered to people who are drinking at harmful levels and all levels of alcohol dependence.

It can be accessed throughout the country through the Improving Access to Psychotherapy (IAPT) programme (www.iapt.nhs.uk), and some non-statutory services (see Chapter 24). Private psychotherapists vary in price and are readily available.

National Institute of Heath and Care Excellence (NICE) guidelines recommend cognitive therapies focusing on alcohol should normally be offered for 60 min once a week for 12 weeks, and can be done as individual therapy or as part of a group. This decision between group and individual therapy is often a pragmatic one based on patient preference and availability.

Other psychotherapies

Other forms of psychotherapies are also useful. These include other behavioural therapies and social network therapies. These can include things such as pattern recognition of drinking, habituating people to cues for drinking and helping them set limits for their drinking.

NICE also recommends behavioural couples therapy, if the patient has a supportive partner, and their relationship is suffering because of alcohol use. This should again be time limited, usually for 60 min a week for 12 weeks. The aim is for a level of drinking (or abstinence) agreed upon by the patient and therapist at the beginning of the therapy.

The type of psychotherapy is guided by a number of considerations: patient choice, how much the patients 'buys in' to the underlying concepts, timing and local availability. The final determination should be between assessing psychotherapist and the patient (Box 22.1).

ABC of Alcohol, Fifth Edition. Edited by Anne McCune.

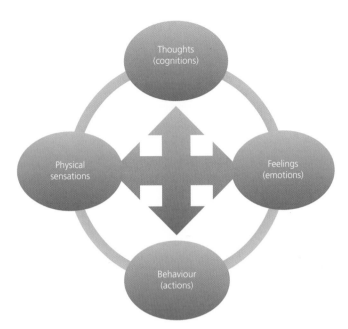

Figure 22.1 Cognitive behavioural therapy. This shows the interplay between thoughts, feelings, behaviour and physical sensations. Influencing one of these factors will influence the others in turn.

Box 22.1 **Summary of psychotherapies**

Cognitive behavioural therapies focused on alcohol-related problems should usually consist of one 60-min session per week for 12 weeks.

Behavioural therapies focused on alcohol-related problems should usually consist of one 60-min session per week for 12 weeks.

Social network and environment-based therapies focused on alcohol-related problems should usually consist of eight 50-min sessions over 12 weeks.

Behavioural couples therapy should be focused on alcohol-related problems and their impact on relationships. It should aim for abstinence, or a level of drinking predetermined and agreed by the therapist and the service user to be reasonable and safe. It should usually consist of one 60-min session per week for 12 weeks.

Source: NICE Guideline 115.

If there is no response to psychotherapies, or if the patient requests it, then consideration can be given to pharmacological help to be given as well as the psychotherapy. In patients with severe alcohol dependence, acamprosate or naltrexone should be offered after assisted withdrawal as routine.

Pharmacology of relapse prevention

Drugs used to improve abstinence don't take the place of the patient's own motivation or desire to change, but can prove a helpful augmentation for some.

Acamprosate

Acamprosate has been shown to increase the rates of abstinence in people who are undergoing treatment for alcohol dependence. Its exact mechanism of action is not clear, but it seems to inhibit excitatory systems in the brain [mediated N-methyl-D-aspartate (NMDA) and glutamate] and increase the gamma-aminobutyric acid (GABA)-mediated inhibitory systems.

While the goal of alcohol treatment may be abstinence, acamprosate has also been shown to reduce the number of alcoholic drinks consumed in people who are still drinking.

It should be considered either as part of a planned withdrawal, or started as soon as the assisted withdrawal is complete. It may be more suitable for people who have a degree of anxiety, or who describe looking for the buzz or high of alcohol addiction (Box 22.2).

Box 22.2 **Before starting medication**

Full physical assessment
Urea and electrolytes
Liver function tests
Gamma GT
Discuss cautions and side effects with the patient

Dosing: patient's weight less than 60 kg 333 mg three times a day orally

patient's weight greater than 60 kg 666 mg three times a day orally

Continuation: for up to 6 months, sometimes longer if clinically appropriate. Discontinuation should be considered if alcohol consumption is unchanged after 4–6 weeks.

Contraindications: severe liver disease (no studies in cirrhosis)

Naltrexone

Naltrexone is an opioid antagonist that can reduce the craving for alcohol. It blocks the effects of endogenous opioid peptides in the brain and influences the dopaminergic reward system in the brain following alcohol intake.

Before starting: Screening should be done for opioid dependence, and recent opioid use by urine drug screens. Liver function tests are needed before and during treatment. Also see Box 22.2.

Dosing: It should be 25 mg for 2 days, then increase to 50 mg daily orally.

A total weekly dose of 350 mg can be given in three divided doses through the week to improve compliance.

A long-acting injectable preparation is also available, although used less widely in the United Kingdom.

Continuation: Patients given naltrexone should stay under monthly supervision for 6 months, after which the frequency of supervision may be reduced. Blood tests don't need to be done regularly for everyone; but in the elderly or people with other comorbidities, on-going monitoring is sensible.

| Cautions: | Caution should be used with hepatic or renal impairment. No studies in cirrhosis. |
| Contraindication: | Opioid dependence. Patients should be given a card to carry with them, notifying any treating doctors about their use of naltrexone in case any opioid analgesia needs to be given in an emergency. |

Disulfram

Disulfram blocks the metabolism of alcohol to produce high concentrations of acetaldehyde. Accumulation of this chemical causes a constellation of reactions including flushing, headache, tachycardia, palpitations nausea and vomiting. If large amounts of alcohol are taken after disulfram, the reaction can also include hypotension and collapse (Box 22.2).

As well as alcoholic drinks, the patient should also be counselled about the presence of alcohol in some medications, confectionary and perfumes as even very small quantities can cause a reaction if taken inadvertently.

Before starting:	The patient must not have ingested any alcohol for at least 24 h prior to starting the disulfram. See also Box 22.2.
Dosing:	Usually 200 mg a day orally Some people may require higher doses to produce an unpleasant enough reaction if they continue to drink.
Continuation:	Patients need to stay under supervision for treatment with disulfram to be effective. Treatment should ideally include a supportive family member or partner to supervise the daily administration of disulfram. Patients should be under formal supervision fortnightly for the first 2 months and then monthly thereafter. Medical review is recommended at 6 monthly intervals.
Cautions:	Do not use in severe liver disease or renal impairment, epilepsy.
Contraindications:	These include cardiac failure, coronary artery disease previous cerebrovascular accident.

Baclofen in chronic liver disease

Baclofen, commonly used as a skeletal muscle relaxant, has GABA-B agonistic properties. It is thought that it is these properties that underlie its action in reducing the craving for alcohol.

Trials of baclofen in patients with cirrhosis aiming for abstinence showed significant improvement over placebo. These findings haven't been consistent across all groups; but in the severely dependent population, it can be effective in controlling cravings for alcohol and maintaining life-saving abstinence. This is the only agent that has been tested in patients with significant liver disease including cirrhosis.

Before starting:	See Box 22.2.
Dosing:	High doses of baclofen have been shown to reduce craving. Doses of up to 120 mg per day are used.
Cautions:	Baclofen is mainly excreted through the kidney, and so caution in renal impairment should be borne in mind.

There's no convincing evidence that either acamprosate or naltrexone are superior in preventing relapse when applied to the UK population. NICE guidance is to offer disulfram after acamprosate or naltrexone, or for patient preference (Box 22.3).

Box 22.3 Drugs not to be used for the treatment of alcohol misuse

Antidepressants
Benzodiazepines (only for withdrawals)

Further reading

Addolorato G, Leggio L, Ferrulli A, Cardone S, Vonghia L, Mirijello A, et al. Effectiveness and safety of baclofen for maintenance of alcohol abstinence in alcohol-dependent patients with liver cirrhosis: randomised, double-blind controlled study. *Lancet* 2007;370(9603): 1915–22.

Lingford-Hughes AR, Welch S, Peters L, Nutt DJ. BAP updated guidelines: evidence-based guidelines for the pharmacological management of substance abuse, harmful use, addiction and comorbidity: recommendations from BAP. *Journal of Psychopharmacology* 2012;26(7): 899–952.

National Institute for Health and Care Excellence. *Alcohol-use disorders: diagnosis, assessment and management of harmful drinking and alcohol dependence* (NICE Guidelines CG115). London: National Institute for Health and Care Excellence, 2011.

Rösner S, Hackl-Herrwerth A, Leucht S, Lehert P, Vecchi S, Soyka M. Acamprosate for alcohol dependence. *Cochrane Database of Systematic Reviews* 2010;9:CD004332. doi:10.1002/14651858.CD004332.pub2.

CHAPTER 23

Alcohol and psychiatry

Nicola Taylor

OVERVIEW

- Harmful alcohol use is a co-morbidity for many types of mental illness.
- Alcohol dependence is a risk factor for suicide.
- Alcohol dependence should be treated first, as this often leads to an improvement in symptoms of mental illness.

Introduction

Harmful alcohol use and dependence is a common co-morbidity of mental disorders. Managing the physical sequelae of alcohol dependence, the psychological consequences and underlying mental health problems takes skill, patience and time.

Alcohol use, mental disorder or both?

Symptoms of all kinds of mental disorder and illness can be caused, exacerbated or hidden by alcohol dependence. If the exact diagnosis is in doubt, then the risk assessment and safety of the patient needs to be the first priority.

Risk assessment

People with alcohol dependence have an increased risk of suicide: up to 20 times in some studies. The exact relationship is complicated. In the short term, alcohol can make people more disinhibited, impulsive and aggressive: all states that have been associated with suicidal behaviour. In the longer term, the social consequences of alcohol dependency – loss of job, function, relationships – are also independent risk factors for self harm and completed suicide (Box 23.1).

As can be seen in Box 23.1, many of the risk factors for completed suicide and self-harm are 'fixed' or non-modifiable by clinicians. It's important to identify the risk factors that we can change – or help the patient to change – to reduce the overall risk.

Box 23.1 **Risk factors for suicide**

- Involvement with psychiatry services, particularly recent discharge from inpatient care
- History of attempts
- Alcohol dependence
- Substance misuse
- Family history of suicide
- Serious physical illness
- Unemployment
- Single
- Male (more completed suicides, women make more attempts)

Key modifiable risk factors for clinicians are the following:

- Alcohol misuse
- Mental illness or disorder
- Chronic pain or illness

Referral to voluntary agencies can also help with social support. Accommodation advice can be found through local councils.

Key message

People who self-harm and express suicidal ideation are at greater risk of completed suicide.

Depression

Alcohol dependence has a high rate of co-morbid depression. Many core symptoms of depression are influenced or hidden by alcohol dependence, and the two can be difficult to unpick.

The feelings of hopelessness and helplessness that are common in depression may make it difficult for a patient to link in with alcohol services, and become empowered to change. It can be a vicious cycle, and engagement with these patients is essential. Careful risk assessment is vital, given the correlation between depression, alcohol and completed suicide. If the risk is high, referral to secondary specialist services is appropriate.

ABC of Alcohol, Fifth Edition. Edited by Anne McCune.
© 2015 John Wiley & Sons, Ltd. Published 2015 by John Wiley & Sons, Ltd.

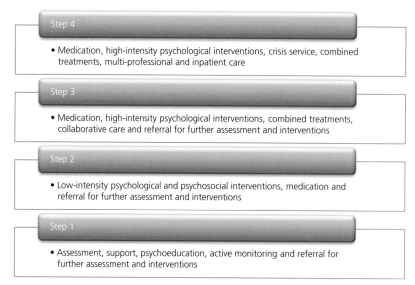

Figure 23.1 Stepped care model of the treatment of depression.

Box 23.2 **Considerations in prescribing antidepressant medication**

- Previous history of GI bleed
- Hepatic impairment
- Chaotic lifestyle and compliance

Box 23.3 **Anxiety and alcohol**

- When did you start drinking?
- Why, can you remember?
- What did alcohol do for you?
- What situations where you in when you started drinking?

Box 23.4 **Indications that the anxiety felt is pathological**

- Severity
- Chronicity
- Autonomy (not caused by a specific trigger)
- Behavioural change
- Functional impairment

If the patient continues to have symptoms of depression after 3–4 weeks of sobriety, then treatment as usual should be offered from the stepped care model (Figure 23.1).

When considering antidepressant medication, special consideration may need to be given if there are physical sequelae of alcohol dependence (Box 23.2).

Anxiety

Alcohol is the most commonly used anxiolytic medication in the country. Self-medicating is common in a range of disorders from post-traumatic stress disorder, to social anxiety disorder. The development of alcohol dependence is easy to trace: using alcohol as a short-term way of reducing anxiety, allowing social functioning or helping someone to sleep can spiral out of control (Box 23.3).

The underlying diagnosis of an anxiety disorder should always be considered. Again, if symptoms persist after 3–4 weeks of sobriety, then treatment as usual should be offered (Box 23.4).

Alcohol hallucinosis

This condition is the presence of auditory hallucinations in external space (the patient will describe them as coming from outside their head). They occur in clear consciousness and are resolved by alcohol use. They can be derogatory and frightening. They respond well to antipsychotics, and have a good prognosis if properly treated. Secondary care assessment may be appropriate to distin-

guish these hallucinations from symptoms more indicative of an ongoing psychotic disorder.

Personality disorder

People with personality disorder have fixed ways of relating to the world, that impact on their functioning in all spheres. These ways of coping and relating cause distress to the patient and often to others around them.

Alcohol can exacerbate the impulsiveness found in emotionally unstable personality disorder and the traits found in antisocial personality disorder. This can in turn lead to acts of self-harm, suicide attempts and violence towards others.

As before, identification and engagement are key. Psychoeducation can be helpful to help people identify patterns, and put in place strategies for harm reduction. For example, making the links between alcohol consumption, illegal behaviour and eventual punishment may be helpful for patients with antisocial personality disorder.

The diagnosis of personality disorder itself is not one of exclusion from psychiatry services, and can respond well to psychotherapy.

The alcohol problems questionnaire

The alcohol problems questionnaire (APQ) is not a screening tool, but it is designed to help monitor the use of alcohol over time. It's reliability and validity have been confirmed. It can be used in supporting patients to monitor their own alcohol use, and examine patterns in their alcohol use and mental health. Positive answers to some of the questions (i.e. those around weight loss, abdominal pain, and pins and needles) should prompt further examination and investigation.

In an emergency

If an intoxicated patient is felt to be a high and immediate risk of suicide, then the following can be considered:

In hospital

- Do they want to leave?
- Do they have the capacity to make this decision?
- If not, what is in their best interest?
- If they do have capacity to make this decision, is consideration of the mental health act appropriate?

In the community

- Are they willing to stay with someone?
- If not, and they are in a public place, consider contacting the police and alerting them to your concerns.

Alcohol and the mental health act

For the purposes of the mental health act, acute intoxication by alcohol is a mental disorder that can result in the detention of a patient for treatment of the mental disorder. In practical terms, this is a rare occurrence: if someone is acutely intoxicated, they may well not have the capacity to make decisions about health care and can be treated in their best interests under the Mental Capacity Act. In the longer term, if people have sequelae of chronic alcohol use, including cognitive impairment, then again this can fall under the auspices of the mental health act, or the mental capacity act. Expert advice from psychiatry services should be sought, and secondary care services involved.

Chronic alcohol dependency

It is important though to note that the Mental Health Act 1983 (amended in 2007) makes it clear the alcohol dependency alone is not a mental disorder for the purposes of the act. This means that no one is able to be detained for treatment of their alcohol dependency alone.

Referral to general psychiatry services

Specialist secondary psychiatric assessment should be sought if:

Symptoms of mental disorders such as depression and anxiety persist after 4 weeks of abstinence, and there is felt to be

---

Assessment of physical health problems in the psychiatry setting

Every admission to a mental health hospital should have a full physical examination including the following:
Stigmata of liver disease
Neurological impairment
Liver function tests
Full blood count (raised MCV may point to chronic alcohol use)
If harmful or dependent levels of drinking are suspected and the patient is malnourished or has decompensated liver disease, then high dose oral thiamine should be given to prevent Wernicke's encephalopathy.

---

significant risk to the persons of health or safety of the safety of others.

Symptoms of mental disorder persist after 4 weeks of abstinence and if these symptoms are not amenable to treatment as usually provided by primary care.

During withdrawal, there are risks associated with the symptoms presenting that may require prescription of antipsychotic medication, or risks are present that may require assessment under the mental health act to be contained.

Cognitive impairment is detected after withdrawal treatment, and function of the patient is impaired.

Specialist psychiatry addiction services

The availability, structure and referral criteria of each specialist psychiatry addiction service differ widely across the country. In general, they are appropriate for:

People who are dependant on alcohol (score more than 20 on the Audit questionnaire, see Chapter 6) AND
- Have significant physical problems related to alcohol
  OR
- Have severe mental illness or personality disorder which when combined with alcohol leads to a significant risk to themselves or others
  OR
- Are pregnant
  OR
- Are living with children who have been identified as being at risk by Child and Young People Services.

People with severe personality disorders and mental illness should already be known and supported by secondary care services, and have a care coordinator.

Alcohol, and psychiatry in the hospital

Liaison psychiatry works at the interface and overlap of psychological and physical illness and disease. Some patients present with physical problems, and while in the hospital are supported in withdrawing from alcohol dependence. If there are specific management problems, or concerns about underlying mental health needs, referral to liaison psychiatry services is appropriate (Box 23.5).

Box 23.5 **Comprehensive assessment in specialist alcohol services**

This should include the following:
Alcohol use – including consumption, dependence and related problems
Collateral history
Physical health problems
Cognitive functioning
Psychological readiness and belief in ability to change.

Box 23.6 **The structure of psychiatry services**

It's almost impossible to generalise across the country about the structure of psychiatry services. Some places will have more comprehensive services than other depending on population, need and provider. However, some common themes might be helpful.

Crisis teams/intensive teams/home treatment teams
These are multidisciplinary teams, usually working 7 days a week who can provide support, assessment and treatment to people in the community as an alternative to admission to a psychiatry hospital

Community mental health teams (CMHTs)
Often split into different functions, these team are again multidisciplinary and work in the community to help people recover from mental illness and disorder.

Care coordinators (usually from CMHTs):
Clinicians from a variety of different backgrounds – including nursing, occupational therapy and social work – who work with patients to assess their needs, and organise appropriate care.

One of the functions of many liaison psychiatry teams is the assessment of people who have self-harmed or attempted suicide. Not infrequently, patients presenting to hospital with these problems are intoxicated. A mental health assessment can be completed while the patient is intoxicated, but this only tells us what the mental state of an intoxicated person is. It is more useful to wait for the patient to 'sober up' when their mental state can be better assessed at the point of discharge, and the patient involved in any plans for follow up or ongoing care (Box 23.6).

Further reading

Department of Health. *Code of Practice Mental Health Act 1983*. London: TSO, 2008.

Drummond DC. The relationship between alcohol dependence and alcohol-related problems in a clinical population. *British Journal of Addiction* 1990;85(3):357–66.

Gunnell D, Frankel S. Prevention of suicide: aspirations and evidence. *BMJ* 1994;308:1227–33.

National Institute for Health and Care Excellence. *Depression in adults: the treatment and management of depression in adults* (NICE Guidelines CG90). London: National Institute for Health and Care Excellence, 2009.

National Institute for Health and Care Excellence. *Alcohol-use disorders: diagnosis, assessment and management of harmful drinking and alcohol dependence* (NICE Guidelines CG115). London: National Institute for Health and Care Excellence, 2011.

National Institute for Health and Care Excellence. *Generalised anxiety disorder and panic disorder (with or without agoraphobia) in adults: management in primary, secondary and community care* (NICE Guidelines CG113). London: National Institute for Health and Care Excellence, 2011.

CHAPTER 24

Other resources, and alcohol and the doctor

Nicola Taylor

OVERVIEW

- There is a wide range of services and help available.
- These services vary greatly throughout the country.
- Knowledge of one or two key resources is useful.

Introduction

There is a huge variety of support, counselling and advice agencies available throughout the country. Many of these will be locally based, and can be found through an internet search or by contacting local substance misuse psychiatry services. All health professionals should be able to act as signposts to information about local provision. Some of the most useful agencies are outlined in the following text.

There are also residential programmes with different acceptance criteria, and therapeutic models. These are more patchy in provision. There are lots of types, but they include three groups:

Abstinence-based residential care

These houses promote an alcohol-free environment. In the past they were known as 'dry houses'. They usually involve a range of counselling, social care and practical help in the recovery from alcohol use.

Houses for ongoing drinkers

These are the 'wet houses': places for people who are not yet ready or able to stop drinking completely. They aim to use whatever they can to improve the health of residents and engagement in appropriate services.

Therapeutic communities

Therapeutic communities can be used with people who have a diverse range of problems. They emphasise the relationship between staff and community members who work and live together, and offer a collaborative reflective environment.

A special group: people who are homeless

Finding oneself homeless and drinking at harmful levels, or dependent on alcohol is the very definition of a vicious circle. Forty per cent of homeless alcohol users believe that a lack of stable accommodation is a barrier to them seeking help with their alcohol use. At the same time, it's not difficult to see how excessive alcohol use can lead to employment problems, debt and all too easily on to homelessness. This is a public health tragedy: the average age of death for a homeless man is 47, and for a woman 43. One-third of those deaths are accounted for by alcohol and drug misuse.

People who are homeless have fewer options to seek help for their alcohol use. Some crisis houses and residential programmes insist on stable accommodation being an acceptance criterion, and so exclude this vulnerable group.

The principles outlined in previous chapters hold true, but their implementation might need a different approach. There's little point in giving someone information about a helpline or website if they don't have access to a phone or computer. The local homeless healthcare centre can be a point of contact and information. Their details are usually found on council websites.

And just because your patient doesn't have access to a computer, it doesn't mean you don't. Find out: print out a map, a bus timetable or anything else that is useful, make sure your patient can understand it and give it to them.

Contact details

There are some organisations that can offer help and support throughout the journey of recovery: from the first inkling that someone has a problem, through decades of abstinence. They are taken from the Royal College of Psychiatrists website: a fantastic and up-to-date source of information.

Drinkline – The National Alcohol Helpline

0800 917 8282 – (England and Wales, Mon–Fri, 9 a.m.–11 p.m.) Drinkline offers free, confidential information and advice on alcohol.

ABC of Alcohol, Fifth Edition. Edited by Anne McCune.
© 2015 John Wiley & Sons, Ltd. Published 2015 by John Wiley & Sons, Ltd.

Alcoholics Anonymous

Helpline: 0845 769 7555; email: helpline@alcoholics-anonymous.org.uk

Contact details for all English AA meetings. There is a quiz to determine whether AA is the right type of organisation for an individual, and a frequently asked question section about AA and alcoholism.

Al-Anon Family Groups UK and Eire

Helpline: 020 7403 0888 (10 a.m.–10 p.m., 365 days a year); email: enquiries@al-anonuk.org.uk

It is a support group for friends and families of alcoholics. It includes a frequently asked questions section, pamphlets and other literature, and information on group meetings in the United Kingdom.

Alcohol Concern

Tel: 020 7928 7377; email: contact@alcoholconcern.org.uk

This site provides information and articles on a range of topics surrounding alcoholism. It includes 18 excellent factsheets crammed with information that would be very useful for professionals such as alcohol and the law a search engine and a good list of alcohol-related links.

Alcohol Focus Scotland

Tel: 0141 572 6700; email: enquiries@alcohol-focus-scotland.org.uk

It is the national volunteer organisation for alcohol issues in Scotland. It provides information about alcohol, including legal matters, frequently asked questions and tips for safe drinking.

Depression Alliance

Tel: 0845 123 23 20; email: information@depressionalliance.org

Information, support and understanding are offered to people who suffer with depression and for relatives who want to help. Self-help groups, information and awareness raising for depression.

Giveupdrinking.co.uk

50 Ways To Leave Your Lager

If you believe you're drinking too much, or you know alcohol is having a detrimental effect on your life, this website can help you.

Alcohol and the doctor

> **OVERVIEW**
>
> • Harmful alcohol use is common in healthcare professionals.
> • It can cause specific problems, with professional implications.
> • There are a wealth of sources of advice and support.

Introduction

What's the definition of someone with an alcohol problem? Someone who drinks more than their doctor.

This old joke highlights some of the difficulties doctors have with alcohol. For many of us, excessive drinking was, and is, felt to be culturally appropriate in undergraduate and early training. Changes in training with less support from the 'firm', disrupted working patterns and increasing stress can all lead to increased alcohol consumption as a way of coping.

Given the nature of most doctors – goal-driven, motivated, perfectionistic – coping with life when we fail to live up to our ideals can be difficult – and alcohol is an easily accessible medication. It's sometimes difficult for doctors to equate their own drinking with that of their patients, but alcohol is damaging at high levels: whether it comes in the form of a bottle of Rioja or supermarket vodka.

The stigma surrounding alcohol dependence makes it difficult for people to admit to a problem, whatever their occupation. There are specialist groups and counselling for doctors and dentists with alcohol and other substance misuse problems, including specialist AA groups. Regulatory bodies are more likely to be supportive if we identify and address the problem ourselves, rather than wait for a problem with our clinical work.

Alcohol and colleagues

If we suspect that a colleague is putting the safety of patients at risk, then we have a duty to report it. This holds true if the risk is generates through alcohol consumption. It might be wise to allow your colleague the opportunity to address this themselves in the first instance, but the employer or the occupational health department must be made aware if patient safety is at risk of being compromised.

If the health care professional with harmful levels of alcohol use or dependence is a patient, then again they should be encouraged to contact their employer or occupational health department. If they decline, then confidentiality is not absolute, and there may be a case for breaking this in the public interest.

A doctor who treats themselves has a fool for a patient, the saying goes. When it comes to alcohol problems, the first steps are the same as for anyone else: be honest, brave and seek help from your GP and alcohol support services.

And remember, if it's difficult for you, then it's difficult for your patients too (Box 24.1).

The Doctors Support Network

This is a confidential support network, for doctors and by doctors to offer help to those with mental health problems.

www.dsn.org.uk/about.html

The Sick Doctors Trust

This is a confidential organisation offering help to doctors and medical students with all levels of alcohol and substance use.

www.sick-doctors-trust.co.uk/

> Box 24.1 **Alcohol and medical students**
>
> Medical students are held to different standards of behaviour because of the status they enjoy. The General Medical Council regulates these standards of behaviour and has published explicit guidance. Medical students don't get to behave as other students might, and to do so can have long-lasting effects on their medical career.

British Doctors and Dentists Group

For doctors, dentist and students who are recovering or want to recover from alcohol and drug addiction.

www.bddg.org

Down Your Drink

It is based at University College London Medical School

www.downyourdrink.org.uk

Email: info@bddg.org

Further reading

Crisis. *Homelessness: a silent killer*. Crisis, 2011. www.crisis.org.uk (accessed 18 September 2014).

General Medical Council. *Good medical practice*. GMC, 2013. www.gmc-uk.org/guidance/index.asp (accessed 18 September 2014).

General Medical Council. *Medical students: professional values and fitness to practise*. GMC, 2013. www.gmc-uk.org/education/undergraduate/professional_behaviour.asp (accessed 18 September 2014).

Index

Note: Page numbers in *italics* refer to Figures; those in **bold** to Tables.

ABC of Alcohol, Fifth Edition. Edited by Anne McCune.
© 2015 John Wiley & Sons, Ltd. Published 2015 by John Wiley & Sons, Ltd.

ABC of Pain

Lesley A. Colvin & Marie Fallon
Western General Hospital, Edinburgh; University of Edinburgh

Pain is a common presentation and this brand new title focuses on the pain management issues most often encountered in primary care. *ABC of Pain*:

- Covers all the chronic pain presentations in primary care right through to tertiary and palliative care and includes guidance on pain management in special groups such as pregnancy, children, the elderly and the terminally ill
- Includes new findings on the effectiveness of interventions and the progression to acute pain and appropriate pharmacological management
- Features pain assessment, epidemiology and the evidence base in a truly comprehensive reference
- Provides a global perspective with an international list of expert contributors

JUNE 2012 | 9781405176217 | 128 PAGES | £24.99/US$44.95/€32.90/AU$47.95

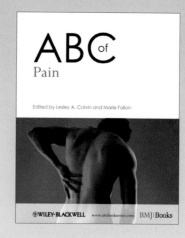

ABC of Urology

3RD EDITION

Chris Dawson & Janine Nethercliffe
Fitzwilliam Hospital, Peterborough; Edith Cavell Hospital, Peterborough

Urological conditions are common, accounting for up to one third of all surgical admissions to hospital. Outside of hospital care urological problems are a common reason for patients needing to see their GP.

- *ABC of Urology, 3rd Edition* provides a comprehensive overview of urology
- Focuses on the diagnosis and management of the most common urological conditions
- Features 4 additional chapters: improved coverage of renal and testis cancer in separate chapters and new chapters on management of haematuria, laparoscopy, trauma and new urological advances
- Ideal for GPs and trainee GPs, and is useful for junior doctors undergoing surgical training, while medical students and nurses undertaking a urological placement as part of their training programme will find this edition indispensable

MARCH 2012 | 9780470657171 | 88 PAGES | £23.99/US$37.95/€30.90/AU$47.95

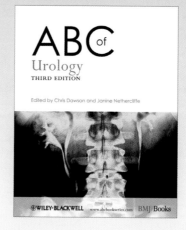

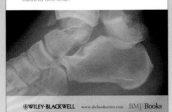

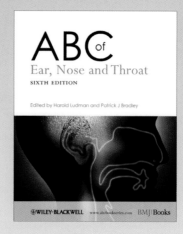
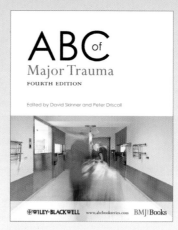

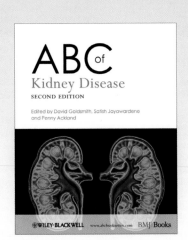